Frederic P. Miller, Agnes F. Vandome,
John McBrewster (Ed.)

British Jamaican

Frederic P. Miller, Agnes F. Vandome,
John McBrewster (Ed.)

British Jamaican

Jamaican diaspora, Office for National
Statistics, History of Jamaica, British
African-Caribbean community, Arrival of
black immigrants in London

Alphascript Publishing

Imprint

All parts of this book are extracted from Wikipedia, the free encyclopedia (www.wikipedia.org).

You can get detailed informations about the authors of this collection of articles at the end of this book. The editors (Ed.) of this book are no authors. They have not modified or extended the original texts.

Pictures published in this book can be under different licences than the GNU Free Documentation License. You can get detailed informations about the authors and licences of pictures at the end of this book.

The content of this book was generated collaboratively by volunteers. Please be advised that nothing found here has necessarily been reviewed by people with the expertise required to provide you with complete, accurate or reliable information. Some information in this book maybe misleading or wrong. The Publisher does not guarantee the validity of the information found here. If you need specific advice (f.e. in fields of medical, legal, financial, or risk management questions) please contact a professional who is licensed or knowledgeable in that area.

Any brand names and product names mentioned in this book are subject to trademark, brand or patent protection and are trademarks or registered trademarks of their respective holders. The use of brand names, product names, common names, trade names, product descriptions etc. even without a particular marking in this works is in no way to be construed to mean that such names may be regarded as unrestricted in respect of trademark and brand protection legislation and could thus be used by anyone.

Cover image: www.ingimage.com
Concerning the licence of the cover image please contact ingimage.

Publisher:
Alphascript Publishing is a trademark of
VDM Publishing House Ltd.,17 Rue Meldrum, Beau Bassin,1713-01 Mauritius
Email: info@vdm-publishing-house.com
Website: www.vdm-publishing-house.com

Published in 2010

Printed in: U.S.A., U.K., Germany. This book was not produced in Mauritius.

ISBN: 978-613-3-85225-9

Contents

Articles

References

Article Licenses

British Jamaican

British Jamaican

Notable British Jamaican people: (1ˢᵗ row): Goldie · Naomi Campbell · Lennox Lewis · Naomie Harris · Wentworth Miller (2ˢᵗ row): Jade Ewen · Deon Burton · Beverley Knight · Delroy Lindo · Diane Abbott (3ˢᵗ row): Chris Eubank · Kelly Holmes · Dennis Seaton · Alesha Dixon · Julian Marley (4ˢᵗ row): Rustie Lee · Benjamin Zephaniah · Shaznay Lewis · Theo Walcott · Alexandra Burke (5ˢᵗ row): Neville Staple · Downtown Julie Brown · Slick Rick · Jamelia · David Haye

Total population
Jamaican-born residents
146,401 (2001 Census)
143,000 (2009 ONS estimate)
Population of Jamaican origin
800,000 (2007 Jamaican High Commission estimate)

Regions with significant populations
London, Birmingham, Liverpool, Manchester, Bristol, Sheffield, Leeds, Newcastle, Brighton, Leicester

Languages
English (British English, Jamaican English), Jamaican Patois

Religion
Christianity, Rastafarian

Related ethnic groups
British African-Caribbean community, Chinese Jamaicans, Jamaicans of African ancestry, Jamaican Americans, Jamaican Canadians, Indo-Jamaicans, Jamaican Australians

British Jamaican is a term that refers to British people who were born in Jamaica or who are of Jamaican descent.[1] [2] The community is well into its fourth generation and consists of around 800,000 individuals, one of the largest Jamaican diasporas on earth.[3] The majority of British people of Jamaican origin were born in the United Kingdom as opposed to Jamaica itself.[4] The Office for National Statistics estimated that in 2009 some 143,000 Jamaican-born people were resident in the UK, with only 47,000 of these retaining Jamaican citizenship.[4]

Jamaicans have been present in the UK since the start of the 20th century, however by far the largest wave of migration occurred after World War II.[3] During the 1950s, Britain's economy was suffering greatly and the nation was plagued with high labour shortages.[3] The British government ultimately looked to its overseas colonies for help and encouraged migration in an effort to fill the many job vacancies.[3] Jamaicans, alongside other Caribbean, South Asian and African groups, came in their hundreds of thousands to the United Kingdom; the majority of Jamaicans settled in London and found work in the likes of London Transport, British Rail and the NHS.[3] The late 20th century saw numerous clashes and rioting involving members of the British Jamaican community and the UK police;

to this day gang culture and violence amongst Black British youths (particularly those of Jamaican descent) has been widely reported in mainstream media.[5] The term 'Yardie' which originated in Jamaica has come to be used to describe British Jamaicans who are associated with gun and knife crime.[5] Despite such troubles, Jamaicans are an extremely well established group in the United Kingdom and British Jamaicans have contributed significantly to the UK music scene and numerous sporting activities such as football and athletics.

History and settlement

The Caribbean island nation of Jamaica was a British colony between 1655 and 1962, these 300 years of English rule changed the face of the island considerably (having previously been under Spanish rule and populated mainly by the indigenous Arawak and Taino communities[6] - now 91.2% of Jamaicans are descended of Sub-Saharan Africans who were brought over as slaves by the British).[6] Jamaica is the third most populous English-speaking nation in the Americas and the local dialect of English is known as Jamaican Patois.[3] The tight-knit link between Jamaica and the United Kingdom remains evident to this day. There has been a long and well established Jamaican community in the UK since near the beginning of the 20th century.[3] Many Jamaicans fought for Britain in World War I, the British West Indies Regiment recruited solely from the British overseas colonies in the Caribbean.

Dozens of Jamaicans disembark the *MV Empire Windrush* at the Port of Tilbury in 1948

Volunteers originally only came from four nations (excluding Jamaica), however as the regiment grew thousands of Jamaican men were recruited and ultimately made up around two thirds of the 15,600 strong regiment.[3] [7] The British West Indies Regiment fought for Britain in the Sinai and Palestine Campaign as well as the East African Campaign. Many of these men became the first permanent Jamaican settlers in the UK after World War II, some of whom also subsequently fought for the country in World War II.[3] [7] Despite this, by far the largest wave of Jamaican migration to the UK including people of all genders and ages occurred in the mid-1900s. A major hurricane in August 1944 ravished eastern Jamaica leading to numerous fatalities and major economic loss after crops were destroyed by flooding. This acted as a push factor in the migration of Jamaicans and at the time by far the largest pull factor was the promise of jobs in the UK.[3] Post-war Britain was suffering from significant labour shortage and looked to its overseas colonies for help, British Rail, the NHS and London transport were noted as being the largest recruiters. On 23 June 1948, the *MV Empire Windrush* arrived in the UK with,amongst other migrants from the Caribbean, 492 Jamaicans onboard whom had been invited to the country to work. Many more followed as the steady flow of Jamaicans to the UK was maintained due to the continuing labour shortage.[3] Between 1955 and 1968, 191,330 Jamaicans settled in the UK.[3] These first generation migrants created the foundation of a community which is now well in to its third if not fourth generation.

Jamaicans continued to migrate to the UK during the 1970s and 1980s, albeit in smaller numbers, the majority of these people came from poor households and went to extreme lengths to get to the UK.[3] There is an uneven distribution of household wealth throughout Jamaica and during the economic crisis of the 1990s lower class Jamaicans continued to migrate in significant numbers. A lot of these later arrivals came from Jamaica's capital and largest city, Kingston where the divide between rich and poor is much more evident than other places on the island.[3] Most first generation immigrants came to the UK in order to seek and improved standard of living, escape violence or to find employment. Jamaicans followed the pattern of other irregular immigrant groups where they tended to work in low paid,

A scene from the April 1981 Brixton riot which is one of the most violent and destructive riots in British history

dirty and often dangerous jobs in order to maintain their independence.[3] Throughout the late 20th century and to this day in fact, the Jamaican community in the UK has been brought into the spotlight due to the involvement of Jamaicans in race-related riots. The first notable event to occur was the 1958 Notting Hill race riots when an argument between local white youths and a Jamaican man, alongside increasing tensions between both communities lead to several nights of disturbances, rioting and attacks.[8] Evidence of institutional racism by London's Metropolitan Police became evident in the high number of Black Britons 'stopped and searched' (under the sus law) alongside the unprovoked shooting of a Jamaican woman in her Lambeth home after police believed she was hiding her criminal son, this event lead to the 1985 Brixton riot.[9] To name one of the more recent riots, the 2005 Birmingham race riots occurred as a result of the alleged rape of a 14-year old Jamaican girl by a group of up to 20 South Asian men including the Pakistani store owner it is reported she initially stole from, unlike earlier race riots this event is evidence that high tensions and violence are happening in the UK not only between Black British and White British people, however all ethnic and national groups.[10] The Murder of Stephen Lawrence occurred in 1993, the London teenager of Jamaican parentage was stabbed to death in a racially motivated attack. The murder was handled in such a bad way by the Metropolitan Police that an inquiry into this established that the force had been institutionally racist, the investigation has been called 'one of the most important moments in the modern history of criminal justice in Britain' and contributed heavily to the creation and passing of the Criminal Justice Act 2003.[11] Many Jamaicans live in the UK having no legal status, having come at a period of less strict immigration policies. Some Jamaican social groups have claimed asylum under the 1951 Convention Relating to the Status of Refugees, this only continued until 2003 when Jamaica was placed on the Non-Suspensive Appeal list when restrictions on UK visas came in to place, making it more difficult for Jamaicans to travel to the UK.[3]

Demographics

Population and distribution

According to the 2001 UK Census 146,401 Jamaican-born people were living in the UK, making them the seventh-largest foreign-born group in the UK at the time.[12] The equivalent figure for 2009 has been estimated at 143,000 by the Office for National Statistics, making them the eleventh-largest foreign-born group.[4] The Jamaican High Commission estimates that there are around 800,000 British people of Jamaican origin in the UK.[3] Jamaicans in the UK are fairly widely dispersed, although there are some locations with much larger numbers and higher concentrations of Jamaican people than others - namely London.[13] The Greater London area is home to some 250,000 Jamaicans, whilst the second largest number which is 45,000 individuals can be found in the West Midlands.[13] 25,000 Jamaicans are thought to live in South West England, 18,000 in the East Midlands, 12,500 in South East England, 14,000 in North West England and 11,500 in Yorkshire and the Humber.[13] Much smaller numbers are located in Wales (3,0000) and Scotland, where the International Organization for Migration suggests that a meer 40 Jamaicans call home.[13] Within the stated regions of the United Kingdom, most people of Jamaican origin can be found in the larger cities and towns. The largest Jamaican communities in the UK are listed below (all figures are 2007 estimates by the IOM, as there isn't a specific 'Jamaican' tick box in the UK census to identify where Jamaicans live within the country).[13]

Year	Numer of Jamaicans granted British citizenship	Naturalisation by residence	Naturalisation by marriage	Registration of a minor child	Registration by other means
1997[14]	732	327	279	114	12
1998[15]	1,370	571	564	221	14
1999[16]	1,437	678	526	226	7
2000[17]	1,882	927	664	281	10
2001[18]	2,070	1,025	710	330	0
2002[19]	2,025	1,035	705	285	0
2003[20]	2,795	1,285	985	520	5
2004[21]	3,180	1,415	1,060	640	65
2005[22]	3,515	1,585	1,080	770	80
2006[23]	2,525	1,110	710	655	55
2007[24]	3,165	1,575	825	725	45
2008[25]	2,715	1,275	695	700	45

- London - 250,000
  Brent, Croydon, Hackney, Lambeth, Lewisham, Southwark and Waltham Forest
- Birmingham - 30,000
  Handsworth, Winson Green, Aston, Ladywood, Newtown and Lozells
- Bristol - 20,000
  St. Paul's and Redfield
- Manchester - 10,000
  Trafford, Moss Side, Cheetham Hill, Chorlton, Didsbury, Wythanshawe, Urmston and Sale
- Gloucester - 4,000
  Barton, Tredworth and Tuffly
- Leeds - 4,000-5,000
  Chapeltown and Harefields
- Leicester - 3,000-4,000
  Highfields and St Matthews
- Sheffield - 2,000
- Liverpool - 1,000-2,000
  Granby and Toxteth
- Preston - 800

Besides the above locations, the IOM has also identified the following towns and cities as having notable Jamaican communities: Bath, Bedford, Bradford, Cardif, Coventry, Derby, Doncaster, Huddersfield, Ipswich, Liskeard, Luton, Middlesbrough, Milton Keynes, Nottingham, Northampton, Swansea, Swindon, Truro and Wolverhampton.[13] The majority of British Jamaicans are in the age range of 18 and 45, and investigation by the IOM in to the ages of community members found that it is more or less on par with the general makeup of the British population. Around 8% of people investigated were under the age of 25, around 13% were in between the ages of 25 and 34. 22% were between 35 and 44, 27% were between 45 and 54 whilst 18% of respondents were aged between 55 and 64. The remainder were 65 years of age or older. As stated earlier, this investigation only involved a few hundred community members it is a balanced representation of the Jamaican community in the UK.[13] Evidence that the Jamaican British community is a long established one is that fact that only around 10% of Jamaicans in the UK came to the country in the decade leading up to 2007.[13] In terms of citizenship, all Jamaicans who came to the UK prior to Jamaican Independence in 1962 were automatically granted British citizenship because Jamaica was an overseas colony of the country. Jamaican immigrants must now apply for citizenship if they wish to become British nationals. The above table shows the number of Jamaicans granted citizenship in recent years.

Religion

The 2001 UK Census showed that 73.7% of Black Caribbeans adhered to the Christian faith, whilst 11.3% of respondents claimed to be atheist. This ranks as a higher percentage of Christians per head compared to Black Africans (68.8%), but a slightly lower percentage than White British Christians (75.7%).[26] Jamaicans and people of Jamaican descent are regular religious worshippers and the majority of them worship across a wide range of mainly Black led Christian denominations as well as in the more mainstream Anglican and Roman Catholic churches. Over recent years the number of regular White worshipers in Anglican churches in particular have decreased significantly, numbers however have been maintained by Black Caribbeans and (mostly Jamaicans) who have taken their places.[13] Other common Christian denominations followed by Jamaicans in the UK include Pentecostalism, the Seventh Day Adventist, Jehovah's Witnesses, the Pilgrims Union Church, the Baptist church and Methodism.[13]

Culture

Cuisine

The earliest Jamaican immigrants to post-war Britain found differences in diet and availability of food an uncomfortable challenge.[27] In later years, as the community developed and food imports became more accessible to all, grocers specialising in Caribbean produce opened in British high streets. Caribbean restaurants can now also be found in most areas of Britain where Jamaicans and other such groups reside, serving traditional Caribbean dishes such as curried goat, fried dumplings and ackee and salt fish (the national dish of Jamaica). "Jerk" is a style of cooking from Jamaica in which meats (including pork and chicken) are dry-rubbed or wet marinated with a very hot spice mixture. The best known Caribbean food brands in the UK are Dunn's River, Tropical Sun, Walkerswood and Grace Foods. Grace Foods is

Scotch bonnet peppers imported from the Caribbean on sale at London's Brixton Market. The peppers are a key ingredient of "Jerk" dishes

originally from Jamaica but is now a multi national conglomerate. In March 2007 Grace Foods bought ENCO Products, owners of the Dunn's River Brand, as well as "Nurishment", a flavoured, sweetened enriched milk drink, and the iconic Encona Sauce Range. Tropical Sun products and ingredients have been widely available in the UK for over 10 years and has a sister brand of Jamaica Sun with products mainly sourced from the Caribbean. Walkerswood is a Jamaican co-operative which has a range of sauces and marinades product.[28]

Media

An investigation by the IOM found that in general Jamaicans in the UK don't have a particular preference of favourite newspaper, many choose to read local newspapers and the national British press (such as *The Guardian* the *Daily Mail* and *Metro*), however the investigation also showed that some 80% of British Jamaicans show an interest in Black or Minority Ethnic newspapers.[29] The *Weekly Gleaner* which as its name suggests is a weekly publication distributed in the UK and contains specific news from the *Jamaica Daily Gleaner*.[29] *The Voice* closely follows in terms of readership, this weekly tabloid newspaper is based in the UK however is owned by the Jamaican GV Media Group and was established by Jamaican-born Val McCalla, the newspaper covers a variety of stories that are aimed solely at the British African-Caribbean community.[29] Other popular newspapers and magazines aimed at the Jamaican and Black British populations in the UK in general include the *New Nation*, *The Big Eye News*, *Pride Magazine*, *The Caribbean Times* and formerly *Black Voice*.[29]

Radio is the most popular form of media within the British Jamaican community, approximately 75% of Jamaicans in the UK listen to the radio on a daily basis or very often.[29] Statistically pirate radio stations (which are stations which have no formal license to broadcast) are by far the most popular within the community. The same investigation as stated above showed that around one quarter of people surveyed preferred to listen to a specific pirate radio station.[29] Most pirate stations are community based, but there are some that broadcast to the whole country, the most frequently listened to pirate stations by British Jamaicans include *Vibes FM*, *Powerjam*, *Irie FM* and *Roots FM*.[29] Out of all legally licensed radio stations in the UK, the single most popular one prevailed as *Premier Christian Radio*, the BBC also has a relatively large Jamaican listening audience whilst local radio stations such as *Choice FM* in London and *New Style Radio 98.7FM* in Birmingham are also popular within the community (both of which are Black orientated).[29]

Music

A wide variety of music has its origins in Jamaica and in the 1960s when the UK's Jamaican community was beginning to emerge there was one hugely popular music genre, ska.[30] The genre which combines elements of Caribbean mento and calypso with American jazz and rhythm and blues became a major part of Jamaican mid-20th century culture, and the popularity of it also became evident in the Jamaican expatriate community in the UK. Despite the presence of Jamaicans in a number of countries at that time (such as the United States), ska music only really triumphed in the UK.[30] In 1962 there were three music labels releasing Jamaican music in the UK (Melodisc, Blue Beat Records and Island Records), as more and more Jamaicans moved to the UK, the country became a more lucrative market for artists than Jamaica itself.[30] "My Boy Lollipop" by Millie was one of the very first ska records to have an impact on the British population in general having charted at #2 on the UK Singles Chart in 1964.[30] Reggae music is another genre that was introduced to the UK through migrating Jamaicans, London-born Julian Marley son of legendary Bob Marley and member of the Rastafari movement is just one of the musicians who helped popularise reggae and Jamaican music in general in the UK.[31] A number of other British Jamaican musicians specialise in reggae and traditional Jamaican music, including Musical Youth[32] and Maxi Priest.[33] It should however be noted that although Reggae music originated in Jamaica, reggae musicians and reggae-influenced musicians now belong to a variety of ethnicites and nationalities in the UK (see white reggae and mixed race reggae). Second, third and fourth generation British Jamaican musicians have helped bridge the gap between traditional Jamaican music and contemporary global music. The X Factor Series 5 winner Alexandra Burke focuses mainly on the R&B, pop, soul genres,[34] Chipmunk primarily focuses on the hip-hop, grime, R&B and pop rap genres[35] whilst Goldie is a popular electronic music artist.[36] This most certainly shows the diverse array of music produced by the current generation of British Jamaican musicians, amongst some other current contemporary British musicians of Jamaican ancestry are Keisha Buchanan,[37] Alesha Dixon,[38] Jade Ewen,[39] Jamelia,[40] Kano[41] and Beverley Knight.[42]

Sport

Linford Christie was the first man to win every major 100m title in world athletics (and to this date the only British man to have done so).[43] Kelly Holmes was one of the success stories of the 2004 Summer Olympics having won multiple gold medals and still holding numerous British records in distance running.[44] Other notable British people of Jamaican origin who have successfully competed in the Olympic Games include Colin Jackson,[45] Louis Smith[46] and Tasha Danvers.[47] Besides athletics and gymnastics, British Jamaicans have also become heavily associated with the combat sport of boxing. Numerous Britons of Jamaican origin have become world renound for their skills in boxing. Frank Bruno is one of the more notable individuals, he won 40 out of 45 of his contests and heald the title of WBC Heavyweight Championship in the mid 1990's.[48] Chris Eubank also held world boxing titles including

Premiership footballer Darren Bent

Middleweight and Super Middleweight champion (Eubank's son, Chris Eubank, Jr. is also a well established boxer). Lennox Lewis of dual British/Canadian citizenship is one of the most successful boxers in the sports history, he is one of only five boxers who have won the Heavyweight championship three times.[49] Errol Christie is also a former boxer, he is the Guinness World Record holder for achieving the most amateur title wins.[50] In more recent times David Haye has become the new face of British Jamaican boxing, Haye has won numerous titles and in 2009 beat Nikolai Valuev to become the current WBA Heavyweight Champion (the fifth Briton to do so, and the third British Jamaican - the other two being Britons of Nigerian origin).[51] A number of the current England national football team have origins in Jamaica, including Darren Bent,[52] Aaron Lennon,[53] Theo Walcott[54] and Shaun Wright-Phillips.[55]

Television and film

An investigation by the IOM in 2007 found that 67% of British Jamaican respondents reported watching television on a daily basis, 10% had no particular preference as to what channels they watched.[56] 31% of respondents claimed to favour the original terrestrial commercial channels such as ITV1, Channel 4 and Five, whilst 23% of people stated a preference to satellite and cable channels such as MTV Base, the Hallmark Channel and Living.[56] There are a number of TV channels in the UK aimed at the Black British community, however none specifically at the British Jamaican community. The same IOM investigation found that minimal numbers of British Jamaicans actually watch these black-orientated channels, this is thought to be down to a heavy focus on Black African culture and issues (as opposed to Afro-Caribbean).[56] In terms of actual members of the British Jamaican community, a number of individuals have found fame in television and film in the UK, and even across the world. Manchester-born Marsha Thomason is noted for her roles in the US shows Las Vegas and Lost,[57] whilst Oxfordshire-born Wentworth Miller of Prison Break fame is also of partial Jamaican descent.[58] Some British Jamaicans to have starred in Hollywood blockbusters include Naomie Harris in Miami Vice and Pirates of the Caribbean[59] and Adrian Lester in The Day After Tomorrow.[60]

See also

- Black British
- Black British population
- British Mixed
- British Indo-Caribbean community
- British African-Caribbean community
- Classification of ethnicity in the United Kingdom
- Jamaicans of African ancestry

References

[1] Conway, Dennis (2005). "Transnationalism and return: 'Home' as an enduring fixture and anchor" (http://books.google.co.uk/ books?id=jM_Yu9Ukud0C&lpg=PA268&dq="British Jamaicans"&pg=PA268#v=onepage&q&f=false). In Potter, Robert B.; Conway, Dennis; Phillips, Joan. *The Experience of Return Migration: Caribbean Perspectives*. Aldershot: Ashgate. p. 268. ISBN 0754643298. .

[2] Dimeo, Paul (2001). "Contemporary developments in Indian football". *Contemporary South Asia* 10 (2): 251–264. doi:10.1080/09584930120083846.

[3] "Jamaica: Mapping exercise" (http://www.iomlondon.org/doc/mapping/IOM_JAMAICA.pdf). London: International Organization for Migration. July 2007. . Retrieved 11 May 2010.

[4] "Estimated population resident in the United Kingdom, by foreign country of birth (Table 1.3)" (http://www.statistics.gov.uk/downloads/ theme_population/Population-by-country-of-birth-and-nationality-Oct08-Sep09.zip). Office for National Statistics. September 2009. . Retrieved 8 July 2010.

[5] Bennetto, Jason (2 August 2000). "Yardies" (http://www.independent.co.uk/news/uk/this-britain/yardies-710989.html). London: The Independent. . Retrieved 31 July 2010.

[6] "The World Factbook: Jamaica" (https://www.cia.gov/library/publications/the-world-factbook/geos/jm.html). Central Intelligence Agency. . Retrieved 11 May 2010.

[7] "Caribbean participants in the First World War" (http://www.mgtrust.org/car1.htm). Memorial Gates Trust. . Retrieved 11 May 2010.

[8] "The 'forgotten' race riot" (http://news.bbc.co.uk/1/hi/uk/6675793.stm). BBC. 21 May 2007. . Retrieved 11 May 2010.

[9] "Riots in Brixton after police shooting" (http://news.bbc.co.uk/onthisday/hi/dates/stories/september/28/newsid_2540000/2540397. stm). BBC. 28 September 1985. . Retrieved 11 May 2010.

[10] "Fear and rumours grip Birmingham" (http://news.bbc.co.uk/1/hi/uk/4373040.stm). BBC. 25 October 2005. . Retrieved 11 May 2010.

[11] "Q&A: Stephen Lawrence murder" (http://news.bbc.co.uk/1/hi/uk/3685733.stm). BBC. 5 May 2004. . Retrieved 11 May 2010.

[12] "Country-of-birth database" (http://www.oecd.org/dataoecd/18/23/34792376.xls). Organisation for Economic Co-operation and Development. . Retrieved 27 February 2009.

[13] "Jamaica: Mapping exercise" (http://www.iomlondon.org/doc/mapping/IOM_JAMAICA.pdf). London: International Organization for Migration. July 2007. . Retrieved 12 May 2010.

[14] "Persons Granted British Citizenship, United Kingdom, 1997" (http://www.homeoffice.gov.uk/rds/pdfs/hosb998.pdf). Home Office. . Retrieved 11 May 2010.

[15] "Persons Granted British Citizenship, United Kingdom, 1998" (http://www.homeoffice.gov.uk/rds/pdfs/hosb699.pdf). Home Office. . Retrieved 11 May 2010.

[16] "Persons Granted British Citizenship, United Kingdom, 1999" (http://www.homeoffice.gov.uk/rds/pdfs/hosb1000.pdf). Home Office. . Retrieved 11 May 2010.

[17] "Persons Granted British Citizenship, United Kingdom, 2000" (http://www.homeoffice.gov.uk/rds/pdfs/hosb901.pdf). Home Office. . Retrieved 11 May 2010.

[18] "Persons Granted British Citizenship, United Kingdom, 2001" (http://www.homeoffice.gov.uk/rds/pdfs2/hosb602.pdf). Home Office. . Retrieved 11 May 2010.

[19] "Persons Granted British Citizenship, United Kingdom, 2002" (http://www.homeoffice.gov.uk/rds/pdfs2/hosb903.pdf). Home Office. . Retrieved 11 May 2010.

[20] "Persons Granted British Citizenship, United Kingdom, 2003" (http://www.homeoffice.gov.uk/rds/pdfs04/hosb0704.pdf). Home Office. . Retrieved 11 May 2010.

[21] "Persons Granted British Citizenship, United Kingdom, 2004" (http://www.homeoffice.gov.uk/rds/pdfs05/hosb0805.pdf). Home Office. . Retrieved 11 May 2010.

[22] "Persons Granted British Citizenship, United Kingdom, 2005" (http://www.homeoffice.gov.uk/rds/pdfs06/hosb0906.pdf). Home Office. . Retrieved 11 May 2010.

[23] "Persons Granted British Citizenship, United Kingdom, 2006" (http://www.homeoffice.gov.uk/rds/pdfs07/hosb0807.pdf). Home Office. . Retrieved 11 May 2010.

[24] "Persons Granted British Citizenship, United Kingdom, 2007" (http://www.homeoffice.gov.uk/rds/pdfs08/hosb0508.pdf). Home Office. . Retrieved 11 May 2010.

[25] "Persons Granted British Citizenship, United Kingdom, 2008" (http://www.homeoffice.gov.uk/rds/pdfs09/hosb0909.pdf). Home Office. . Retrieved 11 May 2010.

[26] "Ethnicity and Religion" (http://www.statistics.gov.uk/downloads/theme_compendia/foer2006/FoER_Main.pdf). Office of National Statistics. . Retrieved 12 May 2010.

[27] "First Impressions of England in 1964" (http://www.movinghere.org.uk/stories/story83/story83.htm?identifier=stories/story83/story83.htm). Moving Here Stories. . Retrieved 12 May 2010.

[28] "Carnival cravings" (http://www.bbc.co.uk/food/news_and_events/events_caribbeancuisine.shtml). BBC. . Retrieved 12 May 2010.

[29] "Jamaica: Mapping exercise" (http://www.iomlondon.org/doc/mapping/IOM_JAMAICA.pdf). London: International Organization for Migration. July 2007. . Retrieved 13 May 2010.

[30] "The History of Jamaican Music: Part 3" (http://www.globalvillageidiot.net/Jamaica3.html). Global Village Idiot. . Retrieved 3 June 2010.

[31] "Julian Marley biography" (http://www.entertainmentvybz.com/2010/01/26/julian-marley-biography/). Entertainmentvybz.com. . Retrieved 3 June 2010.

[32] "Musical Youth" (http://new.uk.music.yahoo.com/blogs/where_are_they_now/1761/musical-youth/?page=9). Yahoo Music. . Retrieved 3 June 2010.

[33] "Maxi Priest is new UB40 frontman" (http://www.expressandstar.com/latest/2008/03/14/maxi-priest-is-new-ub40-frontman/). Express & Star. . Retrieved 3 June 2010.

[34] "Alex's secret brother" (http://www.newsoftheworld.co.uk/showbiz/xfactor/72833/X-Factor-star-Alexandra-Burke-has-a-secret-half-brother.html). NewsoftheWorld. . Retrieved 3 June 2010.

[35] "Chipmunk happy to be a role model" (http://www.newhamrecorder.co.uk/content/newham/recorder/whatson/story.aspx?brand=RECOnline&category=whatsonclubmix&tBrand=northlondon24&tCategory=whatsonnewham&itemid=WeED27 Feb 2009 14:20:19:893). Newham Recorder. . Retrieved 3 June 2010.

[36] "Goldie: A maestro's dirty night at the Proms" (http://entertainment.timesonline.co.uk/tol/arts_and_entertainment/music/proms/article6078109.ece). London: Times Online. 12 April 2009. . Retrieved 3 June 2010.

[37] "Keisha Buchanan" (http://www.imdb.com/name/nm1104784/). IMDb. . Retrieved 3 June 2010.

[38] "Alesha Dixon: Jamaican food" (http://www.hellomagazine.com/celebrities/specials/covers/celebrities-favourite-foods/index.html?pagina=pagina_3_1.html). Hello Magazine. . Retrieved 3 June 2010.

[39] "Sugababe singer Jade Ewen" (http://www.dailyrecord.co.uk/showbiz/celebrity-news/2010/03/20/sugababe-singer-jade-ewen-on-her-blindness-torment-and-death-threats-86908-22125399/). Daily Record. . Retrieved 3 June 2010.

[40] "The 5-minute Interview: Jamelia, Singer-songwriter" (http://www.independent.co.uk/news/people/profiles/the-5minute-interview-jamelia-singersongwriter-397713.html). London: The Independent. 24 October 2007. . Retrieved 3 June 2010.

[41] "Kanosworld" (http://www.kanosworld.com/site/). Kanosworld. . Retrieved 3 June 2010.

[42] "Beverley Knight" (http://www.askmen.com/celebs/women/singer_250/276_beverley_knight.html). Ask Men. . Retrieved 3 June 2010.

[43] "Christie: Legend under fire" (http://news.bbc.co.uk/1/hi/sport/412020.stm). BBC. 4 August 1999. . Retrieved 25 May 2010.

[44] "Kelly Holmes on the perfect 800m" (http://news.bbc.co.uk/sport1/hi/athletics/get_involved/4264442.stm). BBC. 13 December 2005. . Retrieved 25 May 2010.

[45] "Colin Jackson" (http://www.bbc.co.uk/wales/southeast/halloffame/sport/colin_jackson.shtml). BBC. . Retrieved 25 May 2010.

[46] "Louis Smith" (http://www.olympics.org.uk/beijing2008/AthleteProfile.aspx?id=6695). Team GB. . Retrieved 25 May 2010.

[47] "Natasha Danvers" (http://www.olympics.org.uk/beijing2008/AthleteProfile.aspx?id=1000). Team GB. . Retrieved 25 May 2010.

[48] "Frank Bruno" (http://www.100greatblackbritons.com/bios/frank_bruno.html). 100 Great Britons. . Retrieved 25 May 2010.

[49] "Lennox Lewis" (http://www.100greatblackbritons.com/bios/lennox_lewis.html). 100 Great Britons. . Retrieved 25 May 2010.

[50] "How I Put the Black in the Union Jack" (http://www.blacknet.co.uk/UK/UK/how-i-put-the-black-in-the-union-jack-boxer-errol-christies-autobiography-out-now). Blacknet.co.uk. . Retrieved 25 May 2010.

[51] "David Haye" (http://www.guardian.co.uk/sport/davidhayeboxing). London: The Guardian. 17 April 2008. . Retrieved 25 May 2010.

[52] "Bent targets revival at Wigan" (http://news.bbc.co.uk/sport1/hi/football/teams/w/wigan_athletic/7009676.stm). BBC. 24 September 2007. . Retrieved 26 May 2010.

[53] "England Players Profiles - Aaron Lennon" (http://www.englandplayers.net/football/aaronlennon/index.html). Englandlayers.net. . Retrieved 26 May 2010.

[54] Fernandez, Colin (12 September 2008). "Theo Walcott became a national hero" (http://www.dailymail.co.uk/tvshowbiz/article-1054853/Theo-Walcott-national-hero--ask-mum-let-in.html). London: Daily Mail. . Retrieved 26 May 2010.

[55] "Shaun Wright-Phillips" (http://www.shaunwrightphillips.azplayers.com/). azplayers.com. . Retrieved 26 May 2010.

[56] "Jamaica: Mapping exercise" (http://www.iomlondon.org/doc/mapping/IOM_JAMAICA.pdf). London: International Organization for Migration. July 2007. . Retrieved 31 May 2010.

[57] "Biography for Marsha Thomason" (http://www.imdb.com/name/nm0859720/). IMDb. . Retrieved 31 May 2010.

[58] "Biography for Wentworth Miller" (http://www.imdb.com/name/nm0589505/bio). IMDb. . Retrieved 31 May 2010.

[59] "Pleasure island: Actress Naomie Harris returns to Jamaica for latest TV role" (http://www.dailymail.co.uk/travel/article-1228296/Pleasure-island-Actress-Naomie-Harris-returns-Jamaica-latest-TV-role.html). London: Daily Mail. 16 November 2009. . Retrieved 31 May

2010.

[60] "Empire's Children Episode 6 Adrian Lester" (http://www.channel4.com/programmes/empires-children/episode-guide/series-1/episode-6). Channel 4. . Retrieved 31 May 2010.

External links

• UK Caribbean Community site (http://www.itzcaribbean.com)

Jamaican diaspora

"Diaspora" means the scattering of people from their ethnic roots, enforced or voluntary. Thus the **Jamaican diaspora** refers to Jamaicans who have left their traditional homelands, the dispersal of such Jamaicans, and the ensuing developments in their culture. Jamaicans can be found in the far corners of the world but the largest pools of Jamaicans exist in the United States, United Kingdom, Canada, other Caribbean islands, and all across the Caribbean Coast of Central America.

Details

Over the past several decades, close to a million Jamaicans have emigrated, especially to the United States, the United Kingdom and Canada. This emigration appears to have been tapering off somewhat in recent years, however the great number of Jamaicans living abroad has become known as the "Jamaican diaspora". Most Jamaican emigrants have followed a path first to the UK. Many who do not remain in the UK move on to other Commonwealth countries such as Canada. Jamaican emigrants also migrate directly to the United States, Canada, other Caribbean nations, Central & South America (mainly in Panama and Colombia),[1] and even Africa (most notably Egypt and Ethiopia). There has also been emigration of Jamaicans to Cuba[2] and to Nicaragua.[3]

The United Kingdom, and in particular London, has a strong Jamaican diaspora. An estimated 7% of Londoners are of Jamaican heritage. Many are now at least second-, if not third- or fourth-generation Black British Caribbeans. Also a further 2% of people in London are of mixed Jamaican and British origin, the largest mixed-race group of the country and the fastest-growing.

One of the largest and most famous Jamaican expatriate communities is in Brixton, South London. More large Jamaican communities in London are Tottenham and Hackney in North London, Harlesden in North-West London, and Lewisham in South-East London. The highest concentration of Jamaicans are in the Inner-city South London boroughs.

On the last bank holiday of the year during late August the Annual Notting Hill Carnival takes place in west London which is the second biggest street party in the world after Rio Carnival. It spans areas of west London such as Shepherd's Bush, Ladbroke Grove, White City and of course Notting Hill. Many other Caribbean nations have large communities in this part of London such as Trinidad and Tobago, Barbados and Antigua. The Caribbean community including many Jamaicans are involved in the Carnival which starts on Saturday and finishes late on Monday. Jamaicans have many food stalls, soundsystems and floats involved in the procession. Well over a million Londoners come to Notting Hill on the Monday. There is also a much smaller carnival called the Tottenham Carnival which takes place in Tottenham during June, approximately 40,000 people attend. Other Jamaican communities include the areas of St Pauls in Bristol, Chapeltown in Leeds, Moss Side, Longsight and Hulme in Manchester, Toxteth in Liverpool, Burngreave in Sheffield, Handsworth, Lozells, and Aston in Birmingham, and St Ann's, Nottingham.

Concentrations of expatriate Jamaicans are large in a number of cities in the United States, including New York City, Buffalo, the Miami metro area, Atlanta, Orlando, Tampa, Baltimore, Washington, D.C., Philadelphia, Hartford, and Los Angeles. In Canada, the Jamaican population is centred in Toronto, and there are smaller communities in cities such as Hamilton, Montreal, Vancouver and Ottawa. In the United Kingdom, Jamaican communities exist in most large cities where they make up the larger part of the British-Caribbean community. Jamaicans are also present in Ireland, mostly concentrated in Dublin.

New York City is home to a large Jamaican diaspora community, with communities along Flatbush, Nostrand and Utica Avenues in Brooklyn—centred around the neighbourhoods of Prospect Heights, Lefferts Gardens, Flatbush, East Flatbush, Crown Heights, Canarsie, and Flatlands. The Bronx, neighbourhoods and towns such as Wakefield, Eastchester, Baychester, Queens, Westchester County and nearby Stamford, Connecticut also have significant Jamaican ex-pat communities. Flatbush, Nostrand, and Utica Avenues feature miles of Jamaican cuisine, food markets and other businesses, nightlife and residential enclaves.

In Toronto, the Jamaican community is also large. Caribbean areas of the city are located in the neighbourhoods of Rexdale in Etobicoke, Jane and Finch and Lawrence Heights in North York, Malvern in Scarborough, sections of Downtown Toronto, and York, which also includes a Little Jamaica district that is identifiable along Eglinton Avenue West. In recent years, many Jamaicans have been moving out to suburbs such as Mississauga and Brampton. The Jamaican community has had an influence on Toronto's culture. Caribana (the celebration of Caribbean culture) is an annual event in the city. The parade is held downtown on the first Saturday of August, shutting down a portion of Lake Shore Boulevard. Jamaica Day is in July, and the Jesus in the City parade attracts many Jamaican Christians. Reggae and dancehall are popular among Toronto's youth.

More recently many resort and wild-life management skilled Jamaicans have been trending emigration toward such far-flung nations as Australia, New Zealand, the Philippines, Malaysia and Indonesia. The nation continues to have a severe problem with barrel children--those left on their own by parents seeking a better life abroad.

Locations

United Kingdom

UK - around 800,000 Britons of Jamaican origin.[4] Located especially in London, Birmingham, Nottingham, Liverpool, Manchester, Sheffield and Leeds.

United States

US - around 911,000[5] especially in New York City (416,000), South Florida and elsewhere.

Canada

Canada - around 231,000[6] especially in the Toronto metropolitan area (around 160,000),[6] including Brampton (around 31,000).[6]

References

[1] Jamaicans - joshuaproject.com (http://www.joshuaproject.net/peoples.php?peo3=12316)

[2] "Cuba" (http://www.webcitation.org/query?id=1257038432976077). Microsoft Encarta. Archived from the original (http://encarta.msn.com/encyclopedia_761569844_2/Cuba.html) on 2009-11-01. . Retrieved 2008-08-31.

[3] "Nicaragua" (http://www.webcitation.org/5kwrjYMVg). Microsoft Encarta. Archived from the original (http://encarta.msn.com/encyclopedia_761577584_3/Nicaragua.html) on 2009-10-31. . Retrieved 2008-08-31.

[4] "Jamaica Mapping Exercise" (http://www.iomlondon.org/doc/mapping/IOM_JAMAICA.pdf). International Organization for Migration. . Retrieved 2010-04-06.

[5] "Census 2000 Detailed Tables: Ancestry" (http://factfinder.census.gov/servlet/DTTable?_bm=y&-context=dt&-ds_name=DEC_2000_SF3_U&-mt_name=DEC_2000_SF3_U_PCT018&-CONTEXT=dt&-tree_id=403&-redoLog=true&-all_geo_types=N&-geo_id=01000US&-search_results=01000US&-format=&-_lang=en&-SubjectID=14595646). US Census Bureau. . Retrieved 2008-08-31.

[6] "Ethnological Portrait of Canada, 2006 Census" (http://www12.statcan.ca/english/census06/data/highlights/ethnic/pages/Page.cfm?Lang=E&Geo=PR&Code=01&Data=Count&Table=2&StartRec=1&Sort=3&Display=All&CSDFilter=5000). Statistics Canada. . Retrieved 2008-08-31.

Office for National Statistics

Office for National Statistics	
Office for National Statistics logo	
Abbreviation	ONS
Formation	1996
Legal status	Non-Ministerial Government Department
Location	Cardiff Road, Newport, South Wales, NP10 8XG
Region served	UK
Director General	Stephen Penneck
Website	ONS [1]

The **Office for National Statistics (ONS)** is the executive office of the UK Statistics Authority, a non-ministerial department which reports directly to the Parliament of the United Kingdom.

Overview

It is charged with the collection and publication of statistics related to the economy, population and society of the United Kingdom at national and local levels. It functions as the office of the National Statistician, who is also the UK Statistics Authority's Chief Executive and principal statistical adviser to the UK's National Statistics Institute[2] and the 'Head Office' of the Government Statistical Service (GSS). Its main office is in Newport near the United Kingdom Intellectual Property Office and Tredegar House, but another significant office is in Titchfield in Hampshire, and an administrative office on *Myddelton Street* in Islington, the former home of the Family Records Centre. This office moved from *Drummond Gate* in Pimlico in 2008.

History

The ONS was formed on 1 April 1996 by the merger of the Central Statistical Office (CSO) and the Office of Population Censuses and Surveys (OPCS).[3] Following the Statistics and Registration Service Act 2007, the United Kingdom Statistics Authority became a non-ministerial department on the 1 April 2008[4].

Purpose and scope

ONS produces and publishes a wide range of the information about Britain that can be used for social and economic policy-making as well as painting a portrait of the country as its population evolves over time. This is often produced in ways that make comparison with other societies and economies possible. Much of the data on which policy-makers depend is produced by ONS through a combination of a decennial population census, samples and surveys and analysis of data generated by businesses and organisations such as the National Health Service and the register of births, marriages and deaths. Both its publications and its publicly-available raw data, available free, are reported and discussed daily in the media as the basis for the public understanding of the country in which they live.

Applications of data

The reliance on some of these data by government (both local and national) makes ONS material central to debates about the determination of priorities, the allocation of resources and for decisions on interest rates or borrowing. The complexity and degree and speed of change in the society, combined with the challenge of measuring some of these (e.g. in relation to longevity, migration or illness patterns or fine movements in inflation or other aspects of national accounts) give rise to periodic debates about some of its indicators and portrayals. Many of these rely on sources which are outside of ONS, while some of its own sources need to be supplemented, for example between censuses, by updated but less rigorously-obtained information from other sources. Consequently, unexpected or incomplete data or occasional errors or disputes about its analysis can also attract considerable attention.

Independence

Gordon Brown, then Chancellor of the Exchequer, announced on 28 November 2005,[5] that the government intended to publish plans in early 2006 to legislate to render the ONS and the statistics it generates independent of government on a model based on the independence of the Monetary Policy Committee of the Bank of England.[6] This was originally a 1997 Labour manifesto commitment[7] and was also the policy of the Liberal Democrat[8] and Conservative[9] parties. Such independence was also sought by the Royal Statistical Society[10] and the Statistics Commission.[11] The National Statistician would be directly accountable to Parliament through a more widely-constituted independent governing Statistics Board.[12] The ONS would be a non-ministerial government department so that the staff, including the Director, would remain as civil servants but without being under direct ministerial control.[13] The National Statistician, Dame Karen Dunnell, stated that legislation would help improve public trust in official statistics[14] although the ONS already acts independently according to its own published guidelines, the National Statistics Code of Practice,[15] which sets out the key principles and standards that official statisticians, including those in other parts of the government statistical service, are expected to follow and uphold.

The details of the plans for independence were considered in Parliament during the 2006/2007 session and resulted in the Statistics and Registration Service Act 2007.[16] In July 2007, Sir Michael Scholar was nominated by the government to be the three day-a-week non-executive chairman of the Statistics Board which, to re-establish faith in the integrity of government statistics, will take on statutory responsibility for oversight of UK statistics in April 2008 and oversee the Office for National Statistics. It will also have a duty to assess all UK government statistics. Following Gordon Brown's announcement of new constitutional arrangements for public appointments, Sir Michael also became, on 18 July, the first such nominee to appear before the House of Commons Treasury Committee and to have his nomination subject to confirmation by the House.[17] On 7 February 2008, following the first meeting of the shadow board, it was announced that it will be known as the UK Statistics Authority (UKSA).

In addition to Sir Michael Scholar, the non-executive chairman, members of the UK Statistics Authority Board are: Non-executive members, appointed in open competition: Lord Rowe-Beddoe of Kilgetty, deputy chairman responsible for governance of the Office for National Statistics, Professor Sir Roger Jowell CBE, deputy chairman with responsibility for oversight of the UK official statistics system, Colette Bowe, Partha Dasgupta, Moira Gibb CBE, Professor Steve Nickell CBE FBA, Professor David Rhind CBE FRS FBA, and Sir Jon Shortridge KCB. Executive members: Jil Matheson (National Statistician), Richard Alldritt (Head of Assessment) and Stephen Penneck (Director General, Office for National Statistics).

Heads of the Office: National Statistician

Directors are *de facto* Permanent Secretaries but do not use that title. As the ONS previously incorporated the OPCS, the Director was also the Registrar General for England and Wales, although the recent changes saw the transfer of this function away from the ONS. In addition, he or she is *ex officio* the Head of the Government Statistical Service. The first Director of ONS was Professor Tim Holt. Subsequent Directors have had an additional title, the National Statistician. The second Director was Len Cook. He was succeeded by Karen Dunnell on 1 September 2005[18] , then Jil Matheson in September 2009. Following the implementation of the Statistics & Registration Service Act, the General Register Office continues to be part of a ministerially-accountable department and became a part of the Home Office. The title of Registrar-General moved with it and is no longer held by the National Statistician.

Work of the ONS

Where data is broken down by geographical area, this is usually done by the areas defined in the ONS geographical coding system.

Data collection

The principal areas of data collection are:

- Agriculture, Fishing and Forestry
- Commerce, Energy and Industry
- Crime and Justice
- Economy
- Education and Training
- Health and Care (Among numerous regular surveys, such as the General Household Survey, the Labour Force Survey and the UK National Census that takes place every 10 years, ONS runs the England and Wales Longitudinal Survey, which monitors the health, address changes and fertility of a 1% sample of the population of England and Wales over time for statistical purposes).
- Labour Market
- Natural and Built Environment
- Population and Migration
- Public Sector and Other
- Social and Welfare
- Transport, Travel and Tourism

Statisticians are also employed by many other Government departments and agencies, and these statisticians often collect and publish data. They are members of the *Government Statistical Service* and are the professional responsibility of the head of the service, who is also the National Statistician. Each department has a statistical service *Head of Profession*. For example, data on Agriculture, Fishing and Forestry comes primarily from the Department for the Environment, Food and Rural Affairs. Along with economic data on which the Treasury and Bank of England rely for decision-making, many of the statistics that receive widespread media attention are issued by the Home Office, the Department of Health, and the Department for Education and Skills. ONS is also responsible for the maintenance of the *Inter-Departmerntal Business Register* and the *Business Structure Database*.[19]

Former departments

Prior to the establishment of the UK Statistics Authority, the statistical work of ONS, since June 2000, was scrutinized by the Statistics Commission, an independent body with its own chairman and small staff. This ceased to operate from 1 April 2008. The General Register Office and the post of Registrar-General for England & Wales ceased to be part of ONS from that date but remains subject to ministerial accountability within the Home Office.

The Blue Book

Annually, the Office for National Statistics publish their findings in the so-called *Blue Book*. It contains the estimates of the domestic and national product, income and expenditure of the United Kingdom, and is available as hardcopy, as well as a web version.[20]

Education of Statisticians

The Office for National Statistics collaborates with the University of Southampton in the teaching of a MSc in Official Statistics, the programme has been in running since 2003.[21]

Office Locations

The ONS has a head office in the city of Newport, South Wales, and other offices in Islington in London and Titchfield in Hampshire.[22] The Family Records Centre in Myddelton Street in Islington,[22] London, moved to the National Archives in Kew during the first half of 2008, with the building taken over by staff vacating the Pimlico site (1 Drummond Gate).

ONS London office, 1 Drummond Gate

Former Headquarters

The London (Pimlico) office was the head office until April 2006 when the corporate headquarters was moved to Newport[23] following the Lyons Review[24] on public sector relocation. Initially, the London office was in three buildings but due to reductions, London staff are now in Myddelton Street. This London office is expected to house few staff by April 2010 by which time the ONS policy is for its statistical activities to be concentrated in Titchfield and Newport[25]

Gradual move of functions to South Wales

The ONS asserts that recruitment and training of quality staff in South Wales, where data collection and analysis already takes place, will ensure that there is no risk to the quality of its services and that it is managing the risks associated with the changes which it is implementing in a planned and gradual way.[26] However the plan to discontinue all remaining statistical activity in London is proving controversial amid claims that the shift of functions from London and the impending closure of the London office could have serious implications for the future of certain particular sets of statistics. These include health statistics, National Accounts, Retail and Consumer Prices and Labour Market Statistics. These risks derive from the fact that few of the experienced staff working in these highly technical areas are expected to be willing to relocate to Newport, resulting in a substantial loss of expertise and a consequent threat to the continued quality of the statistics.[27] In a submission to the Parliamentary Treasury Sub Committee, the Bank of England too has expressed concern over the relocation of the ONS to Newport, saying, that *"the relocation programme poses serious risks to the maintenance of the quality of macroeconomic data. If substantial numbers of ONS staff are unwilling to relocate, the loss of skilled individuals could have a severe impact on a range of statistics."*[28] [29] The director of ONS has vigorously defended ONS implementation of government policy on civil service relocation and the decision to concentrate staff in the three locations outside London.[30]

Criticism of the ONS

Len Cook, when National Statistician, described himself as the country's most abused civil servant.[31] Occasional errors and revisions accounts for some past criticism while the allocation of Private Finance Initiative expenditure (albeit following OECD and international statistical guidelines according to who carries the risk) has attracted political attention.

Many of the most controversial topics for statistics issued by government do not come from ONS though they are expected to meet *National Statistics* standards. Crime statistics and other data (e.g. health and education) that could be deemed to assess the effectiveness of government policies often attract media scepticism. The compulsory nature of the census (unlike most other surveys by academics and market researchers) differentiates ONS from other data collectors (apart from HM Revenue and Customs). The Office for National Statistics won the 2004 Big Brother Award for the "Most Heinous Government Organisation" from the campaigning organisation Privacy International for its Citizen Information Project. The project is one of several that lead the Information Commissioner to warn that there is a danger of the country "sleepwalking" into a surveillance society.[32] There has also been criticism of the ONS and of the government for its pursuit of government policies for modernization and for relocation to sites outside London. It is not moving to a single site and will continue to perform most of its functions from the two sites in Newport and Titchfield while reducing its London operation to one eventual small location.

See also

- United Kingdom Census 2001
- Departments of the United Kingdom Government
- Northern Ireland Statistics and Research Agency
- List of national and international statistical services

References

[1] http://www.ons.gov.uk
[2] 'National Statistics Institute' and NSI are a standard expression and its acronym used about statistical services in OECD & EU terminology
[3] John Pullinger (1997) *"The Creation of the Office for National Stfstics"* (http://links.jstor.org/ sici?sici=0306-7734(199712)65:3<291:TCOTOF>2.0.CO;2-2&size=LARGE&origin=JSTOR-enlargePage), *International Statistical Review*, Vol. 65, No. 3, pp. 291-308
[4] The Statistics Act: Office for National Statistics (http://www.statistics.gov.uk/about/data/independence/thestatisticsact.asp)
[5] Statement to the House of Commons on the review of the Framework for National Statistics (http://www.publications.parliament.uk/pa/ cm200506/cmhansrd/vo051128/text/51128w20.htm#51128w20.html_spnew7), by the Chancellor of the Exchequer, 28 November 2005.
[6] Budget Statement (http://www.hm-treasury.gov.uk/budget/budget_06/bud_bud06_speech.cfm) made by the Chancellor of the Exchequer, 22 March 2006
[7] Labour Party Manifesto, General Election 1997 (http://www.psr.keele.ac.uk/area/uk/man/lab97.htm), Keele University website.
[8] Liberal Democrats Manifesto General Election 2005 (http://www.libdems.org.uk/media/documents/policies/manifesto2005.pdf).
[9] *"Let Parliament appoint new UK statistics chief"* (http://www.conservatives.com/tile.do?def=news.story.page&obj_id=126557), press release from Conservative Party website.
[10] *"A Vision for National Statistics"* (http://www.rss.org.uk/pdf/A Vision for National Statistics.pdf), Royal Statistical Society.
[11] *"Legislation to build trust in statistics"* (http://www.statscom.org.uk/uploads/files/reports/LegislationToBuildTrust.pdf), a report by the Statistics Commission.
[12] *"Statistics And Registration Service Bill"* (http://www.publications.parliament.uk/pa/cm200607/cmbills/008/en/07008x--.htm), House of Commons Explanatory Note to the Bill, para. 7-8. Retrieved 10 June 2007.
[13] *"Statistics And Registration Service Bill"* (http://www.publications.parliament.uk/pa/cm200607/cmbills/008/en/07008x--.htm), House of Commons Explanatory Note to the Bill, para. 42. Retrieved 10 June 2007.
[14] *"National Statistician welcomes Statistics and Registration Service Bill"* (http://www.statistics.gov.uk/pdfdir/nsa1106.pdf), news release from ONS website.
[15] *"National Statistics Code of Practice"* (http://www.statistics.gov.uk/about/national_statistics/cop/default.asp) ONS website

[16] *"Statistics and Registration Service Bill"* (http://www.publications.parliament.uk/pa/pabills/200607/statistics_and_registration_service. htm), progress of the Bill through the UK Parliament from Parliament website.

[17] *"Whitehall veteran in frame for statistics chief post"* (http://www.ft.com/cms/s/75076a4e-34c7-11dc-8c78-0000779fd2ac.html), Financial Times, 18 July 2007.

[18] *"National Statistician - Director Office for National Statistics"* (http://www.number-10.gov.uk/output/Page8038.asp), 10 Downing Street press notice, 4 August 2005, retrieved 9 June 2007.

[19] (http://www.berr.gov.uk/files/file51198.pdf)

[20] United Kingdom National Accounts (http://www.statistics.gov.uk/downloads/theme_economy/BlueBook2006.pdf) - The Blue Book 2006

[21] MSc in Official Statistics, University of Southampton. (http://www.socstats.soton.ac.uk/moffstat/)

[22] Office for National Statistics: location maps (http://www.statistics.gov.uk/about_ns/locations/onsmaps.asp), www.statistics.gov.uk, retrieved 10 June 2007.

[23] *"Newport to be ONS headquarters"* (http://www.gnn.gov.uk/imagelibrary/downloadMedia.asp?MediaDetailsID=77252), National Statistics news release, 20 September 2004, retrieved 9 June 2007.

[24] *"The Lyons Review: Independent Review of public sector relocation"* (http://www.hm-treasury.gov.uk/consultations_and_legislation/ lyons/consult_lyons_index.cfm#final), HM Treasury website.

[25] *"ONS set to close down London HQ"* (http://news.bbc.co.uk/1/hi/business/6267087.stm), news report from the BBC website.

[26] *"Stats staff 'quitting' over move"* (http://news.bbc.co.uk/1/hi/wales/south_east/6653771.stm), news report from the BBC website, 14 May 2007.

[27] Debate on the Statistics and Registration Service Bill (http://www.publications.parliament.uk/pa/ld200607/ldhansrd/text/70424-0007. htm) in the House of Lords, 24 April 2007, Hansard, Column 597.

[28] *"Bank of England comments on recent ONS performance"* (http://www.bankofengland.co.uk/publications/other/monetary/ treasurycommittee/onsperformance070509.pdf), a submission made by the Bank of England to the Treasury Sub-Committee inquiry into progress on the efficiency programme in the Chancellor's departments, May 2007.

[29] *"Bank warns on ONS move to Wales"* (http://news.bbc.co.uk/1/hi/business/6642897.stm), news report from the BBC website, 10 May 2007.

[30] *"Statistics officers get the measure of relocation"* (http://www.ft.com/cms/s/d664845a-1237-11dc-b963-000b5df10621.html), article by Karen Dunnell, Financial Times, 4 June 2007, retrieved 7 June 2007.

[31] Minutes of evidence given before the Select Committee on Treasury (http://www.publications.parliament.uk/pa/cm200102/cmselect/ cmtreasy/1289/2103009.htm), 30 October 2002.

[32] *"Beware rise of Big Brother state, warns data watchdog"* (http://www.timesonline.co.uk/tol/news/uk/article470264.ece), Times Online, 16 August 2004.

External links

- Office for National Statistics website (http://www.statistics.gov.uk/default.asp)
- UK Statistics Authority (http://www.statisticsauthority.gov.uk)
- The National Statistics Publication Hub (http://www.statistics.gov.uk/hub/index.html)
- Statistics and Registration Service Bill (http://www.hm-treasury.gov.uk/consultations_and_legislation/ statistics_bill/statistics_bill_index.cfm), Treasury website.
- Statistics and Registration Service Bill (http://www.publications.parliament.uk/pa/pabills/200607/ statistics_and_registration_service.htm), Parliament website.
- Palgrave Macmillan, official publisher for the Office for National Statistics (http://www.palgrave.com/ons/)

History of Jamaica

Jamaica, the 3rd largest Caribbean island, was inhabited by Arawak natives. When Christopher Columbus arrived at the island, he claimed the land for Spain. Still, it was not truly colonized until after his death. But only a few decades after Columbus' death almost all Arawaks were disappearing . Spain held the island against many buccaneer raids at the main city, which is now called Spanish Town. Eventually England claimed the island in a raid, but the Spanish did not relinquish their claim to the island until 1670.

Jamaica became a base of operations for buccaneers, including Captain Henry Morgan. In return these buccaneers kept the other colonial powers from attacking the island. Africans were captured, kidnapped, and forced into slavery to work on plantations when sugarcane became the most important export on the island.

Many slaves arrived in Jamaica via the Atlantic slave trade during the same time enslaved Africans arrived in North America. During this time there were many racial tensions, and Jamaica had one of the highest instances of slave uprisings of any Caribbean island.[1] After the

The aftermath of the 1882 Kingston fire.

British crown abolished slavery, the Jamaicans began working toward independence. Since independence there have been political and economic disturbances, as well as a number of strong political leaders.

Spanish rule

The settlers later moved to Villa de la Vega, now called Spanish Town. This settlement became the capital of Jamaica. By the 1640s many people were attracted to Jamaica, which had a reputation for stunning beauty, not only when referring to the island but also to the natives. In fact, pirates were known to desert their raiding parties and stay on the island. For 100 years between 1555 and 1655 Spanish Jamaica was subject to many pirate attacks, the final attack left the island in the hands of the English. The English were also subject to pirate raids after they began their occupation of the island.

The 1907 *Catholic Encyclopedia* states, "A review of the period of Spanish occupation is one which reflects very little credit on Spanish colonial administration in those days. Their treatment of the aboriginal inhabitants, whom they are accused of having practically exterminated, is a grave charge, and if true, cannot be condoned on the plea that such conduct was characteristic of the age, and that as bad or worse was perpetrated by other nations even in later years." This is borne out by the much more detailed history of Spanish Jamaica by Francisco Morales Padrón.

British rule

In 1655, General-at-Sea William Penn and General Robert Venables seized Jamaica without orders in the name of England's Lord Protector Oliver Cromwell, seeking to make up for the disastrous failure of the mission Cromwell had assigned them: to seize Hispaniola. Spanish resistance continued for some years thereafter, in some cases with the help of the maroons, but Spain never succeeded in retaking the island. Under early English rule Jamaica became a haven of privateers, buccaneers, and occasionally outright pirates: Christopher Myngs, Edward Mansvelt, and most famously, Henry Morgan.

A depiction of daily life in Jamaica from the early nineteenth century. Watercolor, ink, and pencil. Created between 1808 and 1816.

The cultivation of sugar cane and coffee by African slave labour made Jamaica one of the most valuable possessions in the world for more than 150 years. The colony's slaves, who outnumbered their white masters by a ratio of 20:1 in 1800, mounted over a dozen major slave conspiracies and uprisings during the 18th century, including Tacky's revolt in 1760. Escaped slaves known as Maroons established independent communities in the mountainous interior that the British were unable to suppress, despite major attempts in the 1730s and 1790s. One Maroon community was expelled from the island after the Second Maroon War in the 1790s, and those Maroons eventually became part of the core of the Creole community of Sierra Leone. The colonial government enlisted the Maroons in capturing escaped plantation slaves. The British also used Jamaica's free people of color, 10,000 strong by 1800, to keep the enslaved population in check. During the Christmas holiday of 1831, a large scale slave revolt known as the Baptist War broke. It was organised originally as a peaceful strike by Samuel Sharpe. The rebellion was suppressed by the militia of the Jamaican plantocracy and the British garrison ten days later in early 1832.

Because the loss of property and life in the 1831 rebellion, the British Parliament held two inquiries. The results of these inquiries contributed greatly to the abolition of slavery as of August 1, 1834 throughout the British Empire. However the Jamaican slaves remained bound to their former owners' service, albeit with a guarantee of rights, until 1838 under what was called the Apprenticeship System. The freed population still faced significant hardships, marked by the October 1865 Morant Bay rebellion led by and Paul Bogle. It was brutally repressed. George William Gordon, a friend of Paul Bogle, was hanged because he was thought to have contributed to the riot even though he was not a part of its organization or execution. The sugar crop was declining in importance in the late 19th century and the colony diversified into bananas.

In 1872 the capital was moved to Kingston, as the port city had far outstripped the inland Spanish Town in size and sophistication.

In 1866 the Jamaican legislature renounced its powers, and the country became a crown colony. Some measure of self-government was restored in the 1880s, when islanders gained the right to elect nine members of a legislative council.

The establishment of Crown Colony rule resulted over the next few decades in the growth of a middle class of low-level public officials and police officers drawn from the mass of the population whose social and political advancement was blocked by the colonial authorities.

The Great Depression had a serious impact both on the emergent middle class and the working class of the 1930s. In the spring of 1938 sugar and dock workers around the island rose in revolt. Although the revolt was suppressed it led to significant changes including the emergence of an organized labour movement and a competitive party system.

Independent Jamaica

Jamaica gained a degree of local political control in the mid-1940's. The People's National Party (PNP) was founded in 1938. Its main rival, the Jamaica Labour Party (JLP) was established five years later. The first elections under universal adult suffrage were held in 1944. Jamaica joined nine other UK territories in the Federation of the West Indies in 1958 but withdrew after Jamaican voters rejected membership in 1961. Jamaica gained independence on August 6, 1962, remaining a member of the Commonwealth of Nations. The first prime minister was Alexander Bustamante of the Jamaica Labour Party.

Initially, power swapped between the People's National Party and the Jamaican Labour Party regularly. Michael Manley was the first PNP prime minister in 1972 and he introduced socialist policies and relations with Cuba. His second term elections marked the start of repeated political violence. When the PNP lost power in 1980 Edward Seaga immediately began to reverse the policies of his predecessor, bringing in privatization and seeking closer ties with the USA. When the PNP and Manley returned to power in 1989 they continued the more moderate policies and were returned in the elections of 1993 and 1998. Manley resigned for health reasons in 1992 and was succeeded as leader of the PNP by Percival Patterson.

Historically, Jamaican emigration has been heavy. In the late 19th and early 20th centuries, many Jamaicans migrated to Central America, Cuba, and the Dominican Republic to work in the banana and canefields. In the 1950s the primary destination was to the United Kingdom; but since the United Kingdom restricted emigration in 1962, major flow has been to the United States and Canada. The heaviest flow of emigration particularly to New York, and Miami occurred during the 1990s and continues to the present day due to high economical crisis. About 100 Jamaicans emigrate to the United States each year; another 200,000 visit annually. New York, Miami, and Fort Lauderdale are among the U.S. cities with the largest Jamaican population. In New York, over half of Jamaican expatriates reside in Brooklyn. Remittances from the expatriate communities in the United States, United Kingdom, and Canada make increasingly significant contributions to Jamaica's economy.

References

- Black, Clinton V. 1983. *The Story of Jamaica*. London: Collins Educational.
- Ledgister, F.S.J. 1998. *Class Alliances and the Liberal-Authoritarian State: The Roots of Post-Colonial Democracy in Jamaica, Trinidad and Tobago, and Surinam*. Trenton: Africa World Press.
- Morales Padrón, Francisco. 1953 2003. *Spanish Jamaica*. Kingston: Ian Randle Publishers.
- Williams, Eric. 1964. *British Historians and the West Indies*. P.N.M. Publishing Company, Port-of-Spain.
- Sawh, Gobin, Ed. 1992. **The Canadian Caribbean Connection:** *Bridging North and South: History, Influences, Lifestyles*. Carindo Cultural Assoc., Halifax.
- Cobourne Trudy, giberish

Notes

[1] "Jamaica History" (http://jamaica-guide.info/past.and.present/history/). . Retrieved 2008-05-11.

Further reading

- Michener, James, A. 1989. *Caribbean*. Secker & Warburg. London. ISBN 0-436-27971-1 (Especially Chap. XI. "Martial Law in Jamaica", pp. 403-442. Semi-fictional but mainly accurate).
- Kurlansky, Mark. 1992. *A Continent of Islands: Searching for the Caribbean Destiny*. Addison-Wesley Publishing. ISBN 0-201-52396-5.
- Barringer, Tim., Forrester, Gillian. and Martinez-Ruiz, Barbaro. 2007. *Art and Empancipation in Jamaica: Isaac Mendes Belisario and His Worlds*. Yale University Press. New Haven and London. ISBN 978-0-300-11661-8

External links

- History of Jamaica (http://www.itzcaribbean.com/jamaicahistory)
- History of Jamaica (http://www.historyofnations.net/northamerica/jamaica.html) - Offers a history of the island from 1494 to the present.
- Jamaica (http://www.newadvent.org/cathen/08270a.htm) - Entry from the 1907 *Catholic Encyclopedia* on Jamaica.

British African-Caribbean community

British African-Caribbean

(British Afro-Caribbean)

Total population
UK, 2001: 565,900[1]
(approximately 1.00% of the British population)
England, 2007: 599,700[2]
(approximately 1.20% of the English population)
(Not including those of partial Afro-Caribbean origin, for example 2007 estimates put the number of people of mixed Afro-Caribbean and White origin in England alone at 282,900)[2]
Regions with significant populations
Greater London · Birmingham · Liverpool · Cardiff · West Midlands · Manchester · Bristol · Nottingham · Leicester · Sheffield
Languages
British English · Caribbean English
Religion
Predominantly Evangelical, Rastafarian minority
Related ethnic groups
African diaspora · Afro-Caribbean · Jamaican British · Guyanese British · Barbadian British · Saint Lucian British · Grenadian British · Montserratian British · Trinidadian British · African American British · Kittitian and Nevisian British · Antiguan British · Vincentian British · Dominican British

The **British African Caribbean communities** are residents of the United Kingdom who are of West Indian background and whose ancestors were primarily indigenous to Africa. As immigration to the United Kingdom from Africa increased in the 1990s, the term has sometimes been used to include UK residents solely of African origin, or as a term to define all Black British residents, though the phrase "African *and* Caribbean" has more often been used to cover such a broader grouping. The most common and traditional use of the term African-Caribbean community is in reference to groups of residents' continuing aspects of Caribbean culture, customs and traditions in the United Kingdom.[Term[·]]

The largest proportion of the African-Caribbean population in the UK are of Jamaican origin; others trace origins to nations such as Trinidad and Tobago, Saint Kitts and Nevis, Barbados, Grenada, Antigua and Barbuda, Saint Lucia,

Dominica, Montserrat, Anguilla, Saint Vincent and the Grenadines, Guyana, which though located on the South American mainland, is very culturally similar to the Caribbean, and was historically considered to be part of the British West Indies, and Belize (formerly British Honduras), in Central America, which culturally is more akin to the English-speaking Caribbean than to Latin America, due to its colonial and still-extant economic ties to the UK.

African-Caribbean communities exist throughout the United Kingdom, though by far the largest concentrations are in London and Birmingham.[3] Significant communities also exist in other population centres, notably Manchester, Bradford, Nottingham, Coventry, Luton, Leicester, Bristol, Leeds, Huddersfield, Sheffield, Liverpool and Cardiff. In these cities, the community is traditionally associated with a particular area, such as, Brixton, Harlesden, Stonebridge, Tottenham, Dalston, Lewisham and Peckham in London, West Bowling and Heaton in Bradford, Chapeltown in Leeds,[4] St. Pauls in Bristol,[5] or Handsworth and Aston in Birmingham or Moss Side In Manchester.

British African-Caribbeans have an extremely high rate of mixed-race relationships, and could in effect become the first UK ethnic group to 'disappear'.[6] Half of all British African-Caribbean men in a relationship have partners of a different race.[6] 2007 estimates for England alone roughly put the full African-Caribbean to partial African-Caribbean heritage ratio at 2:1.[2]

History

Early pioneers

The presence of British African-Caribbean people stems originally from the English involvement in the slave trade. From the 16th century to the 19th century enslaved Africans were shipped by European slave traders to British colonies in the Caribbean and British North America, as well as French, Dutch, Danish, Spanish, and Portuguese colonies. New World slavery was originally focused on the extraction of gold and other precious raw materials. Africans were then later set to work on the vast cotton, tobacco and sugar plantations in the Americas for the economic benefit of these colonial powers and their plantocracy.[7] One impact of the American Revolution was the differing historical development of African American and African-Caribbean people. There are records of small communities in the ports of Cardiff, Liverpool, London and South Shields dating back to the mid-18th century. These communities were formed by freed slaves following the abolition of slavery.[8] Typical occupations of the early migrants were footmen or coachmen.

The only known photograph of Mary Seacole, taken for a carte de visite by Maull & Company in London (c. 1873)

Nineteenth Century

Prominent African-Caribbean people in Britain during the nineteenth century include:

- Robert Wedderburn, (1762-1835/6?), Spencean revolutionary
- William Davidson, (1781-1820), Cato Street Conspirator
- Rev. George Cousens, a Jamaican who became minister of Cradley Heath Baptist Church in 1837
- Mary Seacole (1805 − 1881) the nurse.
- Andrew Watson Footballer
- Walter Tull Footballer and soldier

Early Twentieth Century

The growing Caribbean presence in the British military led to approximately 15,000 migrants arriving in the North-West of England around the time of the First World War to work in munitions factories.[9]

The Jamaican poet and communist activist, Claude McKay came to England following the First World War and became the first Black British journalist, writing for the Workers Dreadnought.

Second World War

In February 1941 345 West Indian workers were brought to work in an around Liverpool.[10] . They were generally better skilled that the local Black British. There was also some tension between them and West Africans who had settled in the area.[11]

The "Windrush generation"

Since World War II many African-Caribbean people migrated to North America and Europe, especially to the United States, Canada, the UK, France, and the Netherlands. As a result of the losses during the war, the British government began to encourage mass immigration from the countries of the British Empire and Commonwealth to fill shortages in the labour market.[12] The 1948 British Nationality Act gave British citizenship to all people living in Commonwealth countries, and full rights of entry and settlement in Britain.[13] Many West Indians were attracted by better prospects in what was often referred to as the mother country.

In 1998, an area of public open space in Brixton was renamed Windrush Square to commemorate the fiftieth anniversary of the arrival of the West Indians.[14]

The ship *MV Empire Windrush* brought the first group of 492 immigrants to Tilbury near London on 22 June 1948. The *Windrush* was en route from Australia to England via the Atlantic, docking in Kingston, Jamaica. An advertisement had appeared in a Jamaican newspaper offering cheap transport on the ship for anybody who wanted to come and work in the UK. The arrivals were temporarily housed in the Clapham South deep shelter in southwest London less than a mile away from Coldharbour Lane in Brixton. Many only intended to stay in Britain for a few years, and although a number returned to the Caribbean to rejoin the RAF, the majority remained to settle permanently.[15] The arrival of the passengers has become an important landmark in the history of modern Britain, and the image of West Indians filing off its gangplank has come to symbolise the beginning of modern British multicultural society.[15] See Windrush image "here" [16]..

There was plenty of work in post-war Britain and industries such as British Rail, the National Health Service and public transport recruited almost exclusively from Jamaica and Barbados.[17] Though Afro-Caribbeans were encouraged to journey to Britain via immigration campaigns created by successive British governments, many new arrivals were to endure intolerance and extreme racism from certain sectors of indigenous British society. This experience was to mark African-Caribbeans' relations with the wider community over a long period.[18] Early African-Caribbean immigrants found private employment and housing denied to them on the basis of race. Housing was in short supply following the wartime bombing, and the shortage led to some of the first clashes with the established white community. Clashes continued and worsened into the 1950s, and riots erupted in cities including London, Birmingham and Nottingham.[12] In 1958, attacks in the London area of Notting Hill by white youths marred relations with West Indian residents, leading to the creation of the annual Notting Hill Carnival, which was initiated in 1959 as a positive response by the Caribbean community.[19]

In 1962, Britain passed the Commonwealth Immigrants Act restricting the entry of immigrants,[12] and by 1972 only holders of work permits, or people with parents or grandparents born in the UK could gain entry - effectively stemming most Caribbean immigration.[13] Despite the restrictive measures, an entire generation of Britons with African-Caribbean heritage now existed, contributing to British society in virtually every field. The number of British persons born in the West Indies had increased from 15,000 in 1951 to 172,000 in 1961 to 304,000 in 1981. The total population of persons of West Indian heritage by 1981 was between 500,000 and 550,000, depending upon the official source used.[20]

Recession and turbulence, 1970s and 1980s

The 1970s and 1980s were decades of comparative turbulence in wider British society; industrial disputes preceded a period of deep recession and widespread unemployment which seriously affected the economically less prosperous African-Caribbean community.Recession[·] Societal racism, discrimination, poverty, powerlessness and oppressive policing sparked a series of riots in areas with substantial African-Caribbean populations.[21] These "uprisings" (as they were described by some in the community) took place in St Pauls in 1980, Brixton, Toxteth and Moss Side in 1981, St Pauls again in 1982, Notting Hill Gate in 1982, Toxteth in 1982, and Handsworth, Brixton and Tottenham in 1985.[22]

Dancers at the Notting Hill Carnival

The riots had a profoundly unsettling effect on local residents, and led the then Home Secretary William Whitelaw to commission the Scarman report to address the root causes of the disturbances. The report identified both "racial discrimination" and a "racial disadvantage" in Britain, concluding that urgent action was needed to prevent these issues becoming an "endemic, ineradicable disease threatening the very survival of our society".[21] The era saw an increase in attacks on Black people by white people. The *Joint Campaign Against Racism* committee reported that there had been more than 20,000 attacks on non-indigenous Britons including Britons of Asian origin during 1985.[23]

Recent history

While individuals with Caribbean heritage excelled in a variety of fields in British society during the 1990s and 2000s, many recurring issues continued to impact the African-Caribbean community as a whole. The police response to the 1993 murder of Black teenager Stephen Lawrence, by assailants that have yet to be convicted, led to an outcry from the community and calls to investigate police conduct. The subsequent government inquiry, the Macpherson Report, was vigorously sought by Stephen's Jamaican-born parents and revealed evidence of institutional racism in the London Metropolitan Police Service, confirming the beliefs of many Black Britons.[24]

The community has suffered from an increasing association with gun-crime, heightened by high profile murders, such as that of two young women shot outside a Birmingham hair salon in 2003. Several media outlets blamed a "gangster rap culture" in the community,[25] though Assistant Chief Constable Nick Tofiluk of the West Midlands Police believed that the use of firearms is not an Afro-Caribbean issue alone, and has been on the rise throughout British society.[26] Tensions between African-Caribbean residents and British Asians in a number of regions have led to confrontations, notably violent disturbances in Birmingham in 2005 where groups from both communities fought and rioted over two nights. There is also evidence of tensions between the African-Caribbean community and the growing number of African immigrants. Some African-Caribbean people have left the UK, seeking a better life aboard, either back in the Caribbean or America.[27]

Statistics

In the UK Census of 2001, 565,876 people classified themselves in the category 'Black Caribbean', amounting to around 1 per cent of the total population.[29] Of the 'minority ethnic' population, which amounted to 7.9 per cent of the total UK population, Black Caribbeans accounted for 12.2 per cent.[29] In addition, 14.6 per cent of the minority ethnic population (equivalent to 1.2 per cent of the total population) identified as mixed race, of whom one third stated that they were of mixed white and Black Caribbean descent.[29] In 2001, 61 per cent of the Black Caribbean group lived in London.[30]

The Census also records respondents' countries of birth and the 2001 Census recorded 146,401 people born in Jamaica, 21,601 from Barbados, 21,283 from Trinidad and Tobago, 20,872 from Guyana, 9,783 from Grenada, 8,265 from Saint Lucia, 7,983 from Montserrat, 7,091 from Saint Vincent and the Grenadines, 6,739 from Dominica, 6,519 from Saint Kitts and Nevis, 3,891 from Antigua and Barbuda, and 498 from Anguilla.[31]

Ridley Road Market in Dalston, London, which sells African-Caribbean music, textiles, and food including goat meat, yams, mangos and spices.[28]

GCSEs

In 2007, 49% of black Caribbean pupils achieved five or more GCSEs at grades A* to C. Compared to just 44% in 2006. 56% of girls achieved five or more GCSEs at A*-C, with 42% of boys doing the same.[32]

The community

In many parts of Britain, African-Caribbean people have been recognised as being part of a distinct community.[3] In the 1950s and 1960s community centres and associations sprung up in some British towns and cities with an aim to serve African-Caribbean populations. One such example was the *African Caribbean Self Help Organisation (ACSHO)* which was formed in 1964 in the district of Handsworth in Birmingham.[33] These centres have often addressed issues that rise within the community, including perceived problems of police harassment and concerns about the housing of Black people, which was viewed as discriminatory during the early decades of mass immigration.Community[›] The centres also allowed African-Caribbean peoples to socialise without risking the potential racial discrimination and aggression of "unfriendly pubs".[34] Many of these associations appointed a Community Relations Officer whose role was to liaise between the community and wider British society including the establishment. Other responsibilities included arranging social events, such as festivals, carnivals and coach trips, which helped bring the communities together.[34] Typical of present day centres is *The Afro Caribbean Millennium Centre* in Birmingham which was established with National Lottery funding to support principally Caribbean people in areas like employment, housing, education, immigration, and cultural issues.[35]

Diane Abbott, born to Jamaican parents, became the first Black woman elected to the House of Commons in 1987

Although the community does not face any official or informal restrictions on political participation, Britons of Caribbean origin are nonetheless under-represented in local and national politics.[3] However there have been some success with Diane Abbott being the frist black person elected to Parliament[36] under Labour and Linda C Douglas being the frist black person to be part of the Labour party National Executive Committee representing the now expelled Militant tendency. British African-West Indians have long asserted that they encounter discriminatory barriers to most middle and higher status occupations, as well as discrimination in hiring practices at all levels of employment. There is also considerable evidence that African-Caribbean people experience differential treatment at the hands of public officials, the British courts and penal system, and the police.[3] Studies have proposed that the isolation of certain regional urban areas by financial institutions such as insurance brokers, disproportionately affects the community to its detriment.[3]

Britain's school system, despite efforts to address issues of discrimination,[37] has often been accused of racism through undermining the self-confidence of all Black children and maligning the culture of their parents.[38] Throughout the 1950s and 1960s, a disproportionate number of Caribbean migrant children were classified as 'educationally subnormal' and placed in special schools and units.[39] By the end of the 1980s, the chances of white school leavers finding employment were four times better than those of Black pupils. In 2000–01, Black pupils were three times more likely than white pupils and ten times more likely than Indian pupils to be officially excluded from school for disciplinary reasons. These chronic problems have contributed to the group being towards at the lower end of the socio-economic spectrum and have continued to be a problem into the 21st century.[40]

African-Caribbean culture in the United Kingdom

Carnivals

African-Caribbean communities organise and participate in Caribbean Carnivals (Caribbean style carnivals) throughout the UK. The best known of these is the annual Notting Hill Carnival, attracting up to 1.5 million people from Britain and around the world, making it the largest street festival in Europe. This is Local London. The carnival began in 1964 as a small procession of Trinidadians in memory of festivals in their home country.

Leeds West Indian Carnival is Europe's oldest West Indian carnival and now attracts around 130,000 people.[41] [42] [43]

Other carnivals include the Leicester Caribbean Carnival and the Birmingham International Carnival.

Food

The earliest Caribbean immigrants to post-war Britain found differences in diet and availability of food an uncomfortable challenge.[44] In later years, as the community developed and food imports became more accessible to all, grocers specialising in Caribbean produce opened in British high streets. Caribbean restaurants can now also be found in most areas of Britain where West Indian communities reside, serving traditional Caribbean dishes such as curried goat, fried dumplings, ackee and salt fish (the national dish of Jamaica), roti (the national dish of Trinidad and Tobago), (Cou-Cou and Flying Fish the national dish of Barbados), Pudding and Souse, as well as another tasty delicacy known as Fish Cakes from Barbados. The spices known as "jerk" and the traditional Sunday West Indian meal of rice and peas

Scotch bonnet peppers imported from the Caribbean on sale at London's Brixton Market. The peppers are a key ingredient of "Jerk" dishes.

The best known Caribbean food brands in the UK are Dunn's River, Tropical Sun, Walkerswood and Grace Foods. Grace Foods is originally from Jamaica but is now a multi national conglomerate. In March 2007 Grace Foods bought ENCO Products, owners of the Dunn's River Brand, as well as "Nurishment", a flavoured, sweetened enriched milk drink, and the iconic Encona Sauce Range. Tropical Sun products and ingredients have been widely available in the UK for over 10 years and has a sister brand of Jamaica Sun with products mainly sourced from the Caribbean. Walkerswood is a Jamaican co-operative which has a range of sauces and marinades product. [45]

Religion

The influx of African-Caribbeans to the United Kingdom was accompanied by religious practices more common to the North American continent. In Britain, many African-Caribbeans continued to practice Non-conformist Protestant denominations with an Evangelical influence such as Pentecostalism and Seventh Day Baptism. African-Caribbeans have supported new churches in many areas of the country, which have grown to act as social centres for the community.[Religion[·]] The manner of worship in some of these churches is more akin to that of African American practices, than to traditional English Catholic or Anglican liturgy. Gospel music also came to play a part in British cultural life. African-Caribbeans played a central role establishing British gospel choirs, most notably the London Community Gospel Choir.

There are around 40,000 African-Caribbean Muslims in the United Kingdom, 30,000 of those reside in London. Muslims of African-Caribbean origins are found in British major cities and town. Some of them, especially those from African countries like Nigeria, Uganda and Sierra Leone are more likely to be born to Muslim families while many, particularly the Caribbean Muslims converted to Islam in various circumstances including marriage and in prison. Sadly, African-Caribbean Muslims partly have a bad reputation, due to some terror suspects who came out of the community. For example, Richard Reid, internationally known as the shoebomber, is of Jamaican descent, and used to live in Brixton. One of the four terrorists who were involved in the 2005 terror attacks in London, Jermaine Lindsey, was also of Jamaican descent. In the 2007 bomb plot, three of the fifteen suspects were of African-Caribbean descent. In South London, there is a Gang which is called Muslim Boys. Its members are of Jamaican descent. Another South London Gang which is formed by African-Caribbean Muslims is Poverty Driven Children.[46]

However, in London, there are mosques, centres and Muslim charitable organisations that belong to people of African-Caribbean origins. For instance, mosque of the Muslim Association of Nigeria is located at 365 Old Kent Road South East London - less than two kilometre from Siera Leoneans' Mosque in Brixton, while London serves as the headquarters of AWQAF Africa, the African Muslim Communities founded by Nigerian Muslim Scholar Dr. Sheikh Adelabu, the President of AWQAf Africa Muslim College in London.

Some British African-Caribbeans continue to practice other religious beliefs such as Rastafarianism, which developed in Jamaica. The Rastafarian belief system, associated personal symbols such as dreadlocks and cultural practices concerning cannabis have influenced British society far beyond the African-Caribbean community, being adopted by both indigenous Britons and others.[47]

Language and dialect

English is the official language of the former British West Indies, therefore African-Caribbean immigrants had few communication difficulties upon arrival in Britain compared to immigrants from other regions.[3] Nevertheless, indigenous Britons were generally unused to the distinct Caribbean dialects, creoles and patois (*patwah*) spoken by many African-Caribbean immigrants and their descendants, which would be particularly problematic in the field of education. In a study by language and education specialist Viv Edwards, *The West Indian language issue in British schools*, language – the Creole spoken by the students – was singled out as an important factor disadvantaging Caribbean children in British schools. The study cites negative attitudes of teachers towards any non-standard variety noting that;

> "The teacher who does not or is not prepared to recognise the problems of the Creole-speaking child in a British English situation can only conclude that he is stupid when he gives either an inappropriate response or no response at all. The stereotyping process leads features of Creole to be stigmatised and to develop connotations of, amongst other things, low academic ability."[48]

As integration continued, African-West Indians born in Britain instinctively adopted hybrid dialects combining Caribbean and local British dialects.[49] These dialects and accents gradually entered mainstream British vernacular, and shades of Caribbean dialects can be heard amongst Britons regardless of cultural origin. A Lancaster University study identified an emergence in certain areas of Britain of a distinctive accent which borrows heavily from Jamaican creole, lifting some words unchanged.[50] This phenomenon, disparagingly named "Jafaican" meaning 'fake Jamaican', was famously parodied by comedian Sacha Baron Cohen through his character Ali G.[50]

Theatre, television and mainstream cinema

The 1970s saw the emergence of independent filmmakers such as Trinidadian-born Horace Ove, the director of *Pressure*, among others.[51] London's Talawa Theatre Company was founded in the 1985 by Jamaican-born Yvonne Brewster, their first production being based on C.L.R. James's historical account of the Haitian Revolution, *The Black Jacobins*.[52] Since the 1980s, the Blue Mountain Theatre's productions have offered a more earthy style of populist comedy, often bringing over Jamaican artists such as Oliver Samuels.[53]

While Guyanese actor Robert Adams became the first African-Caribbean dramatic actor to appear on British television on 11 May 1938 (in a production of Eugene O'Neill's play *The Emperor Jones*), African-Caribbean entertainers were first widely popularised on British television broadcasts with the postwar resumption of BBC television in 1946 (pre-war black entertainers on the BBC - the first in the world - had primarily been African-American stars).[54] The profile of African-Caribbean actors on television, such as Lennie James, Judith Jacob and Diane Parish, has widened substantially since 1970s shows such as *Love Thy Neighbour* (Rudolph Walker) and *Rising Damp* (Don Warrington) when their role was often to act simply as either butt of, or foil to, racist jokes by 'white' characters. The most influential programme in moving away from this formula was the 1989–1994 Channel Four barbershop sitcom *Desmond's*, starring Norman Beaton and Carmen Munroe.

One of the biggest African-Caribbean names in comedy is Lenny Henry, who began his career as a stand-up comedian but whose television sketch shows, where he often caricatured Caribbean émigrés, made him popular enough to headline numerous primetime comedy shows from, for instance, *Lenny Henry* in 1984 to *The Lenny Henry Show* in 2004.[55] The highest professional achievement by a British African-Caribbean actor to date (2006) was Marianne Jean-Baptiste's 1996 nominations for an Academy Award (Oscar), Golden Globe and British Academy Award (bafta) for her feature-film debut role in *Secrets & Lies*.[56]

Literature

Jamaican poet James Berry was one of the first Caribbean writers to come to Britain after the 1948 British Nationality Act. He was followed by writers including Barbadians George Lamming and Edward Kamau Brathwaite, Trinidadians Samuel Selvon, CLR James, Jamaican Andrew Salkey and the Guyanese writer Wilson Harris. These writers viewed London as the centre of the English literary scene, and took advantage of the BBC Radio show *Caribbean voices* to gain attention and be published. By relocating to Britain, these writers also gave Caribbean literature an international readership for the first time and established Caribbean writing as an important perspective within English literature.[58] Some Caribbean writers also began writing about the hardships faced by settlers in post-war Britain. George Lamming addressed these issues with his 1954 novel *The Emigrants*, which traced the journey of migrants from Barbados as they struggled to integrate into British life.[58] By the mid-1980s, a

A shop in Electric Avenue, Brixton. In 1999 the street was hit by a nail-bomb planted by neo-nazi David Copeland. Copeland later stated that he was deliberately targeting the local African-Caribbean community. "Profile: Copeland the killer"[57]. *BBC News.* 2000-06-30. Retrieved 2007-06-24.

more radical wave of writers and poets were addressing the African-Caribbean experience in Britain, promoted by a group of new publishing houses such as Akira, Karia, Dangaroo, and Karnak House.[58]

In 1984, the poet Fred D'Aguiar (born in London to Guyanese parents) won the T. S. Eliot Prize, and in 1994 won the Whitbread First Novel Award for *The Longest Memory*. Linton Kwesi Johnson's rhyming and socio-political commentary over dub beats made him the unofficial poet laureate of the British African-Caribbean community.[59] Another dub poet, Benjamin Zephaniah, born in Birmingham to Jamaican parents, overcame a spell in prison to become a well known writer, and public figure.[60] In 2003 he declined an OBE, stating that it reminded him of 'thousands of years of brutality, it reminds me of how my foremothers were raped and my forefathers brutalised'.[61]

African-Caribbean British writers have achieved recent literary acclaim. In 2004, Andrea Levy's novel *Small Island* was winner of the 2004 Orange Prize for Fiction, one of Britain's highest literary honours. Levy, born in London to Jamaican parents, is the author of four novels, each exploring the problems faced by Black British-born children of Jamaican emigrants.[62] In 2006 Zadie Smith won the Orange Prize for *On Beauty*. Smith's acclaimed first novel *White Teeth* was a portrait of contemporary multicultural London, drawing from her own upbringing with an English father and a Jamaican mother.[63]

The UK also has a modest output of African-Caribbean popular fiction. The most widely known example may be *Yardie*, an Urban fiction written by Victor Headley in 1992. It described the life of a Jamaican courier's carrying cocaine from Jamaica to London. The book was published by Steve Pope and Dotun Adebayo of Xpress books.[64]

Media

The Voice newspaper was the primary African-Caribbean print media outlet in Britain, and was founded in the early 1980s by Val McCalla. Other publications have included the *Gleaner*, *Black Voice*, *Pride Magazine* and *The Caribbean Times*. The growth of such media is aimed to offset the perceived imbalances of 'mainstream' media. In 2006, Sir Ian Blair, the Chief Commissioner of London's Metropolitan Police, joined a long list of commentators in branding the mainstream British media as 'institutionally racist' for its alleged failure to offer a proper balance in reporting affairs related to the community.[65]

Trinidad-born Sir Trevor McDonald is one of the community's best-known journalists, having been the main presenter (newscaster) for the national ITV network for over twenty years.[66] Other notable media figures include Gary Younge, *The Guardian* columnist, and Moira Stuart, the veteran BBC news presenter.[67] Trinidadian-born Darcus Howe has written in *New Statesman* and fronted a number of documentary series including the Channel 4 current affairs programme *Devil's Advocate*. Much of Howe's work is related to the experiences of British African-Caribbeans and racism in wider British society.[68] Other notable producer/directors are Terry Jervis (Jervis Media) and Pogus Caesar (Windrush Productions); both have made multicultural, entertainment and sports programmes for Carlton TV, BBC TV and Channel 4.[69]

The community has a strong tradition of 'underground' 'pirate radio' broadcasters, the most established being London's Lightning Radio, Genesis Radio and Galaxy Radio which play a mix of ragga, reggae, bashment, hip hop and R&B. 'pirate radio' stations like Supreme, Galaxy and Genesis Radio are particularly highly regarded in the Afro Caribbean community for not only playing a variety of music such as Soca, Soul, dancehall, Jazz, Hip Hop, Reveail and Funky House, but also for dedicating time to have *talk shows* and *information shows* often taking an uncompromising stance in view. Thus giving the community the opportunity to phone in and participate in an array of subjects that mainstream radio and media refuse to address.

In 1996, Choice FM received a licence to broadcast in London and Birmingham with a remit to serve the musical tastes of the African-Caribbean community. Sadly, after being bought by PLC (which owns pop station Capital Radio) and more recently Global taking the ownership of the station, many feel that Choice FM has sold out and no longer reflects the community. This is demonstrated by the sacking of talk show host Geoff Schumann. In an article Jeff Shumman said "When I was on Choice, my show— a talk show— had an audience that was higher than any of the station's other shows, and yet I was told, by a white man, that my style wouldn't fit in with the station's future plans.

Generally speaking, a radio show with high ratings is usually the show that a station will keep. But when you want to create the impression that all black people want to do is listen to music, you sack the host that does the talking!" SOURCE: http:// www. voice-online. co. uk/ content. php?show=13728 The people from the Afro-Caribbean community with a sense of identity, dignity and pride have abandoned Choice FM, often criticizing the misrepresentation of the music and the general undermining of not only Afro-Caribbean people, but all black people of African ancestry. http://www.voice-online.co.uk/content.php?show=17687

As a result, many black activists have campaigned tirelessly for the state to stop attacking black 'pirate radio' stations like Power Jam(now deceased) Galaxy Radio and Genesis Radio, as they are the only voice many of the Afro-Caribbean community feel they have to discus issues that concern them; other than just promoting Urban music like what Choice FM has become.

"The thing with me is that I'm not afraid to call myself black. I'm black— I'm not urban." - Geoff Schumann. Presently Geoff Schumann now hosts a talk show on a popular west London 'pirate radio' station with the same format that he had on Choice FM, before the only black owned legal station was sold.

In 2002, the BBC established its digital broadcasting strand 'BBC Radio 1Xtra' to focus on new Black music - which in effect means catering to the tastes of the country's African-Caribbean youth.[70] The Internet has afforded the community the opportunity to publish en-masse, and there are now thousands of websites and blogs produced by or for African-Caribbeans in the UK such as the BBC's Family History page,[71] and The African-Caribbean Network, Blacknet UK, launched in 1996.[72]

Visual arts

One of the most influential African-Caribbeans in the British art world has been Dr. Eddie Chambers.[73] Chambers, along with Donald Rodney, Marlene Smith and curator, artist, critic and academic Keith Piper, founded the BLK Art Group[74] in 1982, when they were initially based in the West Midlands. According to Chambers, significant artists such as the Guyanese-born painters Aubrey Williams and Frank Bowling and the Jamaican sculptor Ronald Moody initially found that, despite achieving worldwide renown, it was difficult to find acceptance in the highest echelons of the art establishment.[75] Chambers worked with Donald Rodney and Sonia Boyce, both of whose work is represented in the permanent collections of the London's Tate Britain museum. In 1986 the Hayward Gallery

Tate Britain gallery which houses works by Donald Rodney and Sonia Boyce

presented the exhibition 'The Other Story' that provided a survey of African-Caribbean, African and Asian artists working in the UK.

Other African-Caribbean artists of note include Faisal Abdu'allah of Jamaican heritage,[76] Guyanan-born Ingrid Pollard,[77] British-based Jamaican painter Eugene Palmer, the sculptor George 'Fowokan' Kelly[78] and Tam Joseph, whose 1983 work *Spirit of Carnival* was a vivid depiction of the Notting Hill Carnival.[79] The movement was also part of the impetus that led to the founding of the Association of Black Photographers by Mark Sealy. In 1999 the filmmaker Steve McQueen (not to be confused with the Hollywood filmstar) won Britain's most prestigious art prize, the Turner Prize, for his video "Deadpan".[80] The artist and producer Pogus Caesar was commissioned by Artangel to direct a film based on McQueen's work. *Forward Ever - Backward Never* was premiered at Lumiere in London 2002. Caesar has also established the OOM Gallery Archives, based in Birmingham, which has in excess of 14,000 images including photographs of contemporary Black British culture.

Academia

There are a number of African-Caribbean academics who are especially prominent in the arts and humanities. Professor Paul Gilroy, of Guyanese/English heritage, is one Britain's leading academics, having taught sociology at Harvard as well as Goldsmiths College and the London School of Economics.[81] The Jamaican-born cultural theorist Professor Stuart Hall has also been a highly influential British intellectual since the 1960s.[82] Dr. Robert Beckford has presented several national television and radio documentaries exploring African-Caribbean history, culture and religion.[83] Other prominent academics include Dr Lez Henry, who currently hosts a fortnightly Talk show on a popular London 'Pirate Radio' station Galaxy 99.5 FM or http://www.afiwestation.com and who is also a former lecturer of Goldsmiths College, and Prof. Harry Goldbourne, a former member of the radical group the Black Unity and Freedom Party, who went on to teach at the University of the South Bank. Although there are hundreds of African-Caribbean teachers in the UK, it has been suggested that their under-representation in inner-city schools is a major factor in the failure, particularly of secondary-level schools, to achieve a satisfactory average of achievement for the community's children (see Bernard Coard and the Swann Report of 1985).[84]

Music

The period of large-scale immigration brought many new musical styles to the United Kingdom. These styles gained popularity amongst Britons of all cultural origins, and aided Caribbean music in gaining international recognition. The earliest of these exponents was the calypso artist Lord Kitchener, who arrived in Britain on the *Windrush* in 1948 accompanied by fellow musician Lord Beginner.[85] Already a star in his native Trinidad, Lord Kitchener got an immediate booking at the only West Indian club in London. Six months later, he was appearing in three clubs nightly, and his popularity extended beyond the West Indian and African nightclub audiences, to include music hall and variety show audiences.[85] Kitchener's recording "London is the place for me" exemplified the experience of the *Windrush generation*.[86] Other calypso musicians began to collaborate with African Kwela musicians and British jazz players in London clubs.[86]

Former Musical Youth Frontman Dennis Seaton in 2005

Jamaican music styles reached Britain in the 1960s, becoming the staple music for young British African-Caribbeans. Tours by ska artists such as Prince Buster and the Skatalites fed the growing British-Caribbean music scene, and the success of Jamaican artists Millie Small, Desmond Dekker and Bob and Marcia propelled Caribbean music and people into mainstream cultural life. British African-Caribbeans followed the changing styles of Jamaican music and began to produce homegrown music appealing to both Black and White communities. In 1969, the British African-Caribbean ska band Symarip recorded "Skinhead Moonstomp" which had a huge effect on the British ska scene. The ska sound and rude boy imagery inspired a generation of white working-class youths (especially mods and skinheads), and later helped spawn Britain's multi-cultural 2 Tone movement in the late 1970s.[87]

As Jamaican ska gave way to the slower styles of rocksteady and the more politicised reggae, British African-Caribbeans followed suit. Sound systems to rival those in Jamaica sprung up throughout communities, and 'Blues parties' - parties in private houses, where one paid at the door - became an institution. The arrival of Bob Marley to London in 1971 helped spawn a Black British music industry based on reggae. His association with the Rastafarian movement influenced waves of young people, reared in Britain, to discover their Caribbean roots. British Barbadian Dennis Bovell became Britain's prominent reggae band leader and producer, working with many international reggae stars, and introducing a reggae flavour to the British pop charts with non-reggae acts such as

Dexys Midnight Runners and Bananarama. Bovell also worked extensively with London-based dub poet Linton Kwesi Johnson.[88]

Successful DJ and musician Goldie, born to Scottish and Jamaican parents [89]

British music with reggae roots prospered in the 1980s and early 1990s. British African-Caribbean artists Musical Youth, Aswad, Maxi Priest and Eddy Grant had major commercial successes, and the multicultural band UB40 helped promote reggae to an international audience. Birmingham-based Steel Pulse became one of the world's foremost exponents of roots reggae and accompanying black consciousness, their debut 1978 album *Handsworth Revolution* becoming a seminal release.[90]

British African-Caribbean music had been generally synonymous with Caribbean styles until the 1990s, although some artists had been drawing on British and American musical forms for several decades. In the 1970s and 1980s, British African-Caribbean artists such as Hot Chocolate and Imagination became leaders of the British disco, soul and R&B scenes.[91] By the mid-1980s British African-Caribbeans were also incorporating American hip hop and House styles, becoming leading figures in Britain's developing dance music culture. This led to an explosion of musical forms. British artists created musical hybrids combining many elements including European techno, Jamaican dancehall, dub, breakbeats and contemporary American R'n'B. These unique blends began to gain international acclaim through the success of Soul II Soul and the multi-racial Massive Attack.[92]

British African-Caribbeans were at the leading edge of the jungle and drum and bass movements of the 1990s. Although the fast-tempo drums and loud intricate bass lines sounded fresh, Caribbean roots could still be detected.[93] Two successful exponents of these new styles were DJs Goldie and Roni Size, both of Jamaican heritage.[89] [94] Later, British African-Caribbean musicians and DJs were at the forefront of the UK garage and Grime scenes.[95]

African-Caribbeans in British sport

British African-Caribbeans are well represented in traditional British sporting pastimes such as football and rugby, and have also represented the nation at the highest level in sports where Caribbeans typically excel in the home countries such as cricket and athletics. Some British African-Caribbeans have gone on to become international sports stars and top global earners in their chosen sporting field.

Athletics

Britain's first Olympic sprint medals came from Harry Edward, born in Guyana, who won two individual bronze medals at the 1920 games in Antwerp.[96] Many years later, sprinter Linford Christie, born in Saint Andrew Parish, Jamaica, won 23 major championship medals, more than any other British male athlete to date. Christie's career highlight was winning a gold medal in the immensely competitive 100 metres event in the 1992 Barcelona Olympics.[97] Welsh Hurdler Colin Jackson, who went to considerable lengths to explore his Jamaican heritage in a BBC documentary, held the 110 metres hurdles world record for 11 years between 1993 and 2004.[98]

Jamaican-born Tessa Sanderson became the first British African-Caribbean woman to win Olympic gold, receiving the medal for her javelin performance in the 1984 Los Angeles Olympics. Denise Lewis, of Jamaican heritage, won heptathlon gold in the 2000 Sydney Olympics,[99] a games where 13 of Britain's 18 track and field representatives had Afro-Caribbean roots.[96] Four years later in the Athens Olympics, Kelly Holmes, the daughter of a Jamaican-born car mechanic, achieved the rare feat of taking gold in both the 800 and 1500 metres races.[100] In the same games, Britain's men's 4 x 100 metre relay team of Marlon Devonish, Darren Campbell, Mark Lewis-Francis and Jason Gardener, all of African-Caribbean heritage, beat the favoured United States quartet to claim Olympic gold.[101]

Boxing

British boxers of a Caribbean background have played a prominent role in the national boxing scene since the early 1980s. In 1995 Frank Bruno, whose mother was a Pentecostal laypreacher from Jamaica, became Britain's first world heavyweight boxing champion in the 20th century.[102] Bruno's reign was shortly followed by British-born Jamaican Lennox Lewis, who defeated Evander Holyfield and Mike Tyson to become the world's premier heavyweight during the late 1990s.[103] Middleweights Chris Eubank, who spent his early years in Jamaica, and Nigel Benn, of Barbadian descent, both claimed world titles and fought a series of brutal battles in the early 1990s.[104] In the Sydney Olympics of 2000, Audley Harrison (who has Jamaican heritage) became Britain's first heavyweight gold medalist.[105] Other boxing champions from the British African-Caribbean community include the welterweight Lloyd Honeyghan, nicknamed 'Ragamuffin Man' in reference to his Jamaican roots, who defeated boxing super-star Donald Curry in 1986.[106]

Cricket

Cricket has long been a popular pastime amongst African-Caribbeans in both the West Indies and the United Kingdom, though this has waned somewhat since its peak during the 1960s-1980s.[107] After the period of widespread immigration, tours of England by the combined West Indian cricket team became cultural celebrations of Caribbean culture in Britain, particularly at cricket grounds such as The Oval in South London.[107] Almost all the great West Indian cricketers became regular features of the domestic county game, including Garfield Sobers, Vivian Richards and Michael Holding. In turn, British cricketers of Caribbean origin also began to make an impact in English cricket. In the 1980s-1990s, players including Gladstone Small (born in Barbados),[108] Devon Malcolm (born in Jamaica)[109] and Phillip DeFreitas (born in Dominica)[110] represented England, making significant contributions to the side.[Cricket[›]]

Motorsport

Lewis Hamilton whose paternal grandparents immigrated from Grenada achieved the highest honour in Motorsport, winning the FIA Formula One World Championship in 2008, only his second season in the sport, after narrowly finishing second in the championship in in his debut season.

Football

The first West Indian-born footballer to play football at a high level in Britain was Andrew Watson, who played for Queens Park (Glasgow) and went on to play for Scotland. Born in May 1857 in British Guyana, Watson lived and worked in Scotland and came to be known as one of the best players of his generation. He played in 36 games for Queens Park and also appeared for the London Swifts in the English FA Cup championship of 1882, making him the first Black player in English Cup history. Watson earned 2 Scottish Cup medals and 4 Charity Cup medals during his career; Who's Who also acknowledged his performances in international matches. Watson's place in football history included a spell in management as Club Secretary for Queens Park - making Watson the first Afro-Caribbean man to reach the boardroom.[111]

Derby County's Michael Johnson, one of a number of British-born players to play for the Jamaica national football team

Manchester United's Rio Ferdinand, whose father came to Britain from St. Lucia,[112] is captain of the English national team.

Other early Caribbean footballers included Walter Tull, of Barbadian descent, who played for the north London club Tottenham Hotspur in the early 20th century. Some years later, Jamaican-born Lloyd 'Lindy' Delapenha made an impact playing for Middlesbrough between 1950–57, becoming a leading goal scorer and the first Black player to win a championship medal.[113] However, it was not until the 1970s that African-Caribbean players began to make a major impact on the game. Clyde Best (West Ham 1969–1976), born in Bermuda,[114] paved the way for players such as Cyrille Regis (born in French Guyana),[115] and Luther Blissett (born in Jamaica).[116] Blissett and Regis joined Viv Anderson to form the first wave of Black footballers to play for the England national team. Although the number of players of African-Caribbean origin in the English league was increasing far beyond proportions in wider society, when Black players represented the English national team, they still had to endure racism from a section of England supporters. When selected to play for England, Cyril Regis received a bullet through the mail with the threat, "You'll get one of these through your knees if you step on our Wembley turf."[115]

By the 1980s the British African-Caribbean community was well represented at all playing levels of the game. John Barnes, born in Jamaica, was one of the most talented players of his generation and one of the few footballers to win every honour in the domestic English game including the PFA Players' Player of the Year.[117] Although Barnes played for England on 78 occasions between 1983 and 1991, his performances rarely matched his club standard.[118] Subsequently, Barnes identified a culture of racism in football during his era as a player.[117] Players of African-Caribbean origin continued to excel in English football, in the 1990s Paul Ince - whose parents were from Trinidad - went on to captain Manchester United, Liverpool F.C. and the English national team. The contribution was reciprocated when a number of British born footballers including Robbie Earle, Frank Sinclair and Darryl Powell represented the Jamaica national football team in the 1998 World Cup finals.

At the turn of the millennium, British-born Black footballers constituted about 13% of the English league,[119] and a number of groups including "Kick It Out" were highlighting issues of racism still in the game.[120] In the 2006 World Cup finals, Theo Walcott, a striker of English and Jamaican parents,[121] became the youngest ever player to join an England world cup squad - a side which included African-Caribbean players in every department, goal-keeping, defence, midfield and attack.England[·]

See also

- British Indo-Caribbean community
- Black British
- Antiguan British
- Jamaican British
- Guyanese British
- Barbadian British
- Saint Lucian British
- Saint Kitts and Nevisian British
- Grenadian British
- Montserratian British
- Trinidadian British
- Vincentian British
- Dominican British
- African British

- African American British
- Sus law
  - Immigration to the United Kingdom
  - British national identity card#Ethnic minorities
- Afro-Caribbean newspapers
  - New Nation
  - The Voice (newspaper)

Notes

^ **Term:** The Oxford English dictionary defines the term "Afro-Caribbean" as a *"a person of African descent living in or coming from the Caribbean."* American Heritage dictionary defines an "Afro-Caribbean [122]" as *"a native or inhabitant of the Caribbean region who is of African ancestry".* •Within the field of phonology, the term British Afro-Caribbean refers exclusively to British citizens of Caribbean ancestry.[49]

•When drawing up anti-racist language guidelines in 1992, the British Sociological Association make a clear distinction between Afro Caribbean, when referring to people of West Indian extraction, and Afro/Caribbean (see [123]).

•The British medical journal's *Glossary of terms relating to ethnicity and race* refers to three primary terms of self identification or identification for people of Sub-Saharan ancestral origins, defining **Afro-Caribbean/African Caribbean** as

> "A person of African ancestral origins whose family settled in the Caribbean before emigrating and who self identifies, or is identified, as Afro-Caribbean (in terms of racial classifications, this population approximates to the group known as Negroid or similar terms)."

The journal also defines **African** as "A person with African ancestral origins who self identifies, or is identified, as African, but excluding those of other ancestry, for example, European and South Asian." and **Black** as "A person with African ancestral origins, who self identifies, or is identified, as Black, African or Afro-Caribbean. In some circumstances the word Black signifies all non-white minority populations, and in this use serves political purposes."[124]

•Usage of the term *"African-Caribbean"* has begun to replace *"Afro-Caribbean"* within media and communications formal style guides (examples can be found in the Guardian newspaper style guide [125] and the University of Bath style guide [126])

^ **Recession:** During the decades of the 1970s and 1980s, unemployment among the children of Caribbean migrants ran at three to four times that of white school leavers.[127] By 1982 the number of all people out of work in Britain had risen above three million for the first time since the 1930s.[128]

^ **Community:** One such community centre was the *Gloucestershire West Indian Association* which was formed in 1962. The formation of this group was in response to a number of issues that arose within the community at this time. These included perceived problems around police harassment and concerns about the housing of Black people on certain council estates in the city, which was viewed as discrimination and segregation.[129] Large centres presently operating include the Leeds West Indian centre[130] and the Manchester West Indian centre[131]

^ **Religion:** Mike Phillips, writing for the UK national archive project, described the influences of the new churches thus; "[they] gave the entire Caribbean community a sense of stability. At a time when migrants were under severe psychological pressure and distrusted the official services, or were misunderstood when they went to them, the Black church groups offered invaluable advice and comfort."[132]

In 2005 The Economist magazine discussed the growth of evangelical churches in London and Birmingham; "Another reason is that Britain's most prominent Afro-Caribbean institutions – the Black evangelical churches – are dominated by the urban poor. That has to do with the way the Caribbean was missionised: the hotter brand of

Christianity gained most converts among the dispossessed, who then re-exported it to Britain."[133]

^ **Cricket:** Phillip DeFreitas, Devon Malcolm and Gladstone Small made 44,40 and 17 test match appearances for England respectively. DeFreitas also played 103 One Day International for England, Malcolm made 10 appearances and Small made 53 appearances in the shorter format. Small and DeFreitas also represented England in the final of the 1987 Cricket World Cup against Australia.[134]

^ **England:** The England football squad for the 2006 world cup also contained Ashley Cole (Barbadian father),[135] Rio Ferdinand (father from St. Lucia)[136] Sol Campbell (Jamaican parents)[99] alongside goalkeeper David James, Jermaine Jenas and Aaron Lennon, all with ancestors from the Caribbean.

References

[1] "The census in England and Wales" (http://www.statistics.gov.uk/census/default.asp). Statistics.gov.uk. . Retrieved 2010-03-26.

[2] Neighbourhood Statistics. "Check Browser Settings" (http://www.neighbourhood.statistics.gov.uk/dissemination/LeadTableView. do?a=7&b=276743&c=london&d=13&e=13&g=325264&i=1001x1003x1004&m=0&r=1&s=1255543520204&enc=1& dsFamilyId=1809). Neighbourhood.statistics.gov.uk. . Retrieved 2010-03-26.

[3] Assessment for Afro-Caribbeans in the United Kingdom (http://www.cidcm.umd.edu/mar/assessment.asp?groupId=20005) Minorities at Risk (MAR) Project. University of Maryland. 2004. Accessed *6 October 2006*

[4] Awareness of Afro-Caribbean Culture (http://www.lhi.org.uk/projects_directory/projects_by_region/yorkshire_the_humber/leeds/ jamaica_society_leeds/awareness_of.html) **Leeds**. Local Heritage Initiative website. "277 Chapeltown Road was, as Melody Walker writes, resurrected from the ruins of urban decay by Jamaicans in the area to become a little piece of Jamaica on British soil." Accessed *14 November 2006*

[5] Yahoo Travel (http://travel.yahoo.com/p-travelguide-2666762-bristol_introduction-i) **Bristol**. "St Paul's is home to the magnificent St Paul's Carnival, an annual street-party of enormous popularity and nation acclaim, which celebrates the African and Caribbean community here." Retrieved 14 November 2006.

[6] Asthana, Anushka; Smith, David (18 January 2009). "Revealed: the rise of mixed-race Britain" (http://www.guardian.co.uk/uk/2009/jan/ 18/race-identity-britain-study). London: The Guardian. . Retrieved 26 July 2010.

[7] Black Britons find their African roots (http://news.bbc.co.uk/1/hi/world/africa/2757525.stm) BBC Online. 14 February 2003. Accessed *6 October 2006*

[8] Culture and Ethnicity Differences in Liverpool - African and Caribbean Communities (http://www.mersey-gateway.org/server. php?show=ConWebDoc.1371) E. Chambré Hardman Archive. Accessed *12 November 2006*

[9] Early immigration (http://www.movinghere.org.uk/galleries/histories/caribbean/working_lives/working_lives.htm#ffw). Migration histories. Accessed *12 November 2006*

[10] 'Liverpool's Black Population During World War II', *Black and Asian Studies Association Newsletter* No. 20, January 1998, p6

[11] 'Liverpool's Black Population During World War II', *Black and Asian Studies Association Newsletter* No. 20, January 1998, p9

[12] Short History of Immigration (http://news.bbc.co.uk/hi/english/static/in_depth/uk/2002/race/short_history_of_immigration.stm) BBC online. Accessed *6 October 2006*

[13] National Archives (http://www.nationalarchives.gov.uk/pathways/citizenship/brave_new_world/citizenship4.htm). Citizenship 1906–2003. Accessed *6 November 2006*

[14] Windrush Square (http://www.icons.org.uk/theicons/icons-atlas/london/windrush-square) Icons: A portrait of England. Accessed *6 October 2006.*

[15] British history : The making of modern Britain (http://www.bbc.co.uk/history/british/modern/windrush_01.shtml) BBC Online : Mike Phillips, 1998. Accessed *4 October 2006.*

[16] http://eee.uci.edu/programs/humcore/images/WestIndies/windrushfaces.jpg

[17] Birmingham's Post War Black Immigrants (http://www.birmingham.gov.uk/GenerateContent?CONTENT_ITEM_ID=2392& CONTENT_ITEM_TYPE=0&MENU_ID=0) Birmingham.gov.uk. *Birmingham council* website. Accessed *8 October 2006.*

[18] Four decades of UK race law BBC online (http://news.bbc.co.uk/1/hi/uk/4510062.stm). Accessed *6 October 2006.*

[19] Carnival's roots (http://www.bbc.co.uk/london/content/articles/2005/07/25/carnival_history_feature.shtml) BBC online. Accessed *11 November 2006*

[20] General Timeline of Blacks in Britain (http://www.bunchecenter.ucla.edu/diaspora/research_topics/british_blacks.htm) Centre for African American Studies. University of California, Los Angeles. *Accessed 7 October 2006*

[21] Q&A: The Scarman Report 27 (http://news.bbc.co.uk/1/hi/programmes/bbc_parliament/3631579.stm) BBC Online. April 2004. Accessed *6 October 2006.*

[22] A Different Reality: minority struggle in British cities (http://www.warwick.ac.uk/CRER/differentreality/timeline.html) University of Warwick. Centre for Research in Ethnic Relations. Accessed *6 October 2006*

° The 1981 Brixton Uprisings (http://www.eco.utexas.edu/~hmcleave/357Limpossibleintro.pdf#search="riots uprisings brixton") "The Riot not to work collective". "...*What has changed since last year's uprisings*". London 1982. Accessed *6 October 2006*

[23] Law and Order, moral order: The changing rhetoric of the Thatcher government. online (http://socialistregister.com/socialistregister.com/files/SR_1987_Taylor.pdf). Ian Taylor. *Accessed 6 October 2006*

[24] The Lawrence inquiry (http://news.bbc.co.uk/1/hi/special_report/1999/02/99/stephen_lawrence/285357.stm). BBC online. *Accessed 11 November 2006*

[25] Totally off target (http://www.guardian.co.uk/comment/story/0,,1026112,00.html) Guardian Unlimited. 21 August 2003. *Accessed 5 November 2006*

[26] Gun crime spreads 'like a cancer' across Britain (http://observer.guardian.co.uk/crimedebate/story/0,,1056411,00.html) Guardian online. *Accessed 5 November 2006*

[27] Turning on each other (http://www.guardian.co.uk/race/story/0,11374,1278275,00.html) Darcus Howe. Guardian online. *Accessed 5 November 2006*

[28] African directory (http://www.bbc.co.uk/africalives/africandirectory/category_c5_s28.shtml) BBC Online. *Accessed 16 November 2006*

[29] "Population size: 7.9% from a minority ethnic group" (http://www.statistics.gov.uk/cci/nugget.asp?id=273). Office for National Statistics. 2003-02-13. . Retrieved 2009-02-21.

[30] "Regional Distribution: 45% of minority ethnic people live in London" (http://www.statistics.gov.uk/cci/nugget.asp?id=263). Office for National Statistics. 2003-02-13. . Retrieved 2009-03-01.

[31] "Country-of-birth database" (http://www.oecd.org/dataoecd/18/23/34792376.xls). Organisation for Economic Co-operation and Development. . Retrieved 2009-02-21.

[32] Leppard, David; Watt, Holly (16 November 2008). "Black women now outstrip whites on pay" (http://business.timesonline.co.uk/tol/business/career_and_jobs/article5162672.ece). *The Times* (London). . Retrieved 27 April 2010.

[33] African Caribbean Self Help Organisation website (http://acsho.org.uk/index.html). *Accessed 4 March 2007.*

[34] Building a Community (http://www.irespect.net/Untold Stories/Caribbean/Building a Community.htm) Gloucestershire County Council website. *Accessed 9 October 2006.*

[35] Afro Caribbean Millennium Centre website (http://www.acmccentre.com/acmc.shtml).*Accessed 18 November 2006.*

[36] "BBC Radio 4 - Factual - Desert Island Discs - Diane Abbott" (http://www.bbc.co.uk/radio4/factual/desertislanddiscs_20080518.shtml). Bbc.co.uk. . Retrieved 2010-03-26.

[37] Inner London Education Authority Television Service Teachers Notes: West Indian English Online (http://www.movinghere.org.uk/deliveryfiles/LMA/ILEA_S_LR_11_144/0/1.pdf). 1974 education file on the particular problems of Caribbean children attending English schools. *Accessed 6 October 2006*

[38] Schools still failing Black children (http://www.irr.org.uk/2005/december/ha000017.html) iRR news. 21 December 2005. *Accessed 6 October 2006*

[39] Migration histories (http://www.movinghere.org.uk/galleries/histories/caribbean/growing_up/growing_up.htm) "Moving here" website. Mike Phillips. *Accessed 6 October 2006*

[40] Race head criticises schools' record (http://news.bbc.co.uk/2/hi/uk_news/education/2691873.stm), BBC news website. *Accessed 21 December 2006*

[41] "Legacies - Immigration and Emigration - England - Leeds - Partying towards equality" (http://www.bbc.co.uk/legacies/immig_emig/england/leeds/index.shtml). BBC. 2003-11-13. . Retrieved 2010-03-26.

[42] (http://www.leedscarnival.co.uk/index.php?option=content&task=view&id=66&Itemid=2)

[43] Bellamy, Alison. "Leeds prepares for carnival fever" (http://www.yorkshireeveningpost.co.uk/news/Leeds-prepares-for-carnival-fever.5562668.jp). Yorkshire Evening Post. . Retrieved 2010-03-26.

[44] First Impressions of England in 1964 (http://www.movinghere.org.uk/stories/story83/story83.htm?identifier=stories/story83/story83.htm) Migration histories. "The food which was served to us in seemingly enormous but bland quantities". Accessed *21 November 2006.*
° Hardship (http://www.movinghere.org.uk/stories/story462/story462.htm?identifier=stories/story462/story462.htm) Migration histories. "It was really hard, and cold, the food wasn't nice, I used to cry, I wanted to go home." Accessed *21 November 2006*

[45] Caribbean food in Britain (http://www.bbc.co.uk/food/news_and_events/events_caribbeancuisine.shtml) BBC Online. Accessed *21 November 2006.*

[46] (http://news.bbc.co.uk/2/hi/uk_news/4762591.stm); (http://journals.aol.co.uk/kenningtonnews/KenningtonNews/entries/2006/01/07/student-was-shot-by-muslim-boys-gang/2035); (http://www.independent.co.uk/news/uk/crime/special-investigation-are-muslim-boys-using-profits-of-crime-to-fund-terrorist-attacks-502831.html)

[47] Rastafarianism (http://www.movinghere.org.uk/galleries/histories/caribbean/culture/religion_role3.htm#) Migration histories website. Accessed *6 October 2006*

[48] Pace in the UK (http://www.hawaii.edu/satocenter/pace/5-special.htm) (*pidgin and creole English*). Accessed *9 October 2006.*

[49] British Afro-Caribbean English: A bibliography (http://privatewww.essex.ac.uk/~patrickp/aavesem/BrACEbib.htm) Compiled by Peter L. Patrick. Retrieved 6 October 2006.

[50] 'Jafaican' is wiping out inner-city English accents (http://www.dailymail.co.uk/pages/live/articles/news/news.html?in_article_id=382734&in_page_id=1770&in_a_source) Daily Mail. 12 April 2006. Retrieved 6 October 2006.

[51] BFI website (http://www.bfi.org.uk/booksvideo/video/catalogue/index.php/page/item_view/code/439) "Pressure" description. Accessed *1 June 2007.*

[52] Yvonne Brewster profile (http://www.100greatblackbritons.com/bios/yvonne_brewster.html). 100 Great Black Britons. Accessed *8 October 2006.*

° New Black theatre companies (http://www.movinghere.org.uk/galleries/histories/caribbean/culture/theatre4.htm) Migration histories. Accessed *8 October 2006.*

[53] Blue Mountain Theatre website (http://www.bluemountaintheatre.com/NewFiles/whatson.html) Accessed *8 October 2006.*

[54] Untold London website (http://www.untoldlondon.org.uk/news/ART42059.html) (Museum of London). Retrieved 26 February 2007.

[55] Lenny Henry BBC shows history (http://www.bbc.co.uk/comedy/guide/talent/h/henry_lenny.shtml). BBC online. Accessed *22 December 2006.*

[56] Marianne Jean-Baptiste profile (http://film.guardian.co.uk/Player/Player_Page/0,,68701,00.html) Guardian online. Accessed *7 October 2006.*

[57] http://news.bbc.co.uk/1/hi/uk/781755.stm

[58] Black British Literature since Windrush (http://www.bbc.co.uk/history/british/modern/literature_01.shtml) by Onyekachi Wambu BBC online. Accessed *24 November 2006*

[59] Linton Kwesi Johnson takes his place (http://www.theage.com.au/articles/2002/07/19/1026898910975.html) "Johnson is credited with coining the term dub poetry for the fusion of verse and bass-heavy rhythms" - "He has even been called the alternative poet laureate". The Age newspaper online. 19 July 2002. Accessed *6 October 2006*

[60] Benjamin Zephaniah : A poet to be seen and heard (http://www.britishcouncil.org/argentina-arts-zephaniah_about.htm) British council website. Argentina. Accessed *6 October 2006*

[61] Rasta poet publicly rejects his OBE (http://www.guardian.co.uk/uk_news/story/0,3604,1094118,00.html) Guardian online. 27 November 2003. Accessed *6 October 2006*

[62] www.contemporarywriters.com Author Profile (http://www.contemporarywriters.com/authors/profile/?p=auth149) Andrea Levy. Accessed *6 October 2006*

[63] www.contemporarywriters.com Author Profile (http://www.contemporarywriters.com/authors/?p=auth257) Zadie Smith. Accessed *6 October 2006*

[64] Online (http://fds.oup.com/www.oup.co.uk/pdf/0-19-818428-X.pdf) *A New English Literature 1990–2000.* Oxford University Press. Accessed *22 November 2006*

[65] Met chief accuses media of racism (http://news.bbc.co.uk/1/hi/england/london/4651368.stm) BBC news online. 26 January 2006. Accessed *7 October 2006.*

[66] Trevor McDonald, profile (http://www.museum.tv/archives/etv/M/htmlM/mcdonaldtre/mcdonaldtre.htm) Museum of Broadcast communications. "McDonald is not only one of the most respected elder statesmen of news broadcasting". Accessed *6 October 2006.*

[67] Young writes from the perspective of an African descendant (http://www.blackbritain.co.uk/lifestyle/details.aspx?i=45&c=Book+Review&h=Stranger+in+a+Strange+Land+by+Gary+Younge) Black Britain website. "Throughout his book, [Gary Younge] never lets you forget that he has this unique African Caribbean/British outlook on life in the land of the free." Accessed *17 November 2006*

° Honorary degree for Moira Stuart (http://news.bbc.co.uk/1/hi/scotland/edinburgh_and_east/5177274.stm) BBC Online. "Ms Stuart's maternal grandparents, both from the Caribbean, met while they were studying medicine at Edinburgh University." Accessed *17 November 2006.*

[68] Darcus Howe profile (http://www.awigp.com/default.asp?numcat=darcus) The new West Indian. Accessed *17 November 2006*

[69] Terry Jervis profile (http://www.100greatblackbritons.com/bios/terry_jervis.html) "Successful black producer" 100 Great Black Britons. Accessed *17 November 2006.*

[70] text**'survey=no&url=www.bbc.co.uk/1xtra/index.shtml&js=yes** (http://www.bbc.co.uk/1xtra/index.shtml?'"''Italic] 1Xtra BBC Online. Accessed *17 November 2006.*

[71] Caribbean Family History (http://www.bbc.co.uk/history/familyhistory/get_started/caribbean_01.shtml) BBC Online. Accessed *17 November 2006*

[72] Blacknet UK (http://www.blacknet.co.uk) Accessed *17 November 2006*

[73] Eddie Chambers Biography (http://www.calling.org.uk/pages/commentary/chambers/Chambers_bio.php) by Richard Hylton. "As a facilitator and mentor to many in the visual arts, the importance of his contribution cannot be overstated". Accessed *22 December 2006*

[74] Marlene Smith recounts founding of BLK Art Group on Tate Britain website. Online (http://www.tate.org.uk/britain/exhibitions/rodney/q1.htm). Accessed *23 February 2007.*

[75] Eddie Chambers articles (http://www.eddiechambers.com/articles/moffat.html). Accessed *8 October 2006.*

[76] Faisal Abdu'Allah gallery (http://universes-in-universe.de/car/sharjah/2003/art/abdu-allah/english.htm) Universes in Universe - Worlds of Art. Accessed *8 October 2006.*

[77] Ingrid Pollard: Postcards Home (http://www.foto8.com/reviews/V3N1/pics_postcards.html) foto 8 website. Accessed *21 December 2006*

[78] The Chronicle - Fowkan (http://www.thechronicle.demon.co.uk/archive/7_8_31fo.htm) Accessed *16 March 2006*

[79] Art Buzz (http://www.meppublishers.com/online/caribbean-beat/archive/index.php?id=cb77-2-36) Caribbean beat. Accessed *8 October 2006.*

° Migration Histories website (http://www.movinghere.org.uk/galleries/histories/caribbean/culture/culture.htm). Accessed *8 October 2006.*

[80] Deadpan McQueen takes the Turner (http://www.guardian.co.uk/turner1999/Story/0,,196434,00.html) Guardian Unlimited. Accessed *8 November 2006*.

[81] Paul Gilroy profile (http://learning.berkeley.edu/cipolat/PDF/ISF100A/Lectures/Gilroy.pdf). Berkeley education website. Accessed *13 October 2006*

[82] A Conversation With Stuart Hall (http://www.umich.edu/~iinet/journal/vol7no1/Hall.htm). The Journal of the International Institute. Accessed *13 October 2006*

[83] For Empire, read exploitation (http://observer.guardian.co.uk/race/story/0,,768964,00.html). Guardian online. Accessed *13 October 2006*.

[84] The need to develop effective educational strategies for young people of African descent (http://www.ritesofpassage.org/df99-articles/mis-education.htm) By Makeda J. Graham

[85] Calypso kings (http://arts.guardian.co.uk/nottinghillcarnival2002/story/0,,773465,00.html). Guardian Online. 28 June 2002. Accessed *6 October 2006*.

[86] London is the place for me (http://www.nthposition.com/londonistheplacefor.php) Review by Ian Simmons. NthPosition.com. Accessed *6 October 2006*

[87] Bring back the skins (http://www.skinheadnation.co.uk/traditionalskinheads.htm) Skinhead nation.co.uk. Accessed *6 October 2006*

[88] Dennis Bovell profile (http://www.lkjrecords.com/dennisbovell.htm) LJK records website. Accessed *6 October 2006*

[89] Goldie profile (http://metropolis.co.jp/tokyo/524/clubs.asp) City Guide by Don Crispy. Japan Today magazine. "Born to a Scottish-Jamaican couple in England and put up for adoption, Goldie was raised in various foster homes". Accessed *8 October 2006*

[90] Handsworth Evolution programme (http://www.the-drum.org.uk/event_info.php?id=328&eid=47) The Drum national centre for Black British arts and culture. "Steel Pulse exploded onto the UK reggae scene in the late 70s with their seminal album - Handsworth Revolution". Accessed *6 October 2006*.
↑Allmusic. "Handsworth Revolution" Review (http://www.allmusic.com/cg/amg.dll?p=amg&sql=10:auddyl38xpeb) "Steel Pulse's debut album set the band decisively apart from its British colleagues". Accessed *6 October 2006*.

[91] Errol Brown profile (http://www.100greatblackbritons.com/bios/errol_brown.html) 100 Great Black Britons. "(Hot Chocolate frontman) Errol Brown was born in Jamaica and moved to Britain when he was 12". Accessed *6 October 2006*.
° St Lucia celebrates 27 years of Independence (http://www.socanews.com/artman_new/publish/Features/1674.shtml) Soca News. 7 February 2006. "In the UK, many of the younger generation of St Lucian parentage continue to excel in various fields including [Imagination singer] Leee John (singer/songwriter)". Accessed *6 October 2006*.

[92] Soul II Soul (http://www.bbc.co.uk/cgi-perl/music/muze/index.pl?site=music&action=biography&artist_id=28344) Music profiles. BBC Online. Accessed *6 October 2006*
° Massive attack (http://www.bbc.co.uk/music/profiles/massiveattack.shtml) Music profiles. BBC Online. Accessed *6 October 2006*

[93] Type of club genre (http://www.uk-clubbing-directory.co.uk/pages/genre_types.asp) UKCD.com - Clubbing. "Jungle sped up breakbeats to 200 beats per minute and added ragga vocals from the Caribbean and heavy bassline". Accessed *6 October 2006*.
° Story of Reggae UK Urban and Dance. BBC online. (http://niceup.com/history/bbc/ukurbandance.html). "When the UK started making its own dance music, the dub and remix techniques and bass-heavy sound balances of reggae dictated how things shaped up – drum'n'bass didn't even bother to think up a new name for itself. The later styles, jungle and UK garage, borrowed heavily from dancehall in terms of attitude and presentation". Accessed *6 October 2006*

[94] Roni Size Concert preview (http://metropolis.co.jp/tokyomusicconcerts/concert/348/tokyomusicconcertsinc.htm) Tokyo music concerts. "Born to Jamaican immigrant parents, Size was weaned on the sounds of hip hop and reggae". Accessed *8 October 2006*.

[95] Story of Reggae UK Urban and Dance. BBC online. (http://niceup.com/history/bbc/ukurbandance.html). Accessed *6 October 2006*.

[96] Fast and loose (http://www.guardian.co.uk/Archive/Article/0,4273,4057249,00.html) Guardian Online. Accessed *14 November 2006*

[97] Caribbean online (http://www.afiwi.com/people2.asp?id=200&name=Linford+Christie&coun=0&cat=1&options=&keywords=&alpha_index=&offset=) Linford Christie profile. Accessed *17 November 2006*

[98] Who do you think you are? (http://www.bbc.co.uk/pressoffice/proginfo/tv/wk38/feature_whodoyouthink.shtml) BBC Online. Accessed *14 November 2006*

[99] Yardies who built Britain (http://www.guardian.co.uk/comment/story/0,3604,769705,00.html) Guardian online. 6 August 2002. Accessed *6 October 2006*

[100] Kelly Holmes: The Autobiography (Kelly Holmes) ISBN 1-85227-224-4

[101] New kid on the blocks (http://observer.guardian.co.uk/osm/story/0,,749439,00.html) Guardian Unlimited "The Brit pack, almost all of whom are Afro-Caribbean, includes Christian Malcolm, Dwain Chambers and Darren Campbell, but even in this exalted company Lewis-Francis is seen as exceptional." Accessed *17 November 2006*
Fast and loose (http://www.guardian.co.uk/Archive/Article/0,4273,4057249,00.html) Guardian Online. "Now the second and even third generation of Caribbean-rooted British male sprinters is at hand, many coached by athletes from the first wave". Accessed *14 November 2006*

[102] Caribbean Hall of Fame (http://caribbean.halloffame.tripod.com/Frank_Bruno.html) Frank Bruno biography. 2001. Accessed *6 October 2006*

[103] The Lennox Lewis interview (http://www.playboy.com/arts-entertainment/features/hboboxing/lennoxlewis/). Playboy online. April 2002. Accessed *6 October 2006*

[104] 100 Great Black Britons (http://www.100greatblackbritons.com/bios/nigel_benn-chris_eubanks.html). Chris Eubank biography. Accessed *6 October 2006*

° The Rubank-Benn-Watson rivalry (http://www.eastsideboxing.com/news/Benn-Eubank-Watson.php) Eastsideboxing.com. Accessed 6 October 2006

[105] Harrison hits out at Beeb (http://news.bbc.co.uk/sport1/hi/boxing/2526861.stm) BBC Sport. 29 November 2002. Accessed 6 October 2006

[106] The Time Tunnel: Honeyghan-Curry Remembered (http://www.eastsideboxing.com/boxing-news/Honeyghan2301.php) Eastsideboxing.com. Accessed 6 October 2006

[107] Not-cricket cricket (http://www.catalystmagazine.org/Default.aspx.LocID-0hgnew0e8.RefLocID-0hg01b001006001.Lang-EN.htm) Catalyst magazine. "Test match ticket prices have risen beyond most working class pockets and, some years ago, the ground authorities banned the drums, whistles and klaxons that once created an atmosphere of Caribbean carnival at the Kennington Oval, particularly. The ban has since been slightly relaxed, but probably too late. First, and even some second, generation Caribbean immigrants went to cheer the all-conquering West Indies team, now in decline." Accessed 21 November 2006

[108] Gladstone Small player profile (http://content-usa.cricinfo.com/ci/content/player/20217.html). cricinfo.com. Accessed 6 October 2006

[109] Devon Malcolm player profile (http://content-usa.cricinfo.com/england/content/current/player/16885.html). cricinfo.com. Accessed 6 October 2006

[110] Phil DeFreitas player profile (http://content-usa.cricinfo.com/ci/content/player/11865.html). cricinfo.com. Accessed 6 October 2006

[111] First Black footballer Andrew Watson inspired British soccer in 1870s (http://www.black-history-month.co.uk/articles/andrew_watson.html) Black history month.co.uk. Accessed 6 October 2006

[112] (http://www.thefa.com/WorldCup2006/NewsAndFeatures/Postings/2006/06/WorldCup_Rioready.htm)

[113] Football Unites, Racism Divides (http://www.furd.org/default.asp?intPageID=269) Official website. Biography of Lloyd 'Lindy' Delapenha.Accessed 6 October 2006

[114] FIFA Order of Merit Presented to Clyde Best (http://www.bfa.bm/headline.php?storyId=72) Bermuda Football Association homepage. Accessed 6 October 2006

[115] Football Unites, Racism Divides (http://www.furd.org/default.asp?intPageID=34) Cyril Regis. Accessed 6 October 2006

[116] Englishmen Abroad: Luther Blissett (http://www.thefa.com/Features/EnglishDomestic/Postings/2003/07/54903.htm) F.A. com. Accessed 6 October 2006

[117] Society has to change - Barnes (http://news.bbc.co.uk/sport1/hi/tv_and_radio/world_football/2399629.stm) Alan Green talks to John Barnes. BBC Online. 4 November 2002. Accessed 6 October 2006

[118] John Barnes profile. Football-England (http://www.football-england.com/john_barnes.html) "His international career began when there was a definite hooligan element among England's support. There was also a definite racist element. Famously, a group of travelling supporters was heard remarking, after Barnes had scored his wonderful goal in Brazil, that England had only won 1-0 because his goal didn't count. It is true that the consistent brilliance he showed for Liverpool always eluded him in an England Shirt but for everybody who thought the problem lay with him there was as many again who felt it was the inadequacy of his teammates." Accessed 21 November 2006

[119] Football Unites Racism Divides (http://www.furd.org/default.asp?intPageID=69) Accessed 26 October 2006.

[120] Kick It Out is football's anti-racism campaign. (http://www.kickitout.org/index.php?id=4) Accessed 26 October 2006.

[121] England's teenaged star Walcott linked to Jamaica (http://www.jamaicaobserver.com/sports/html/20060610T220000-0500_106677_OBS_ENGLAND_S_TEENAGED_STAR_WALCOTT_LINKED_TO_JAMAICA_.asp) The Jamaica Observer. 11 June 2006. Accessed 26 October 2006.

[122] http://www.bartleby.com/61/98/A0129800.html

[123] http://www.c-sap.bham.ac.uk/subject_areas/sociology/handbook/sectionJ/J6.doc

[124] Glossary of terms relating to ethnicity and race: for reflection and debate (http://jech.bmjjournals.com/cgi/content/full/58/6/441) R Bhopal. Journal of Epidemiology and Community Health. Accessed 6 October 2006

[125] http://www.guardian.co.uk/styleguide/page/0,,184844,00.html

[126] http://www.bath.ac.uk/marketing/style/

[127] Working lives (http://www.movinghere.org.uk/galleries/histories/caribbean/working_lives/working_lives.htm) Migration histories. Accessed 8 October 2006

[128] UK unemployment tops three million (http://news.bbc.co.uk/onthisday/hi/dates/stories/january/26/newsid_2506000/2506335.stm) On this day. BBC online 1982. Accessed 8 October 2006

[129] Voices: Our Untold Stories. African Caribbean Stories (http://www.bbc.co.uk/gloucestershire/untold_stories/african/wi_association.shtml) BBC online. Accessed 6 October 2006

[130] Leeds West Indian centre (http://www.skiddle.com/whatson/guide.php/skiddle/LEEDS/THE_WEST_INDIAN_CENTER_(LEEDS)/) Details. Accessed 6 October 2006

[131] Manchester City Council West Indian centre (http://www.manchester2002-uk.com/meeting/afro.html) Details. Accessed 6 October 2006

[132] Worship for Caribbeans in Britain (http://www.movinghere.org.uk/galleries/histories/caribbean/culture/religion_role2.htm#) Migration histories. Accessed 6 October 2006

[133] The suburbs turn Black (http://economist.com/displaystory.cfm?story_id=4064660) Economist.com. 9 June 2005. Accessed 6 October 2006

[134] Australia v England scorecard 1987 (http://www.cricketweb.net/worldcup2007/scorecards/WCFinal1987.txt) Cricket web.net. Accessed 6 October 2006

[135] Defender cast in unwanted role of target man (http://football.guardian.co.uk/Columnists/Column/0,,1360980,00.html) Guardian online. 27 November 2004. Accessed 6 October 2006

[136] England's Ferdinand looks forward to World Cup clash against Trinidad (http://www.caribbeannetnews.com/2005/12/12/looks.shtml) Caribbean net news. 12 December 2005. Accessed 6 October 2006

Further reading

- A Land of Dreams : A Study of Jewish and Afro-Caribbean Migrant Communities in England (http://www. fircroft.ac.uk/Land_of_Dreams.html), by Simon Taylor, Routledge; 1 edition (April 1993). ISBN 0-415-08447-4
- *Black and British (Paperback)*, by David Bygott, Oxford University Press (18 April 1996). ISBN 0-19-913305-0
- *In Search of a Better Life: Perspectives on Migration from the Caribbean*, by Ransford W. Palmer, Praeger Publishers (21 May 1990). ISBN 0-275-93409-8
- *The History of African and Caribbean Communities in Britain*, by Hakim Adi, Wayland London 1995. ISBN 0-7502-1517-8
- *Windrush: The Irresistible Rise of Multi-Racial Britain*, by Mike Phillips & Trevor Phillips, HarperCollins Publishers, Incorporated 1998. ISBN 0-00-255909-9
- Young Blacks, Political Groups and the Police in Handsworth (http://www.theplebeian.net) An examination of police attempts to isolate young Blacks and attempts by leftist political groups to attract Black youth into their political orbit that preceded the Handsworth protests of 1985.

External links

- The Black Presence in Britain (http://www.blackpresence.co.uk/)
- The Voice Newspaper (http://www.voice-online.co.uk/)
- OOM Gallery (http://www.oomgallery.net/)
- Digital Handsworth (http://www.digitalhandsworth.org.uk/)
- Black Youth Empowerment UK (http://www.byempowerment.blogspot.com/)
- Reassessing what we collect website - The Caribbean Community in London (http://www.museumoflondon. org.uk/English/Collections/OnlineResources/RWWC/Themes/1102/) History of Caribbean London with objects and images
- Windrush settlers arrive in Britain, 1948 - treasures of The National Archives (UK). (http://www. nationalarchives.gov.uk/museum/item.asp?item_id=50)
- Windrush settlers arrive in Britain, 1948 – Transcript (http://www.nationalarchives.gov.uk/museum/ additional_image_types.asp?extra_image_type_id=2&image_id=69)

Carnivals

- Leeds Carnival (http://www.leedscarnival.co.uk)
- London Notting Hill Carnival (http://www.londoncarnival.co.uk)
- Luton Carnival (http://www.luton.gov.uk/carnival)

Community sites

- UK Black Community website (http://www.blacknet.co.uk)
- African Caribbean Coventry website (http://www.limelightmagazine.com/front.htm)
- itzcaribbean.com (http://www.itzcaribbean.com/)
- Afro Caribbean Millennium Centre (http://www.acmccentre.com/acmc.shtml) Caribbean (http://www. calibbian.com/privacy.htm) Website for the Birmingham based community centre
- Community Action Project (http://www.cap-centre.com/) Sandwel based community centre website

• African and Caribbean Black Community Network (http://www.blackcnet.com)

Arrival of black immigrants in London

The history of black immigrants in London.

Prehistoric

The original inhabitants of London arrived about 400,000 years ago, descended from migrants from Africa. A further wave of immigration occurred about 40,000 years ago. They were able to walk across the sea on account of a land bridge [1]

Roman London

Archeologists have found a spoon and a lamp with representations of African people dating from Roman times.[1]

16th century

Early in the 16th century Africans arrived in London when Catherine of Aragon travelled to London and brought a group of her African attendants with her. Around the same time African named trumpeters, who served Henry VII and Henry VIII, came to London. When

William Hogarth's engraving *Four Times of the Day: Noon* (1738) shows a black London resident.

trade lines began to open between London and West Africa, Africans slowly began to become part of the London population. The first record of an African in London was in 1593. His name was Cornelius. London's residents started to become fearful of the increased black population. At this time Elizabeth I declared that black "Negroes and black Moors" were to be arrested and expelled from her kingdom, although this did not lead to actual legisation.[2] [3]

17th-18th centuries

During this era there was a rise of black settlements in London. Britain was involved with the tri-continental slave trade between Europe, Africa and the Americas. Black slaves were attendants to sea captains and ex-colonial officials as well as traders, plantation owners and military personnel. This marked growing evidence of the black presence in the northern, eastern and southern areas of London. There were also small numbers of free slaves and seaman from West Africa and South Asia. Many of these people were forced into beggary due to the lack of jobs and racial discrimination.[4] [5]

Around the 1750s London became the home of many of Blacks, Jews, Irish, Germans, and Huguenots. The number of Blacks in London reached between 10,000 to 15,000 during the 1760s. Evidence of the number of Black residents in London has been found through registered burials. The whites of London had widespread views that Black people in London were less than human; these views were expressed in slave sale advertisements. Some Black people in London resisted through escape. Leading Black activists of this era included Olaudah Equiano, Ignatius Sancho and

Quobna Ottobah Cugoano.

With the support of other Britons these activists demanded that Blacks be freed from slavery. Supporters involved in this movements included workers and other nationalities of the urban poor. London Blacks vocally contested slavery and the slave trade. At this time the slavery of whites was forbidden, but the legal statuses of these practices were not clearly defined. Free black slaves could not be enslaved, but blacks who were bought as slaves to Britain were considered the property of their owners. During this era Lord Mansfield declared that a slave who fled from his master could not be taken by force or sold abroad. This verdict fueled the numbers of Blacks that escaped slavery, and helped send slavery into decline. During this same period many slave soldiers who fought on the side of the British in the American Revolutionary War arrived in London. These soldiers were deprived of pensions and many of them became poverty-stricken and were reduced to begging on the streets. The Blacks in London lived among the whites in areas of Mile End, Stepney, Paddington and St Giles. The majority of these people did not live as slaves, but as servants to wealthy whites. Many became labeled as the "Black Poor" defined as former low wage soldiers, seafarers and plantation workers.[6]

During the late 18th century there were many publications and memoirs written about the "black poor". One example is the writings of Equiano, who became an unofficial spokesman for Britain's Black community. A memoir about his life is entitled, *The Interesting Narratives of the Life of Olaudah Equiano*. Equiano became a landowner in Cambridgeshire and married Susannah Cullen, from Soham [7]. Both his daughters were born and baptised there.

19th century

Coming into the early 19th century, more groups of black soldiers and seaman were displaced after the Napoleonic wars and settled in London. These settlers suffered and faced many challenges as did many Black Londoners. In 1807 the British slave trade was abolished and the slave trade was abolished completely in the British empire by 1834. The number of blacks in London was steadily declining with these new laws. Fewer blacks were brought into London from the West Indies and parts of Africa.[6]

The 19th century was also a time when "scientific racism" flourished. Many white Londoners claimed that they were the superior race and that blacks were not as intelligent as whites. They tried to hold up their accounts with scientific evidence, for example the size of the brain. Such claims were later proven false, but this was just one more obstacle for the blacks in London to hurdle over. The late 19th century effectively ended the first period of large scale black immigration to London and Britain. This decline in immigration gave way to the gradual incorporation of blacks and their descendents into this predominantly white society.

During the mid-19th century there were restrictions on African immigration. In the later part of the 19th century there was a build up of small groups of black dockside communities in towns such as Canning Town,[8] Liverpool, and Cardiff. This was a direct effect of new shipping links that were established with the Caribbean and West Africa. As these small groups of black communities made their lives as a part of London many of the London-born blacks began to make a significant mark on London life. There was a continuous influx of African students, sportsmen, and businessmen mixed with this dominant white society. These black-born Londoners were gaining professional positions as doctors, politicians and activists. Slowly they were being accepted into London and British society.

World War I

World War I was another growth period for blacks in London. Their communities grew with the arrival of merchant seaman and soldiers. At the same time there is also a continuous presence of small groups of students from Africa and the Caribbean slowly immigrating into London. These first communities which housed London's first black immigrants survive and now are among the oldest black communities of London.

World War II

World War II marked another growth period for black immigrants into London and Britain societies. Many blacks from the Caribbean and West Africa arrive in small groups as wartime workers, merchant seaman, and servicemen from the army, navy, and air forces. It is estimated that approximately twenty thousand black Londoners lived in communities concentrated in the dock side areas of London, Liverpool and Cardiff. One of these black Londoners, Learie Constantine, who was a welfare officer in the RAF, was refused service at a London hotel. He stood up for his rights and later was awarded damages. This particular example is used by some to illustrate the slow change from racism towards acceptance and equality of all citizens in London.[9]

Post-war period

During the mid nineteen hundreds the first groups of Britain's post war Caribbean immigrants settled in London. There were about four hundred and ninety two immigrants that were passengers on the SS Empire Windrush. These passengers settled in the area of Brixton which is now a prominently black district in Britain. From the 1950s into the 1960s there was a mass migration of workers from all over the English-speaking Caribbean, particularly Jamaica, who settled in Britain. These immigrants were invited to fill labour requirements in London's hospitals, transportation venues and railway development. They are widely viewed as having been a major contributing factor to the rebuilding of the post-war urban London economy.

In 1962 the Commonwealth Immigrants Act was passed in Britain along with a succession of other laws in 1968, 1971, and 1981 that severely restricted the entry of Black immigrants into Britain. During this period it is widely argued that emergent blacks and Asians struggled in Britain against racism and prejudice. In 1975 a new voice emerged for the black London population; his name was David Pitt and he brought a new voice to the House of Lords. He spoke against racism and for equality in regards to all residents of Britain. With this new tone also came the opportunity for the black population to elect four Black members into Parliament.

By the end of the 20th century the number of black Londoners numbered half a million, according to the 1991 census. An increasing number of these black Londoners were London- or British-born. Even with this growing population and the first blacks elected to Parliament, many argue that there was still discrimination and a socio-economic imbalance in London among the Blacks. In 1992 the number of blacks in Parliament increased to six and in 1997 they increased their numbers to nine. There are still many problems that Black Londoners face; the new global and high tech information revolution is changing the urban economy and some argue that it is driving unemployment rates among blacks up relative to non-blacks, something which, it is argued, threatens to erode the progress made thus far.[6]

As of June 2007, the black population of London is 802,300 or 10.6% of the population of London. 4.3% of Londoners are Caribbean, 5.5% of Londoners are African and a further 0.8% are from other black backgrounds including American and Latin American. There are also 117,400 people who are mixed black and white.[10]

References

[1] The African Community in London (http://www.museumoflondon.org.uk/English/Collections/OnlineResources/RWWC/Themes/ 1078/), Museum of London website accessed 7 August 2010

[2] Bartels, Emily (22 March 2006). "Too many Blackamoors: deportation, discrimination, and Elizabeth I" (http://www.accessmylibrary.com/ coms2/summary_0286-15698891_ITM). *Studies in English Literature, 1500-1900.* . Retrieved January 2008.

[3] Davies, Carole Boyce (2008). *Encyclopedia of the African diaspora: origins, experiences, and culture.* ABC-CLIO Ltd. ISBN 1851097007.

[4] Banton, Michael (1955), *The Coloured Quarter.* Jonathan Cape. London.

[5] Shyllon, Folarin, "The Black Presence and Experience in Britain: An Analytical Overview", in Gundara and Duffield eds. (1992), *Essays on the History of Blacks in Britain.* Avebury, Aldershot.http://www.chronicleworld.org

[6] File, Nigel and Chris Power (1981), *Black Settlers in Britain 1555-1958.* Heinnemann Educational. http://www.chronicleworld.org

[7] http://equiano.soham.org.uk/intro.htm

[8] Geoffrey Bell, *The other Eastenders : Kamal Chunchie and West Ham's early black community* (Stratford: Eastside Community Heritage, 2002)

[9] Rose, Sonya (May 2001). "Race, empire and British wartime national identity, 1939–45" (http://www.blackwell-synergy.com/action/ showPdf?submitPDF=Full+Text+PDF+(247+KB)&doi=10.1111/1468-2281.00125&cookieSet=1). *Historical Research* **74** (184): 224. doi:10.1111/1468-2281.00125. .

[10] Resident Population Estimates by Ethnic Group, All Persons (http://www.neighbourhood.statistics.gov.uk/dissemination/ LeadTableView.do?a=3&b=276743&c=london&d=13&e=13&g=325264&i=1001x1003x1004&m=0&r=1&s=1217082648365& enc=1&dsFamilyId=1809)

See also

- Historical immigration to Great Britain
- Black British

Demographics of Jamaica

This article is about the **demographic features of the population of Jamaica**, including population density, ethnicity, education level, health of the populace, economic status, religious affiliations and other aspects of the population.

Demographic statistics

The following demographic statistics are from the CIA World Factbook unless otherwise referenced.

Population

2,682,100 (2007 est.[1]), 2,804,334 (July 2008 est.)

Age structure

0–14 years: 33.1% (male 464,297/female 449,181)
15–64 years: 59.6% (male 808,718/female 835,394)
65 years and over: 7.3% (male 90,100/female 110,434) (2006 est.)

Population growth rate

0.8% (2006 est.)

Birth rate

20.82 births/1,000 population (2006 est.) There were a total of 45,600 births in 2007. (46,300 in 2006 and 47,000 in 2005 resulting in a birth rate of 17.0 per 1000 in 2007.[1]

Death rate

6.55 deaths/1,000 population (2006 est.)[Note: Birth-Death+Net mig=Pop increase --> 20.82-X-6.27=8 --> X=6.55]

Net migration rate

-6.27 migrant(s)/1,000 populations (2006 est.)

Sex ratio

Practic: 1.05 male(s)/female
under 15 years: 1.03 male(s)/female
15-64 years: 0.97 male(s)/female
65 years and over: 0.82 male(s)/female
total population: 0.98 male(s)/female (2006 est.)

Infant mortality rate

total population: 15.98 deaths/1,000 live births
male: 16.66 deaths/1,000 live births
female: 15.27 deaths/1,000 live births (2006 est.)

Life expectancy at birth

total population: 73.24 years
male: 71.54 years
female: 75.03 years (2006 est.)

Total fertility rate

2.41 children born/woman (2006 est.)

Nationality

noun: Jamaican(s)
adjective: Jamaican

Ethnic groups

This topic is somewhat contentious with several respected sources giving different figures. In alphabetic order these are:

- **CIA Fact Book**: black 91.2%, mixed 6.2%, other or unknown 2.6% (2001 census).[2]
- **University of the West Indies**: 76.3% African descent, 15.1% Afro-European, 3.4% East Indian and Afro-East Indian, 3.2% Caucasian, 1.2% Chinese and 0.8% Other.[3]

Religions

Protestant 62.5% (including Church of God 23.7%, Seventh-Day Adventist 10.8%, Pentecostal 9.5%, Baptist 7.2%, Anglican 3.6%) Roman Catholic 2.6%, Other or unspecified 14.2% None 20.9%

Languages

English (official), Jamaican Creole (most widely spoken language)

Literacy

definition: age 15 and over has ever attended school
total population: 87.9%
male: 84.1%
female: 91.6% (2003 est.)

External links

- CIA World Factbook -- Jamaica [4]

References

[1] Henry, Balford (March 30, 2008). "An estimated 17,000 Jamaicans passed on last year but..." (http://web.archive.org/web/ 20080506062808/http://www.jamaicaobserver.com/news/html/ 20080329T180000-0500_134008_OBS_AN_ESTIMATED_____JAMAICANS_PASSED_ON_LAST_YEAR_BUT____.asp). The Jamaica Observer. Archived from the original (http://www.jamaicaobserver.com/news/html/ 20080329T180000-0500_134008_OBS_AN_ESTIMATED_____JAMAICANS_PASSED_ON_LAST_YEAR_BUT____.asp) on 2008-05-06. . Retrieved 2008-05-11.

[2] https://www.cia.gov/library/publications/the-world-factbook/geos/jm.html#People

[3] University of the West Indies (http://www.uwi.edu/territories/jamaica.aspx)

[4] https://www.cia.gov/library/publications/the-world-factbook/geos/jm.html

Lists of UK locations with large ethnic minority populations

This article lists United Kingdom locations with large and/or significant ethnic minority communities. The overwhealming majority of ethnic minority individuals in the UK reside in the larger cities, most specifically London. The British capital is home to 50 non-indigenous communities which have a population of more than 10,000 (therefore laying claim to being the most diverse city in the world).[1] Despite this, there are many many other towns and cities across the country which have larger ethnic minority populations per head. Examples being the 25% Indian population of Leicester[2] and the 28% Portuguese population of Thetford.[3]

Afghan communities

All below figures are 2007 estimates by the IOM.[4]

- London - 5,000-11,000
- Birmingham - 500-8,000
- Manchester - 150-2,000
- Southampton - 200-800
- Glasgow - 300
- Sheffield - 200-300
- Coventry - 230
- Bradford - 150
- Wolverhampton - 120
- Cardiff - 50-100
- Lincoln - 70-80

Bangladeshi communities

All data below is based on 2007 estimates and is for Bangladeshi people in the UK regardless of birthplace (excluding those of partial Bangladeshi origin).[5]

- London - 174,900 (2.3% of the city's population)
  - Tower Hamlets - 63,400 (29.4%)
  - Newham - 23,200 (9.3%)
  - Camden - 12,800 (5.5%)
- Birmingham - 23,700 (2.3%)
- Oldham - 11,200 (5.1%)
- Luton - 8,700 (4.6%)
- Bradford - 5,900 (1.2%)
- Newcastle upon Tyne - 3,100 (1.1%)

Protest march by Bangladeshis to Downing Street with murdered Altab Ali's coffin, 1978

Black British communities

All data below is based on 2007 estimates and is for Black British people in the UK regardless of birthplace (Including Black Africans, Caribbeans and other Black groups, but excluding those of partial Sub-Saharan African origin).[6]

- London - 802,300 (10.6% of the city's population)
- Birmingham - 67,500 (6.7%)
- Manchester - 25,100 (5.5%)
- Leeds - 16,600 (2.2%)
- Luton - 16,200 (8.6%)
- Leicester - 14,300 (4.9%)
- Sheffield - 14,000 (2.6%)
- Nottingham - 13,700 (4.8%)
- Sandwell - 12,400 (4.3%)
- Bristol - 12,300 (2.9%)
- Wolverhampton - 11,400 (4.8%)
- Coventry - 10,000 (3.3%)
- Milton Keynes - 9,100 (4.0%)
- Liverpool - 8,500 (1.9%)

Afro-Caribbean communities

All data below is based on 2007 estimates and is for Black Caribbean people in the UK regardless of birthplace (excluding other Black groups and those of partial Afro-Caribbean origin).[7]

Afro-Caribbean Leicester

- London - 321,300 (4.3% of the city's population)
  - Lewisham - 28,400 (11.0%)
  - Croydon - 26,800 (7.9%)
  - Lambeth - 25,600 (9.4%)
  - Brent - 24,100 (8.9%)
  - Hackney - 18,200 (8.7%)
  - Haringey - 17,700 (7.9%)

  - Southwark - 17,500 (6.4%)
  - Waltham Forest - 16,700 (7.5%)
  - Newham - 15,900 (6.4)
- Birmingham - 44,700 (4.4%)
- Manchester - 8,700 (1.9%)
- Nottingham - 8,400 (2.9%)
- Wolverhampton - 8,200 (3.5%)
- Luton - 8,000 (4.2%)
- Leeds - 6,900 (0.9%)
- Bristol - 5,400 (1.3%)
- Sheffield - 5,100 (1.0%)

Jamaican British

All below figures are 2007 estimates by the IOM.[8]

- London - 250,000
- Birmingham - 30,000
- Bristol - 20,000
- Manchester - 10,000
- Gloucester - 4,000
- Leeds - 4,000-5,000
- Leicester - 3,000-4,000
- Sheffield - 2,000
- Liverpool - 1,000-2,000
- Preston - 800

Congolese communities

All below figures are 2006 estimates by the IOM.[9]

- London - 13,000-17,000
- Manchester - 1,800-2,500
- Birmingham - 1,500-2,000
- Glasgow - 450-600
- Newcastle - 300-400
- Bristol - 180-200
- Newport - 100-150
- Cardiff - 100-150
- Southampton - 100
- Sheffield - 100

Ghanaian communities

All below figures are 2009 estimates by the IOM.[10]

- London - 20,000
- Cardiff - 12,000
- Liverpool - 9,000
- Southampton - 8,000
- Milton Keynes - 5,000
- Bracknell - 1,500

Ivorian communities

All below figures are 2008 estimates by the IOM.[11]

- London - 3,000-4,500
- Birmingham - 2,000-3,000
- Newcastle - 400-1,000
- Glasgow - 100-200

Tanzanian communities

All below figures are 2009 estimates by the IOM.[12]

- London - 20,000-25,000
- Birmingham - 4,500-5,000
- Reading - 3,500-4,000
- Manchester - 3,000-3,500
- Milton Keynes - 2,500-3,000
- Northampton - 1,500-2,000
- Coventry - 1,500-2,000
- Leicester - 1,500-2,000
- Slough - 800-1,000
- Leeds 700-800
- Glasgow - 300-350
- Cardiff - 200-250
- Edinburgh - 100-150

Zimbabwean communities

All below figures are 2006 estimates by the IOM.[12]

- London - 40,000
- Luton - 20,000
- Leeds - 20,000
- Slough - 10,000
- Milton Keynes - 10,000
- Manchester - 10,000
- Sheffield - 10,000
- Birmingham - 10,000
- Wolverhampton - 5,000
- Coventry - 5,000
- Leicester - 5,000
- Glasgow - 5,000
- Edinburgh - 3,000
- Liverpool - 3,000
- Bristol - 2,000
- Oxford - 1,000
- Cardiff - 1,000

Chinese communities

All data below is based on 2007 estimates and is for Chinese people in the UK regardless of birthplace (excluding those of partial Chinese origin).[13] Exceptions come in the form of IOM 2006 estimates.

- London - 114,800 (1.5% of the city's population)
- London - 100,000-200,000[14]

  - Barnet - 8,000 (2.4%)
  - Southwark - 7,900 (2.9%)
  - Westminster - 7,700 (3.3%)
  - Camden - 6,700 (2.9%)
  - Tower Hamlets - 5,500 (2.5%)
  - Kensington and Chelsea - 5,100 (2.9%)
  - Islington - 4,600 (2.5%)
  - Ealing - 4,500 (1.5%)
  - Greenwich - 3,700 (1.7%)
  - Lewisham - 3,600 (1.4%)
  - Lambeth - 3,600 (1.3%)
  - Haringey - 3,500 (1.6%)
  - Newham - 3,500 (1.4%)
  - Brent - 3,500 (1.3%)
- Manchester - 12,300 (2.7%)
- Manchester - 35,000-80,000[14]
- Birmingham - 12,300 (1.2%)
- Birmingham - 60,000[14]
- Liverpool - 7,400 (1.7%)
- Liverpool - 25,000-35,000[14]
- Glasgow - 11,000-30,000[14]
- Edinburgh - 15,000[14]
- Leeds - 10,100 (1.3%)
- Sheffield - 6,700 (1.3%)
- Oxford - 4,500 (3.0%)
- Cambridge - 3,900 (3.3%)
- Newcastle upon Tyne - 3,600 (1.3%)
- Belfast - 1,100 (1.2%)
- Belfast - 2,000[14]

London's Chinatown, located in the Soho area of the West End of London.

Ethiopian communities

All below figures are 2006 estimates by the IOM.[15]

- London - 25,000-30,000
- Leeds - 12,500
- West Midlands conurbation - 3,000-5,000
- Greater Manchester - 2,000-3,000
- Sheffield - 1,500
- East Midlands Nottingham/ Leicester Urban Area - 1,000-2,000
- Newcastle - 1,000
- Glasgow - 1,000
- Cardiff - 500
- Edinburgh - 500

Filipino communities

- London - 120,000[16]
- Cambridge - 3,000-5,000[17]

Iraqi communities

All data below is based on estimates and is for Iraqi people in the UK regardless of birthplace.[18]

- London - 125,000 (1.8% of city's population)
- Birmingham - 35,000 (3.5%)
- Manchester - 18,000 (4.0%)
- Cardiff - 9,000 (2.8%)
- Glasgow - 5,000 (0.9%)
- Derby - 2,000 (0.9%)
- Plymouth - 2,000 (0.8%)

Iraqi London

Italian communities

- London - 39,000 Italian born people only[19]
- Manchester - 25,000 Italians and British born Italians[20]
- Bedford - 14,000 (20% of town's population is of Italian origin)[21]
- Liverpool - 6,000 Italian born people only[22]
- Bristol - 6,000 Italian born people only[23]
- Glasgow - 4,000 Italian born or British born Italian[24] [Estimated 100,000 within Scotland] [25]

Latin American communities

Bolivian communities

All below figures are 2007 estimates by the IOM.[26]

- London - 15,000-20,000
  - Southwark - 6,000-8,000
  - Haringey - 3,000-4,000
  - Camden - 2,000-3,000
  - Lewisham - 2,000-3,000
  - Lambeth - 1,000-2,000
- Newcastle - 500-2,000
- Edinburgh - 200-1,000

Brazilian communities

All below figures are 2007 estimates by the IOM unless stated otherwise.[27]

- London - 130,000-160,000[28]
- West Midlands conurbation - 20,000
- Norfolk/ East Anglia - 15,000
- Brighton - 10,000
- Greater Manchester/ Liverpool Urban Area - 10,000

Colombian communities

All below figures are 2007 estimates by the IOM.[29]

- London - 100,000-120,000
- Brighton - 2,000-5,000
- Newcastle upon Tyne - 100-300
- Swansea - 50-150
- Edinburgh - 50-150
- Manchester 50-200
- Leeds - 50-100

Colombian London

Ecuadorian communities

All below figures are 2008 estimates by the IOM.[30]

- London - 100,000
- Birmingham - 300
- Manchester - 200

Malaysian communities

All below figures are 2009 estimates by the IOM.[4]

- London - 48,000
- Manchester - 18,000
- Sheffield - 12,000
- Leeds - 12,000

- Birmingham - 12,000
- Liverpool - 6,000
- Southampton - 1,200
- Bristol - 1,200

Pakistani communities

All data below is based on 2007 estimates and is for Pakistani people in the UK regardless of birthplace (excluding those of partial Pakistani origin).[31]

- London - 179,100 (2.4% of city's population, see Pakistani community of London)
  - Newham - 23,000 (9.2%)
  - Redbridge - 17,800 (7.0%)
  - Waltham Forest - 17,500 (7.8%)
  - Ealing - 12,400 (4.0%)
  - Brent - 12,200 (4.5%)
  - Hounslow - 10,200 (4.6%)
  - Croydon - 9,400 (2.8%)
  - Harrow - 6,100 (2.8%)
  - Barnet - 5,900 (1.8%)
  - Wandsworth - 5,400 (1.9%)
- Birmingham - 113,000 (11.2%)
- Bradford - 80,000 (16.1%)
- Glasgow - 30,000
- Kirklees - 28,600 (7.1%)
- Manchester - 28,100 (6.1%)
- Luton - 20,100 (10.6%)
- Leeds - 18,200 (2.4%)
- Sheffield - 17,400 (3.3%)
- Rochdale - 17,200 (8.4%)
- Oldham - 15,300 (7.0%)
- Slough - 14,600 (12.2%)
- Blackburn - 12,600 (9.0%)
- Pendle - 11,800 (13.1%)
- Calderdale - 11,500 (5.7%)
- Derby - 10,800 (4.5%)
- Nottingham - 10,500 (3.6%)
- Walsall - 10,300 (4.0%)
- Sandwell - 9,900 (3.4%)
- Wycombe - 9,100 (5.7%)
- Dudley - 7,900 (2.6%)
- Peterborough - 7,400 (4.6%)
- Bolton - 7,300 (2.8%)
- Coventry - 7,100 (2.3%)
- Stoke-on-Trent - 7,000 (2.9%)
- Bury - 6,600 (3.6%)
- Bristol - 6,000 (1.4%)
- Hyndburn - 5,900 (7.2%)

- Leicester - 5,800 (2.0%)
- Rotherham - 5,700 (2.2%)
- Middlesbrough - 5,500 (4.0%)
- Newcastle upon Tyne - 5,200 (1.9%)
- Trafford - 4,700 (2.2%)
- Wakefield - 4,700 (1.5%)
- Wolverhampton - 4,500 (1.9%)
- Aylesbury - 4,300 (2.4%)
- Stockport - 3,900 (1.4%)
- Watford - 3,700 (4.6%)
- Crawley - 3,400 (3.4%)

Polish communities

- Inverness - 10,000 (17%) 2001 Estimate
- London - 120,000[32]
- Leicester - 30,000[33]
- Southampton - 20,000[34]
- Peterborough - 10,000[35]
- Slough - 10,000[36]
- Reading - 8,000[37]
- Swindon - 7,000[38]
- Blackpool - 5,000[39]
- Carlisle - 1,600[40]

Portuguese communities

- London - 25,000 Portuguese born only,[41] plus a large percentage of the total half a million Portuguese British community
  - Stockwell (Little Portugal) in Lambeth - 27,000
- Thetford - 6,000[3]
- West Midlands conurbation - 1,000 Portuguese born only[42]
- Channel Islands

Russian communities

All below figures are 2007 estimates by the IOM.[43]

- London - 300,000
- Manchester - 40,000
- Cambridge - 13,000
- Brighton - 13,000
- Bristol - 13,000
- Birmingham - 13,000

South African communities

All below figures are 2008 estimates by the IOM.[44]

- London - 200,000-300,000
  - Putney - 5,500
  - Leytonstone - 5,000
  - Wandsworth - 5,000
  - Hampstead - 4,000
  - Leyton - 3,500
  - Canada Water - 3,000
  - Wimbledon - 3,000
  - Waltham Forest - 2,500
  - Canary Wharf - 2,000
  - North Finchley - 2,000
  - Ealing - 2,000
  - Fulham - 2,000
  - Merton - 2,000
  - Finchley - 1,500
  - Southwark - 1,500
- Manchester - 5,000
- Bristol - 3,500
- Cambridge - 2,500
- Brighton - 2,500
- Birmingham - 2,500
- Guildford - 2,000
- Oxford - 2,000
- Reading - 1,000
- Cardiff - 500
- Edinburgh - 500

Somali communities

All below figures are 2006 estimates by the IOM.[45]

- London - 70,000
- Birmingham - 35,000
- Leicester - 15,000
- Cardiff - 10,000
- Sheffield - 10,000
- Liverpool - 9,000

Sudanese communities

All below figures are 2006 estimates by the IOM.[45]

- London - 10,00-25,000
- Brighton - 3,000-18,000
- West Midlands conurbation - 4,000-5,000
- Manchester - 2,000
- Glasgow - 1,500
- Edinburgh - 1,000

Ukrainian communities

All below figures are 2007 estimates by the IOM.[46]

- London - 48,000
- Manchester - 12,000
- Bradford - 6,000
- Nottingham - 6,000

Vietnamese communities

All below figures are 2008 estimates by the IOM.[47]

- London - 30,000-35,000
- Leeds/ West Yorkshire - 10,000
- Birmingham - 3,000-4,000
- Manchester - 2,500-3,000
- South Wales - 2,000
- Liverpool - 1,500
- Leicester - 1,000
- Surrey - 700-1,000
- Nottingham - 500
- Northampton - 500
- Cambridge - 500
- Portsmouth - 400-500
- Southampton - 400-500

Yemeni communities

See: Yemeni communities in the United Kingdom

See also

- Demography of the United Kingdom
- Ethnic groups of the United Kingdom
- Ethnic enclave
- Lists of U.S. cities with large ethnic populations

References

[1] Benedictus, Leo (2005-01-21). "Every race, colour, nation and religion on earth" (http://www.guardian.co.uk/uk/2005/jan/21/britishidentity1). London: The Guardian. . Retrieved 2010-04-22.

[2] Neighbourhood Statistics - Neil Sillitoe. "Indians in Leicester" (http://www.neighbourhood.statistics.gov.uk/dissemination/LeadHome.do;jessionid=ac1f930bce6bcf78fc81679419397d18967b152469c?m=0&s=1217013755765&enc=1&nsjs=true&nsck=true&nssvg=false&nswid=1259). Neighbourhood.statistics.gov.uk. . Retrieved 2010-08-10.

[3] "Portuguese in Thetford" (http://spamandchips.net/portuguese/index.htm). Spamandchips.net. . Retrieved 2010-08-10.

[4] "Afghanistan Mapping Exercise" (http://www.iomlondon.org/doc/mapping/IOM_AFGHANISTAN.pdf). International Organization for Migration. . Retrieved 2010-04-21.

[5] Neighbourhood Statistics - Neil Sillitoe. "Bangladeshi people in the UK" (http://www.neighbourhood.statistics.gov.uk/dissemination/LeadHome.do;jessionid=ac1f930bce6bcf78fc81679419397d18967b152469c?m=0&s=1217013755765&enc=1&nsjs=true&nsck=true&nssvg=false&nswid=1259). Neighbourhood.statistics.gov.uk. . Retrieved 2010-08-10.

[6] Neighbourhood Statistics - Neil Sillitoe. "Black British people in the UK" (http://www.neighbourhood.statistics.gov.uk/dissemination/LeadHome.do;jessionid=ac1f930bce6bcf78fc81679419397d18967b152469c?m=0&s=1217013755765&enc=1&nsjs=true&nsck=true&nssvg=false&nswid=1259). Neighbourhood.statistics.gov.uk. . Retrieved 2010-08-10.

[7] Neighbourhood Statistics - Neil Sillitoe. "Black Caribbean people in the UK" (http://www.neighbourhood.statistics.gov.uk/dissemination/LeadHome.do;jessionid=ac1f930bce6bcf78fc81679419397d18967b152469c?m=0&s=1217013755765&enc=1&nsjs=true&nsck=true&nssvg=false&nswid=1259). Neighbourhood.statistics.gov.uk. . Retrieved 2010-08-10.

[8] "Jamaica Mapping Exercise" (http://www.iomlondon.org/doc/mapping/IOM_JAMAICA.pdf). International Organization for Migration. . Retrieved 2010-04-20.

[9] "DRC Mapping Exercise" (http://www.iomlondon.org/doc/mapping/IOM_DRC.pdf). International Organization for Migration. . Retrieved 2010-04-21.

[10] "Ghana Mapping Exercise" (http://www.iomlondon.org/doc/mapping/IOM_GHANA.pdf). International Organization for Migration. . Retrieved 2010-04-21.

[11] "Ivory Coast Mapping Exercise" (http://www.iomlondon.org/doc/mapping/IOM_IVORY_COAST.pdf). International Organization for Migration. . Retrieved 2010-04-21.

[12] "Tanzania Mapping Exercise" (http://www.iomlondon.org/doc/mapping/IOM_TANZANIA.pdf). International Organization for Migration. . Retrieved 2010-04-21.

[13] Neighbourhood Statistics - Neil Sillitoe. "Chinese people in the UK" (http://www.neighbourhood.statistics.gov.uk/dissemination/LeadHome.do;jessionid=ac1f930bce6bcf78fc81679419397d18967b152469c?m=0&s=1217013755765&enc=1&nsjs=true&nsck=true&nssvg=false&nswid=1259). Neighbourhood.statistics.gov.uk. . Retrieved 2010-08-10.

[14] "China Mapping Exercise" (http://www.iomlondon.org/doc/mapping/IOM_CHINA.pdf). International Organization for Migration. . Retrieved 2010-04-21.

[15] "Ethiopia Mapping Exercise" (http://www.iomlondon.org/doc/mapping/IOM_ETHIOPIA.pdf). International Organization for Migration. . Retrieved 2010-04-21.

[16] Filipinos in London (http://www.manilatimes.net/national/2007/sept/24/yehey/opinion/20070924opi4.html)

[17] "Filipinos in Cambridge" (http://www.guardian.co.uk/uk/2006/jan/23/britishidentity.features114). London: Guardian. 2006-01-23. . Retrieved 2010-08-10.

[18] Iraqis in the UK (http://www.iomlondon.org/doc/mapping/Iraqi Mapping Exercise Final Report.pdf)

[19] "Italians in London" (http://news.bbc.co.uk/1/shared/spl/hi/uk/05/born_abroad/countries/html/italy.stm). BBC News. 2005-09-07. . Retrieved 2010-08-10.

[20] Green, David (2003-11-29). "Italians in Manchester" (http://news.bbc.co.uk/1/hi/england/manchester/3223776.stm). BBC News. . Retrieved 2010-08-10.

[21] "Italians in Bedford" (http://www.bbc.co.uk/legacies/immig_emig/england/beds_herts_bucks/index.shtml). Bbc.co.uk. . Retrieved 2010-08-10.

[22] Neighbourhood Statistics. "Italians in Liverpool" (http://www.neighbourhood.statistics.gov.uk/dissemination/LeadTableView.do?a=3&b=276787&c=Liverpool&d=13&e=13&g=359393&i=1001x1003x1004&m=0&r=1&s=1217013995015&enc=1&dsFamilyId=85). Neighbourhood.statistics.gov.uk. . Retrieved 2010-08-10.

[23] Neighbourhood Statistics. "Italians in Bristol" (http://www.neighbourhood.statistics.gov.uk/dissemination/LeadTableView.do?a=3&b=276834&c=Bristol&d=13&e=13&g=398712&i=1001x1003x1004&m=0&r=1&s=1217014024140&enc=1&dsFamilyId=85). Neighbourhood.statistics.gov.uk. . Retrieved 2010-08-10.

[24] "Italians in Glasgow". BBC News.

[25] [[cite weblhttp://en.wikipedia.org/wiki/Italian_Scots

[26] "Mapping Exercise: Bolivia" (http://www.iomlondon.org/doc/mapping/Bolivia Mapping Report.pdf). International Organization for Migration. July 2007. . Retrieved 2009-02-02.

[27] "Brazil Mapping Exercise" (http://www.iomlondon.org/doc/mapping/IOM_BRAZIL.pdf). International Organization for Migration. . Retrieved 2010-04-20.

[28] Evans, Yara; Wills, Jane; Datta, Kavita; Herbert, Joanna; McIlwaine, Cathy; May, Jon; Osvaldo de Araújo, José; França, Ana Carla and França, Ana Paula (September 2007). "Brazilians in London: A report for the Strangers into Citizens Campaign" (http://www.geog.qmul. ac.uk/globalcities/reports/docs/brazilians.pdf). Queen Mary, University of London. . Retrieved 2010-04-20.

[29] "Colombia Mapping Exercise" (http://www.iomlondon.org/doc/mapping/IOM_COLOMBIA.pdf). International Organization for Migration. . Retrieved 2010-04-21.

[30] "Ecuador Mapping Exercise" (http://www.iomlondon.org/doc/mapping/IOM_ECUADOR.pdf). International Organization for Migration. . Retrieved 2010-04-21.

[31] Neighbourhood Statistics - Neil Sillitoe. "Pakistani people in the UK" (http://www.neighbourhood.statistics.gov.uk/dissemination/ LeadHome.do;jessionid=ac1f930bce6bcf78fc81679419397d18967b152469c?m=0&s=1217013755765&enc=1&nsjs=true&nsck=true& nssvg=false&nswid=1259). Neighbourhood.statistics.gov.uk. . Retrieved 2010-08-10.

[32] "Polish in London" (http://www.visitlondon.com/maps/multicultural_london/polish/index). Visitlondon.com. . Retrieved 2010-08-10.

[33] Leicester's Polish Community (2008-01-17). "Polish in Leicester" (http://www.bbc.co.uk/leicester/content/articles/2008/01/17/ polish_community_feature.shtml). Bbc.co.uk. . Retrieved 2010-08-10.

[34] Peter HenleyPolitics Editor, BBC South (2006-06-16). "Polish in Southampton" (http://news.bbc.co.uk/1/hi/england/5080924.stm). BBC News. . Retrieved 2010-08-10.

[35] The Polish phenomenon (2007-12-20). "Polish in Peterborough" (http://www.bbc.co.uk/lookeast/content/articles/2007/12/04/ poland_special_041207_feature.shtml). Bbc.co.uk. . Retrieved 2010-08-10.

[36] Peter Lo. "Polish in Slough" (http://www.article99.com/real-estate/real-estate-investing/article.php?art=9534). Article99.com. . Retrieved 2010-08-10.

[37] Cacciottolo, Mario (2006-10-13). "Polish in Reading" (http://news.bbc.co.uk/1/hi/uk/6045568.stm). BBC News. . Retrieved 2010-08-10.

[38] Polish in Swindon (http://www.agwsha.nhs.uk/board/july04/Agenda_Item_6.1_Vic_SOC_Final_10_June_20041.pdf/)

[39] "Polish in Blackpool" (http://www.blackpoolgazette.co.uk/blackpoolnews/Polish-Gazette-in-the-TV.1874795.jp). Blackpoolgazette.co.uk. . Retrieved 2010-08-10.

[40] "Polish in Carlisle" (http://www.carlisle.gov.uk/). Carlisle.gov.uk. . Retrieved 2010-08-10.

[41] "Portuguese in London" (http://news.bbc.co.uk/1/shared/spl/hi/uk/05/born_abroad/countries/html/portugal.stm). BBC News. 2005-09-07. . Retrieved 2010-08-10.

[42] Neighbourhood Statistics. "Portuguese in Birmingham" (http://www.neighbourhood.statistics.gov.uk/dissemination/LeadTableView. do?a=3&b=276800&c=Birmingham&d=13&e=13&g=373272&i=1001x1003x1004&m=0&r=1&s=1217270997781&enc=1& dsFamilyId=85). Neighbourhood.statistics.gov.uk. . Retrieved 2010-08-10.

[43] "Russia Mapping Exercise" (http://www.iomlondon.org/doc/mapping/IOM_RUSSIA.pdf). International Organization for Migration. . Retrieved 2010-04-21.

[44] "South Africa Mapping Exercise" (http://www.iomlondon.org/doc/mapping/IOM_SOUTH_AFRICA.pdf). International Organization for Migration. . Retrieved 2010-04-21.

[45] "Somalia Mapping Exercise" (http://www.iomlondon.org/doc/mapping/IOM_SOMALI_MR.pdf). International Organization for Migration. . Retrieved 2010-04-21.

[46] "Ukraine Mapping Exercise" (http://www.iomlondon.org/doc/mapping/IOM_UKRAINE.pdf). International Organization for Migration. . Retrieved 2010-04-21.

[47] "Vietnam Mapping Exercise" (http://www.iomlondon.org/doc/mapping/IOM_VIETNAM.pdf). International Organization for Migration. . Retrieved 2010-04-21.

Jamaican cuisine

Cuisine of Jamaica includes a mixture of cooking techniques, flavors, spices and influences from the indigenous people on the island, and the Spanish, British, Africans, Indians, and Chinese who have inhabited the island. It is also influenced by the crops introduced into the island from tropical Southeast Asia. Jamaican cuisine includes various dishes from the different cultures brought to the island with the arrival of people from elsewhere. Other dishes are novel or a fusion of techniques and traditions. In addition to ingredients that are native to Jamaica, many foods have been introduced and are now grown locally. A wide variety of seafood, tropical fruits and meats are available.

Jerk, a distinctly Jamaican style of barbecued meat and chicken, is now one of the most popular Jamaican foods worldwide.

Some Jamaican cuisine dishes are variations on the cuisines and cooking styles brought to the island from elsewhere. These are often modified to incorporate local produce. Others are novel and have developed locally. Popular Jamaican dishes include curry goat, fried dumplings, ackee and salt fish (cod) (the national dish of Jamaica), fried plantain, "jerk", steamed cabbage and "rice and peas" (pigeon peas or kidney beans). Jamaican Cuisine has been adapted by African, British, French, Spanish, Chinese and Indian influences. Jamaican patties and various pastries and breads are also popular as well as fruit beverages and Jamaican rum.

Jamaican cuisine has spread with emigrations, especially during the 20th Century, from the island to other nations as Jamaicans have sought economic opportunities in other areas.

History

Cuisine of the Tainos

Christopher Columbus visited Jamaica multiple times towards the end of the 15th century and the beginning of the 16th century, once even shipwrecked off the north coast for two years (1503–1504). During these visits he described a way the Arawaks (the indigenous inhabitants of Jamaica) preserved meat by adding peppers, allspice and sea salt to make what is now known as Jamaican jerk spice.

Development of the cuisine

The Spanish, the first European arrivals to the island contributed dishes such as the vinegary concoction escovitched fish (Spanish escabeche). Later, Cantonese/Hakka influences developed the Jamaican patty, an empanada styled turnover filled with spiced meat. African cuisine developed on the island as a result of waves of slavery introduced by the European powers. More Chinese and East Indian influences can also be found in Jamaican cuisine, as a result of indentured labourers who replaced slaves after emancipation brought their own culinary talents (especially curry, which Jamaican chefs sometimes use to season goat meat for special occasions).

Women selling desserts in Kingston, Jamaica, c. 1899

African cuisine, Indian cuisine and American cuisine, Chinese cuisine and British cuisine are not new to the island. Through many years of British colonialism the cuisine developed many habits of cooking particular to a trading colony. The natives of Jamaica drink the most tea per capita in the Caribbean to this day as a result .

Popular ingredients

- Ackee
- Allspice (locally known as "pimento")
- Avocado (locally known as "pear")
- Black pepper
- Breadfruit
- Callaloo
- Cassava (locally known as "yuca")
- Chayote (locally known as "chocho")
- Coconut
- Coconut milk
- Escallion
- Green Banana
- Ginger
- Pigeon peas (locally known as "gungo peas")
- Plantain
- Scotch bonnet (pepper)
- Taro (locally known as "dasheen" or "coco")
- Jerk spice
- Yam (vegetable)
- Garlic

Curry goat with rice and beans

Gizzada pastry with coconut, sugar, nutmeg and vanilla

- Dried and salted cod (locally known as "salt fish")
- Salt beef
- Thyme
- Oxtail
- Cow feet
- Pig tail and ears
- Guava
- Passion fruit
- Soursop
- Sugar cane
- Ketchup
- Onion
- Browning Sauce
- Boniato (locally known as "sweet potato")
- Calabaza (locally known as "pumpkin")
- Anatto
- Gungo pea
- Kidney bean
- Roselle (plant) (locally known as "sorrel")

- Tamarind
- Acerola (locally known as "cherry")
- Lima bean
- Chondrus crispus
- Tahitian apple (locally known as "June plum")
- Jackfruit
- Pineapple
- Malay apple (locally known as "apple" or "Otaheite apple")
- banana
- Vinegar

Popular dishes

A Jamaican breakfast is said to include ackee and saltfish, seasoned callaloo, boiled green bananas, and fried dumplings.[1]

Main courses

- Ackee and saltfish
- Jerk chicken - grilled Jerk-spiced chicken/pork
- Curry goat and Curried Mutton
- Jamaican patties (beef, chicken, vegetarian, cheese, curry)
- Brown Stew Chicken, Brown Stew Beef
- Escoveitch fish (like Spanish cuisine escabeche)
- Oxtail
- Corned Beef and cabbage
- Saltfish with cabbage or callaloo
- Steamed fish
- Jamaican spiced bun

Stamp and Go and callaloo fritters

Soups

- Mannish Water (Head and "man meat" of Goat soup) - said to be an aphrodisiac. Traditionally eaten at New Year's Eve
- Coconut Rundown - spicy mackerel and coconut stew
- Fish tea

Ackee and saltfish

Side dishes

- Rice and peas - rice stewed with beans and coconut milk.
- Pilau - a dish containing rice, chicken, pork, shellfish, and vegetables, similar to Paella
- Red Peas Soup
- Stewed Peas
- Callaloo
- Cabbage
- Pepperpot Soup
- Okra (also Okra and saltfish stew)
- Pigfoot

- Cowfoot
- Solomon gundy
- Spinners - dumplings shaped by "spinning" them in the hands.[2]

Breads and pastries

- Coco bread
- Bulla cakes
- Hard dough bread
- Bammy

A Jamaican patty wrapped in coco bread

Dinner plate with black beans, shredded beef, jerk chicken, rice and plantain

Beverages

- Carrot juice with spices such as nutmeg and vanilla
- Guinness punch with spices such as nutmeg and vanilla
- Ginger beer
- Irish Moss (also called sea moss) a milkshake like beverage said to be an aphrodisiac.[3]
- Limeade
- Mango juice
- Peanut punch
- Sorrel drink
- Tamarind drink
- Bush tea
- Tamarind Fizz
- Cucumber juice
- Otaheiti Apple Juice
- Sour Sop juice

Hot Chocolate Sky Juice Suck-Suck

- Ting soda

Irish Moss drink in can and over ice

Desserts

Mango and soursop ice Cream are two popular desserts. Jamaican ice cream is traditionally made with coconut milk, rather than milk or cream as used elsewhere. The most popular Jamaican ice cream flavours are grapenut and rum raisin.

Other popular desserts include potato pudding, gizzada (a small tart shell with sweet spiced coconut filling), grater cake, toto (dessert) (a small coconut cake), banana fritters, coconut drops, plantain tart. Duckunoo is a Ghanaian dish made with sweetened starch (usually cornmeal but can also be cassava) wrapped and boiled in a banana leaf. Also called "blue drawers'. Asham is ground or powdered sweetened parched corn. There is also Bustamante Backbone, named after the first Prime Minister Alexander Bustamante.

Ting grapefruit soda, bottled

Export

Jamaican cuisine has been brought to the United States including a large number of restaurants in some of New York's boroughs and other metropolitan areas like Atlanta, Georgia, and cities in Florida. Many Jamaicans work in hospitals, and Golden Krust Caribbean Bakery & Grill is a chain of about 120 franchised restaurants spread through many states with many of them owned by nurses. The eatery specializes in Jamaican patties and supplies them to schools and prisons in New York. Darden Restaurants has also opened a Caribbean food chain.

External links

- Jamaican Food and Recipes [4]
- Jamaica Recipes [5] (includes description of Jamaican Cuisine)

References

[1] Deborah S. Hartz Authentic Jamaican breakfast (http://news.google.com/newspapers?id=bp0TAAAAIBAJ&sjid=PgcEAAAAIBAJ& pg=1279,382584&dq=stamp+and+go+jamaica) Aug 1, 1991 Ocala Star-Banner page 44

[2] Dictionary of Jamaican English (http://books.google.com/books?id=_lmFzFgsTZYC&pg=PA72&lpg=PA72&dq=parched+corn+balls+ Jamaica&source=bl&ots=N6LqvhRysa&sig=3KxXrpRKwXiChEfh7czjvfRhQU4&hl=en&ei=DmWMSrXNOY6sswPyrbC6CQ&sa=X& oi=book_result&ct=result&resnum=3#v=onepage&q=spinners&f=false) By Frederic Gomes Cassidy, Robert Brock Le Page page 420

[3] http://pqasb.pqarchiver.com/newsday/access/104297272.html?dids=104297272:104297272&FMT=ABS&FMTS=ABS:FT& type=current&date=Feb+04%2C+1987&author=SYLVIA+CARTER&pub=Newsday+(Combined+editions)&desc=A+TASTE+OF+ THE+ISLANDS&pqatl=google

[4] http://www.foodjamaica.net

[5] http://www.caribbeanchoice.com/recipes/countryrecipe.asp?country=Jamaica

Caribbean music in the United Kingdom

Music of Jamaica
Kumina - Niyabinghi - Mento - Ska - Rocksteady - Reggae - Sound systems - Lovers rock - Dub - Dancehall - Dub poetry - Toasting - Raggamuffin - Roots reggae - Reggae fusion

Anglophone Caribbean music
Anguilla - Antigua and Barbuda - Bahamas - Barbados - Bermuda - Caymans - Grenada - Jamaica - Montserrat - St. Kitts and Nevis - St. Vincent and the Grenadines - Trinidad and Tobago - Turks and Caicos - Virgin Islands

Other Caribbean music
Aruba and the Dutch Antilles - Cuba - Dominica - Dominican Republic - Haiti - Hawaii - Martinique and Guadeloupe - Puerto Rico - St. Lucia - United States - United Kingdom

Music from Trinidad

Large-scale Caribbean migration to England began in 1948. The Empire Windrush carried almost 500 passengers from Jamaica, including Lord Kitchener, a calypso singer from Trinidad. By chance, a local newsreel company filmed him singing "London Is The Place For Me" as he got off the ship. In 2002, "London Is The Place For Me: Trinidadian Calypso, 1950-1956" was finally released in Britain. The 1951 Festival of Britain brought the Trinidad All Steel Percussion Orchestra (TAPSO) and Roaring Lion to public attention. The smart set in Oxford and Cambridge adopted both calypso and steelband for debutante parties. In 1959, Trinidadian Claudia Jones started the Notting Hill Carnival. They brought Mighty Sparrow and others directly from Trinidad. Edric Connor had arrived in England from Trinidad in 1944. He starred in a West End musical called "Calypso" in 1948. A white Danish duo, Nina and Frederick, recorded several calypsos from 1958 to 1962, scoring in the charts. Cy Grant (from Guyana) sang a song by Lord Kitchener in the TV drama "A Man From the Sun" in 1956. It told the story of Caribbean migrants. From 1957 to 1960, Cy Grant sang calypsos on the BBC TV news programme Tonight. In 1962 English comedian Bernard Cribbins had a hit with "Gossip Calypso".

Reggae and ska

Cecil Bustamante Campbell (Prince Buster) was born in 1938 in Orange Street, Kingston, Jamaica. In 1961 he signed to Blue Beat records.

In 1962, Jamaica won its independence and Island Records was founded. One of the record label's producers, Chris Blackwell, brought Millie Small to Britain in 1963. Her high-pitched, slightly nasal voice had wide appeal with "My Boy Lollipop", which reached number 2 in the UK. It was perceived as a novelty pop song, not the start of a boom in ska. It was not until 1969 that reggae artists began to receive significant airplay. Dave and Ansell Collins, Ken Boothe and John Holt had hits.

Trojan Records was founded in 1967, named after producer Duke Reid, known as "The Trojan." It brought Jamaican recordings to Britain. Their first hit was Jimmy Cliff's "Wonderful World, Beautiful People" in 1969. The label had 28 other hits.

The first Jamaican performers to reach number one in Britain were Desmond Dekker and the Aces with "Israelites" in 1969. The second act was Althea & Donna with "Up Town, Top Ranking" in 1977. Bob Marley came from Jamaica to London and recorded "Catch a Fire" in 1972, returning to record "Exodus" and "Kaya" in 1977. Eddy Grant was born in Guyana in 1948 and grew up in Brixton. He was part of The Equals, the first multi-racial group to reach number 1 in the UK, with "Baby come Back" in 1968. He took Caribbean music further in the direction of rock than anyone else. His gritty voice took "Electric Avenue" to the top 10 twice. His studio in Barbados has been used by Sting and Elvis Costello.

Roots and Dub

Roots reggae was increasingly popular with the UK's black working class youth from the 1970s onwards, its message of Rastafari and overcoming injustice striking a chord with those on the receiving end of racism and poverty. Jamaicans who had settled in the UK (and their children who had been born here) were instrumental in setting up a network of reggae soundsystems. The most popular soundsystems included Jah Shaka, Coxsone Outernational, Fatman, Jah Tubbys and Quaker City.

A number of producers such as Dennis Bovell and Mad Professor began to record UK and Jamaican artists and release their records.

Bands such as Aswad, Steel Pulse and Misty In Roots released records and played gigs throughout the UK.

As roots music's popularity waned in Jamaica in the 1980s, soundsystems such as Jah Shaka kept the faith in the UK, influencing a new generation of producers, soundsystems and artists such as The Disciples, Iration Steppas, Jah Warrior and The Rootsman. This scene has been referred to as "UK Dub".

The 1990s saw a resurgence of interest in 70s roots reggae and dub with a number of UK-based specialist labels such as Pressure Sounds, Soul Jazz and Blood & Fire being set up to re-release classic recordings.

Punky Reggae Party

Punky Reggae Party is a song written by Bob Marley as a positive response to the emerging UK punk scene.

Roots and Dub music gained popularity with UK punks in the mid-70s, with Don Letts playing reggae records alongside punk ones at the Roxy nightclub and Johnny Rotten citing Dr Alimantado's "Born for a Purpose" as one of his favourite records in a radio interview. After the Sex Pistols split, Rotten was sent to Jamaica by Virgin Records as a talent scout for their Frontline reggae sub-label.

The Clash started out as a straight-ahead punk rock group, but their first album covered "Police & Thieves", a reggae track by Junior Murvin. Their bass player Paul Simonon was a reggae enthusiast. Increasingly the group took significant influence from reggae, on tracks such as The Guns of Brixton, which used themes of impoverished criminality and a renegade lifestyle, with a punky edge. Their track "White Man In Hammersmith Palais" was written about the group's experience at a reggae dance. Jamaican reggae producer Lee Perry was brought in to produce the tune "Complete Control".

The Ruts recorded the reggae-inspired Babylon's Burning.

Towards the end of the 70s, punk and reggae groups would appear on the same bills at Rock Against Racism events.

Lovers rock

While most of the developments in the music took place in Jamaica (dub, toasting, dancehall, ragga) there was one form that was born in Britain. Lovers rock, developed in the 1970s, was a smooth, soulful version of reggae, spearheaded by Dennis Brown.

Early years of lovers rock was London 'Blues Parties', 14-year-old Louisa Mark's "Caught you in a Lie" with backing group Matumbi and Lloyd Coxsone on production.

The early years of 'lovers rock' have two main resonances: 'London blues parties' and discs by girl singers who sounded as if they were still worrying about their school reports. The record that kick-started the phenomenon was the 14-year-old Louisa Marks plaintive reading of Robert Parker's soul hit, "Caught You In A Lie". With Matumbi as backing group and production by sound-system man Lloyd Coxsone (b. Lloyd Blackwood, Jamaica), this appeared on Coxsone's Safari imprint in 1975 and was impressive enough to see release in Jamaica by Gussie Clake. Several of Louisa Marks's subsequent titles, including "All My Loving" (Safari) and "Six Sixth Street" (Bushays). repeated the success and have remained favourites at revive sessions ever since.

Louisa Marks's hit was followed by Ginger Williams "Tenderness" (Third World), and a genre was born-essentially Philly/Chicago soul ballads played over fat reggae basslines. The style was consolidated by the husband and wife team of Dennis and Eve Harris who had a big hit with the white singer T.T. Ross's massively popular "Last Date" (Lucky), another key record, and set up a new imprint, Lover's Rock, Giving the genre its name.

Later labels like Fashion Records and Ariwa would go on to take lovers rock to more sophisticated plains and beyond the music's original market of working-class teenagers. and while the music media largely ignored their performers-singers like Peter Hunnigale, Sylvia Tella, Michael Gordon and Keith Douglas they have deservedly scored hit after hit with audiences who trust what they hear rather than read.

White reggae

The influence of reggae was felt in rock almost immediately, but usually surfaced as a tangential reference in some stars' isolated songs. The early Beatles song 1964 "I Call Your Name," for instance, has a ska break; a few years later, they would appropriate the reggae rhythm for 1968 "Ob-La-Di, Ob-La-Da."[1]

Chris Andrews (born 1942) was a songwriter for Sandie Shaw. The song "Yesterday Man" was inappropriate for her, so he sang it himself and it went to #3 in the British singles charts in 1965. At the time, the musical style was called bluebeat, a music genre that is now recognized by most as ska or reggae. He followed this with "To Whom It Concerns" (#13 in 1965) and "Something On My Mind" (number 41 in 1966).

Paul McCartney bought Jamaican-imported singles, but this was not obvious in The Beatles' repertoire until "Ob-La-Di, Ob-La-Da" on the *White Album*. There was a gentle reggae beat in some of his later solo singles, such as "Another Day" and "Silly Love Songs". The first British top ten album to contain several reggae songs was Peter Frampton's "Frampton Comes Alive" in 1976. Other pop hits include "Sugar Sugar" by the Archies (number 1 in 1969) and "I can see clearly now" by Johnny Nash (number 5 in 1972). Also in the mid-1970s, art-rockers 10cc released a few reggae-styled singles, including "Dreadlock Holiday".

Ska/reggae artist Judge Dread (named after a Prince Buster character) released his first single in 1972; the somewhat X-rated "Big Six", which went to #11. Judge Dread (born Alexander Hughes) continued his popularity with other rude songs, chiefly enjoyed by skinheads, who had always been avid fans of ska and reggae. Skinheads were preceded by the mods, who were the first real white supporters of ska/bluebeat in the 1960s. Georgie Fame, a mod R&B favourite, popularised a ska feel in his music at times.

The Police's first reggae single was "Roxanne", followed by "Don't Stand So Close to Me", "Walking on the Moon" and others. Sting's somewhat interesting Jamaican accent attracted criticism, but the band was commercially successful. Blondie's "The Tide is High" was perhaps the first big white reggae hit in Britain and also draws on the lovers-rock elements of reggae. Both Harry Belafonte and Nina and Frederick had hits with "Mary's Boy Child", but it was Boney M who gave this slow ballad a reggae rhythm in 1978 and took it to #1 for four weeks.

Mixed race reggae

More long-term success was achieved by UB40, of Birmingham. They started life performing reggae-influenced material of their own creation, but their biggest contribution is perhaps their covers of reggae originals. Kingston Town, Many Rivers to Cross and Here I Am (Come & Take Me) are a few of the more famous. Their chart-topping cover of Red Red Wine was an accident of sorts - they knew a reggae version of the song, but were unaware that the American pop singer Neil Diamond was its original author.

2-Tone

2 Tone Records, founded in 1979, combined ska, reggae and rock which some say developed into punk rock, spawning the 2 Tone movement with bands such as The Specials, The Selecter and Madness. The 2-Tone sound continued and evolved into the 1980s, with bands such as The Hot Knives, The Loafers and Potato 5.

Gospel Music

Gospel music although a subgenre of black music in the UK today also arrived in England in the early post war years along with the large scale immigrant influx and their wide variety of musical tastes. Pioneers in this field include an 8-piece a cappella family from Trinidad called the Singing Stewarts who were the first to appear on a major British record label in the late 1960s. They impressed many English audiences with their unique interpretation of Negro Spiritual and traditional Gospel songs. Based in the Midlands, Birmingham, they appeared on Numerous Radio Shows and participated in the prestigious Edinburgh festival, again increasing awareness of this genre. In later years and decades when black people began to settle in the UK, groups such as The Doyleys, Paradise, Lavine Hudson and the, Bazil Meade inspired, London Community Gospel Choir began to drive the music much further towards the mainstream and out of the comfort zone of the black churches.

See also

- British Afro-Caribbean community

References

[1] Reggae [Relation to Rock & Roll] Richie Unterberger

External links

- Caribbean Music London (http://www.itzcaribbean.com/caribbean-music-london.php)

Music of Jamaica

Music of Jamaica
Kumina - Niyabinghi - Mento - Ska - Rocksteady - Reggae - Sound systems - Lovers rock - Dub - Dancehall - Dub poetry - Toasting - Raggamuffin - Roots reggae - Reggae fusion
Anglophone Caribbean music
Anguilla - Antigua and Barbuda - Bahamas - Barbados - Bermuda - Caymans - Grenada - Jamaica - Montserrat - St. Kitts and Nevis - St. Vincent and the Grenadines - Trinidad and Tobago - Turks and Caicos - Virgin Islands
Other Caribbean music
Aruba and the Dutch Antilles - Cuba - Dominica - Dominican Republic - Haiti - Hawaii - Martinique and Guadeloupe - Puerto Rico - St. Lucia - United States - United Kingdom

The **music of Jamaica** includes Jamaican folk music and many popular genres, such as mento, ska, rocksteady, reggae, dub music, dancehall, reggae fusion and related styles. Jamaica's music culture is a fusion of elements from the United States (rhythm and blues, rock and roll, soul), Africa and neighboring Caribbean islands such as Trinidad and Tobago (calypso and soca). Reggae is especially popular through the international fame of Bob Marley. Jamaican music's influence on music styles in other countries includes the practice of toasting, which was brought to New York City and evolved into rapping, For years, and still today, Jamaican Music, such as slangs and beats has been copied into other cultures because of the originality and creativity within the islands vibe. British genres as Lovers rock and jungle music are also influenced by Jamaican music.

Folk music

108 Jamaican folk songs was published 1907 at Walter Jekyll's Jamaican Song and Story.[1] *Unlike much other Jamaican music, these folk songs are in the public domain. They served as the basis for much research in Jamaican folk music and folklore, and several (along with other folk songs) were arranged by Olive Lewin and published by Oxford University Press. Several melodies in the Jekyll and Lewin collections, such as "Linstead Market", were adapted to other styles, including mento.it is a pop*

Mentos

Mento was recorded in Jamaica in the 1950s due to the efforts of Stanley Motta, who noted the similarities between Jamaican folk and Trinidadian calypso, which was becoming popular around the world. For decades, mento bands toured the big hotels in Jamaica.[2] While mento never found as large an international audience as calypso, some mento recordings, such as by Count Lasher, Lord Composer and George Moxey, are now widely-respected legends of Jamaican music. Although mento has largely been supplanted by successors like reggae and dub, the style is still performed, recorded, and released internationally by traditionalist performers like the Jolly Boys.

Sound systems

Mobile sound systems that played American hits became popular in the 1950s in Kingston, Jamaica. Major figures in the early sound system scene included Duke Reid, Prince Buster and Sir Coxsone Dodd. In 1958, due to a shortage of new material, the first local rhythm and blues bands, most influentially the duo Higgs and Wilson (Joe Higgs and Roy Wilson), began recording to fulfil the local demand for new music. Rupert E. Brown was the original owner of the "King Attarney" sound system, which was popular from 1975 to 1976. His only album was *Dubbing to the King In A Higher Rank*. The DJ crew that worked for King Attarney was Danny Dread, U-Roy, and Ranking Trevor.

Jazz

From early in the 20th century, Jamaica produced many notable jazz musicians. In this development the enlightened policy of the Alpha School in Kingston, which provided training and encouragement in music education for its pupils, was very influential. Also significant was the brass band tradition of the island, strengthened by opportunities for musical work and training in military contexts. However, limited scope for making a career playing jazz in Jamaica resulted in many local jazz musicians leaving the island to settle in London or in the United States. Among the most notable Jamaican jazz instrumentalists who made successful careers abroad was alto saxophonist Joe Harriott, now regarded internationally as one of the most original and innovative of jazz composers. Also internationally successful were trumpeters Dizzy Reece, Leslie 'Jiver' Hutchinson and Leslie Thompson, bassist Coleridge Goode, guitarist Ernest Ranglin and pianist Monty Alexander. Harriott, Goode, Hutchinson and Thompson built their careers in London, along with many other instrumentalists, such as pianist Yorke de Souza and the outstanding saxophonist Bertie King, who later returned to Jamaica and formed a mento-style band. Reece and Alexander worked in the US. Saxophonist Wilton 'Bogey' Gaynair settled in Germany working mainly with Kurt Edelhagen's orchestra.

Ska

Ska originated in the late 1950s in Jamaica. Some of the first songs identified as ska were "Manny-O" by Joe Higgs (1958), "Easy Snapping" by Theophilus Beckford (1959), and "Oh! Carolina" by the Folkes Brothers (1960). "Simmer Down", a huge ska hit, was recorded by The Wailers in 1963.[3] [4] Perhaps the best-known of the original ska bands were The Skatalites, whose career spanned decades and transcended Jamaican musical genres. The Skatalites' music launched the careers of Tommy McCook, virtuoso trombonist Don Drummond and tenor saxophonist, and fellow Alpha Boys School graduates Roland Alphonso, Jackie Mittoo, and Lester Sterling.[5] .

At first primarily instrumental, ska's rhythms generally didn't lend well to vocal stylings. However, some popular singers such as Desmond Dekker, Toots Hibbert and Bob Marley got their start by singing in this style. This new style was widely embraced by Jamaican youths, and soon became popular in the United Kingdom and around the world. In 1963 Chris Blackwell brought teenage singer Millie Small to Great Britain. She exploded on the scene with My Boy Lollipop, which climbed the charts to #2 in both Great Britain and the United States.[6]

Live touring bands launched the careers of many ska, rocksteady and reggae artists. Tommy McCook had been part of the band of Aubrey Adams based at the Courtleigh Manor hotel in Kingston before becoming one of the founding members of the Skatalites.[5] Drummer Lloyd Knibb, also of The Skatalites, had done the hotel circuit playing for the Val Bennett, Len Hibbert and Cecil Lloyd bands.[7] One of the most successful music groups in Jamaica was Billy Vernon and the Celestials, the resident band at the Yellow Bird Club in Montego Bay. They toured many of the island's leading hotels. Their work was a blend of ska, mento and jump up, and featured hits such as "Ska Suzanna", "Yellow Bird" and "Wings Of A Dove". A number of artists, including Errol "E.T." Webster, also known as "Errol T," got their start in the music business with Billy Vernon and the Celestials." [8]

Chris Blackwell's Island Records became the biggest label promoting Jamaican music to the international market. Due to its affiliation with the record industry in the UK and First world funding, Island had the distribution to vastly increase exposure of Jamaican music to the global pop market, especially in the UK, where a significant population of Jamaican expatriates had relocated on the invitation of the British government. Blackwell's early group of artists included Millie Small, singer of the first major Jamaican music UK radio hit, 1964's "My Boy Lollipop" which settled high in the UK Singles Chart.

Ska's popularity grew steadily in Jamaica alongside Rastafari, which spread rapidly in impoverished urban areas, and among the often politically radical music scene. The lyrics of ska songs began to focus on Rastafarian themes; slower beats and chants entered the music from religious Rastafarian music, and ska soon evolved into rocksteady.

DJs and toasting

Along with the rise of ska came the popularity of DJs like Sir Lord Comic, King Stitt and pioneer Count Matchuki, who began talking stylistically over the rhythms of popular songs at sound systems. In Jamaican music, the DJ is the one who talks (known elsewhere as the MC) and the selector is the person who chooses the records. The popularity of DJs as an essential component of the sound system created a need for instrumental songs, as well as instrumental versions of popular vocal songs.

In the late 1960s, producers like King Tubby and Lee Perry began stripping the vocals away from tracks recorded for sound system parties. With the bare beats and bass playing and the lead instruments dropping in and out of the mix, DJs began toasting, or delivering humorous and often provoking jabs at fellow DJs and local celebrities. Over time, toasting became an increasingly complex activity, and became as big a draw as the dance beats played behind it. In the early 1970s, DJs such as DJ Kool Herc took the practice of toasting to New York City, where it evolved into rap music.

Rocksteady

Rocksteady was the music of Jamaica's rude boys by the mid-1960s, when The Wailers and The Clarendonians dominated the charts, taking over from pioneers like Alton Ellis (who is believed to have invented rocksteady). Desmond Dekker's "007" brought international attention to the new genre. The mix put heavy emphasis on the bass line, as opposed to ska's strong horn section, and the rhythm guitar began playing on the upbeat. Session musicians like Supersonics, Soul Vendors, Jets and Jackie Mittoo (of the Skatalites) became popular during this period.

Reggae

By the early 1970s, rocksteady had evolved into reggae, which combines elements from American soul music with the traditional shuffle and one-drop of Jamaican mento. Reggae quickly became popular around the world, due in large part to the international success of artists like Bob Marley, Peter Tosh and Bunny Wailer. Marley was viewed as a Rastafarian messianic figure by some fans, particularly throughout the Caribbean, Africa, and among Native Americans and Australian Aborigines. His lyrics about love, redemption and natural beauty captivated audiences, and he gained headlines for negotiating truces between the two opposing Jamaican political parties (at the One Love Concert), led by Michael Manley (PNP) and Edward Seaga (JLP). Reggae music was intricately tied to the expansion of the Rastafarian religion, and its principles of pacifism and pan-Africanism. Musicians like Gregory Isaacs, The Congos and Burning Spear — and producers like Lee "Scratch" Perry — solidified the early sound of reggae.

Dub

By 1973, dub music had emerged as a distinct reggae genre, and heralded the dawn of the remix. Developed by record producers such as Lee "Scratch" Perry and King Tubby, dub featured previously-recorded songs remixed with prominence on the bass. Often the lead instruments and vocals would drop in and out of the mix, sometimes processed heavily with studio effects. King Tubby's advantage came from his intimate knowledge with audio gear, and his ability to build his own sound systems and recording studios that were superior to the competition. He became famous for his remixes of recordings made by others, as well as those he recorded in his own studio. Following in Tubby's footsteps came artists such as U-Roy and Big Youth, who used Rasta chants in songs. Until the end of the 1970s, Big Youth-inspired dub music with chanted vocals dominated Jamaican popular music. At the very end of the decade, dancehall artists like Ranking Joe, Lone Ranger and General Echo brought a return to U-Roy's style.

Other 1970s developments

Other popular music forms that arose during the 1970s include: Briton (Linton Kwesi Johnson's dub poetry); Sly & Robbie's rockers reggae, which drew on Augustus Pablo's melodica, becoming popular with artists such as The Mighty Diamonds and The Gladiators; Joe Gibbs' mellower rockers reggae, including music by Culture and Dennis Brown; Burning Spear's distinctive style, as represented by the albums *Marcus Garvey* and *Man in the Hills*; and harmonic, spiritually-oriented Rasta music like that of The Abyssinians, Black Uhuru and Third World. In 1975, Louisa Marks had a hit with "Caught You in a Lie", beginning a trend of British performers making romantic, ballad-oriented reggae called lovers rock.

Reggae and ska had a massive influence on British punk rock and New Wave bands of the 1970s, such as The Clash, Elvis Costello and the Attractions, The Police, The Slits, and The Ruts. Ska revival bands such as The Specials, Madness and The Selecter developed the 2 Tone genre.

Dancehall and ragga

During the 1980s, the most popular music styles in Jamaica were dancehall and ragga. Dancehall is essentially speechifying with musical accompaniment, including a basic drum beat (most often played on electric drums). The lyrics moved away from the political and spiritual lyrics popular in the 1970s and concentrate more on less serious issues. Ragga is characterized by the use of computerized beats and sequenced melodic tracks. Ragga is usually said to have been invented with the song "Under Mi Sleng Teng" by Wayne Smith. Ragga barely edged out dancehall as the dominant form of Jamaican music in the 1980s. DJ Shabba Ranks and vocalist team Chaka Demus and Pliers proved more enduring than the competition, and helped inspire an updated version of the rude boy culture called raggamuffin.

Dancehall was sometimes violent in lyrical content, and several rival performers made headlines with their feuds across Jamaica (most notably Beenie Man versus Bounty Killer). Dancehall emerged from pioneering recordings in the late 1970s by Barrington Levy, with Roots Radics backing and Junjo Lawes as producer. The Roots Radics were the pre-eminent backing band for the dancehall style. Yellowman, Ini Kamoze, Charlie Chaplin and General Echo helped popularize the style along with producers like Sugar Minott.

The 1980s saw a rise in reggae music from outside of Jamaica. During this time, reggae particularly influenced African popular music, where Sonny Okusuns (Nigeria), John Chibadura (Zimbabwe), Lucky Dube (South Africa) and Alpha Blondy (Ivory Coast) became stars. The 1980s saw the end of the dub era in Jamaica, although dub has remained a popular and influential style in the UK, and to a lesser extent throughout Europe and the US. Dub in the 1980s and 1990s has merged with electronic music.

Variations of dancehall continued to be popular into the mid 1990s. Some of the performers of the previous decade converted to Rastafari, and changed their lyrical content. Artists like Buju Banton experienced significant crossover success in foreign markets, while Beenie Man, Bounty Killer and others developed a sizable North American following, due to their frequent guest spots on albums by gangsta rappers like Wu-Tang Clan and Jay-Z. Some ragga musicians, including Beenie Man, Shabba Ranks and Capleton, publicly converted to a new lyrical style, in the hope that his new style of lyrics would not offend any one particular social group. ..and is a very beautiful place to be.

Reggae fusion

Reggae fusion emerged as a popular subgenre in the late 1990s. It is a mixture of reggae or dancehall with elements of other genres such as hip hop, R&B, jazz, rock 'n roll or indie rock.[9] It is closely related to ragga music. It originated in Jamaica, North America and Europe

Non-Rastafarian Jamaican religious music

The Bongo Nation is a distinct group of Jamaicans possibly descended from the Congo. They are known for Kumina, which refers to both a religion and a form of music. Kumina's distinctive drumming style became one of the roots of Rastafarian drumming, itself the source of the distinctive Jamaican rhythm heard in ska, rocksteady and reggae. The modern intertwining of Jamaican religion and music can be traced back to the 1860s, when the Pocomania and Revival Zion churches drew on African traditions, and incorporated music into almost every facet of worship. Later, this trend spread into Hindu communities, resulting in baccra music.

The spread of Rastafari into urban Jamaica in the 1960s transformed the Jamaican music scene, which incorporated drumming (played at grounation ceremonies) and which has led to today's popular music. Many of the above mentioned music and dance have been stylised by the National Dance Theatre Company of Jamaica led by Prof. Rex Nettleford artistic director (ret, prof and vice chancellor of The University of the West Indies) and Marjorie Whyle Musical Director (Caribbean Musicologist, pianist, drummer, arranger lecturer at the University of the West Indies). Since 1962, this volunteer company of dancers and musicians have had many of these dances in its core repertoire and have performed worldwide to large audiences, including The British Royal family.

Other developments

Other trends included minimalist digital tracks, which began with Dave Kelly's "Pepper Seed" in 1995, alongside the return of love balladeers like Beres Hammond. American, British, and European electronic musicians used reggae-oriented beats to create further hybrid electronic music styles. Dub, world music, and electronic music continue to influence music in the 2000s.

JaFolk Mix is a term coined by Jamaican musician Joy Fairclough, to mean the mix of Jamaican Folk Music with any foreign and local styles of music and the evolution of a new sound created by their fusion. This is the latest Jamaican Music stylistic development of the late 20th century and 21st century. Jamaican music continues to influence the world's music. Many efforts at studying and copying Jamaican music has introduced the world to this new form of music as the copied styles are performed with accents linguistically and musically slanted to that of the home nation in which it is being studied, copied and performed.

Footnotes

[1] (http://books.google.com/books?id=mNwb65fmvqUC&pg=PA108&lpg=PA108&dq="Leah+and+Tiger"&source=web&
ots=Ltp89l2Cre&sig=VY3mLKgEHgBsStMleE03lVCcNK8&hl=en&sa=X&oi=book_result&resnum=1&ct=result#PPR3,M1)

[2] Mento Music: Hotel Bands (http://www.mentomusic.com/hotel.htm)

[3] Burnin' Vernon's Original Ska Page (http://burninvernon.8m.com)

[4] A History of Reggae Music (http://www.scaruffi.com/history/reggae.html)

[5] History of Jamaican Music 1953-1973 (http://niceup.com/history/ja_music_59-73.html)

[6] Millie (Small) (http://www.45-rpm.org.uk/dirm/millie.htm)

[7] Skatalites drummer Lloyd Knibb interview by Carter Van Pelt & Dan Batman (4/23/98) (http://incolor.inebraska.com/cvanpelt/knibb.
html)

[8] E.T.Webster (http://members.tripod.com/mrmsrecords/et.html)

[9] Big D (2008-05-08). "Reggae Fusion" (http://www.reggae-reviews.com/fusion.html). Reggae-Reviews. . Retrieved 2008-06-07.

References

- Goode, Coleridge and Roger Cotterrell, *Bass Lines: A Life in Jazz*. London: Northway Books, 2002. ISBN 0-9537040-2-5

- Manuel, Peter, with Kenneth Bilby and Michael Largey. *Caribbean Currents: Caribbean Music from Rumba to Reggae (2nd edition)*. Temple University Press, 2006. ISBN 1-59213-463-7.

- Mthembu-Salter, Gregory and Peter Dalton. "The Loudest Island in the World". 2000. In Broughton, Simon and Ellingham, Mark with McConnachie, James and Duane, Orla (Ed.), *World Music, Vol. 2: Latin & North America, Caribbean, India, Asia and Pacific*, pp 430–456. Rough Guides Ltd, Penguin Books. ISBN 1-85828-636-0

- Mthembu-Salter, Gregory and Peter Dalton. "Lovers and Poets -- Babylon Sounds". 2000. In Broughton, Simon and Ellingham, Mark with McConnachie, James and Duane, Orla (Ed.), *World Music, Vol. 2: Latin & North America, Caribbean, India, Asia and Pacific*, pp 457–462. Rough Guides Ltd, Penguin Books. ISBN 1-85828-636-0

- O'Brien Chang, Kevin and Wayne Chen. *Reggae Routes: The Story of Jamaican Music*. Temple University Press. Philadelphia.

- Jahn, Brian and Tom Weber. *Reggae Island: Jamaican Music in the Digital Age*. Da Capo Press. Kingston. ISBN 0-306-80853-6

- Robertson, Alan, *Joe Harriott: Fire in his Soul*. London: Northway Books, 2003. ISBN 0-9537040-3-3

- Staple, Neville. *Original Rude Boy*. 2009. Aurum Press. ISBN 978-1-84513-480-8

- Thompson, Leslie with Jeffrey Green, *Swing from a Small Island: The Story of Leslie Thompson*. London: Northway Books, 2008. ISBN 978-09557888-2-6

External links

- Jamaican Mento Music (http://www.mentomusic.com/)
- Jamaican Song and Story (http://books.google.com/books?id=mNwb65fmvqUC&pg=PA108&lpg=PA108& dq="Leah+and+Tiger"&source=web&ots=Ltp89l2Cre&sig=VY3mLKgEHgBsStMleE03lVCcNK8&hl=en& sa=X&oi=book_result&resnum=1&ct=result#PPR3,M1").
- Historical Notes for Collection 1: African-American and Jamaican Melodies (http://imslp.org/wiki/ User:Clark_Kimberling/Historical_Notes_1)
- Ashe Performing Arts Company, Jamaica (http://www.asheperforms.com/)
- Pogus Caesar: photographs of Jamaican singers, producers and DJs (http://www.oomgallery.net/gallery. asp?location=6&c=251)
- DaFlava Internet Radio (http://www.daflavaradio.com/index)

List of Jamaican British people

This list is incomplete.

This is a list of notable **Jamaican British people.**

- Diane Abbott, Labour Party MP also the first black woman to be elected to the House of Commons of the United Kingdom
- David Haye, Boxer
- Jo Hamilton, Musician
- Zaraah Abrahams, Actress currently starring in Waterloo Road
- Akala, Rapper and electro/rock/alternative artist
- Cliff Akurang, Footballer currently with Barnet
- Asher D, Rapper once part of Daddy Freddy
- Giles Barnes, Football midfielder currently with Derby County
- John Barnes, Former footballer
- Rikki Beadle-Blair, Actor, director, screenwriter and playwright
- Peter Beckford, Acting Governor of Jamaica in 1702
- Melissa Bell, former lead singer of Soul II Soul
- Trevor Benjamin, Footballer currently with Northwich Victoria
- Darren Bent, Footballer currently with Sunderland
- Narada Bernard, Footballer currently with Maidenhead United
- Noel Blake, Former footballer
- Valerie Bloom, MBE, Poet and a novelist
- Walter Boyd, Footballer currently with Arnett Gardens
- Yvonne Brewster, OBE, Stage director, teacher and writer
- Constance Briscoe, One of the UK's first black female judges
- Errol Brown, Singer, songwriter, and frontman of Hot Chocolate
- Downtown Julie Brown, Actress and MTV VJ
- Selwyn Brown, Keyboardist and backup vocalist of Steel Pulse
- VV Brown, Up and coming recording artist, songwriter and producer
- YolanDa Brown, Saxophonist, Presenter,songwriter
- Frank Bruno, Former boxer who was once the WBC Heavyweight championship
- Keisha Buchanan, Singer, songwriter, and a founding member of the Sugababes
- Deon Burton, Football striker currently with Charlton Athletic
- Dawn Butler, Labour part MP
- Alexandra Burke, Singer and winner of X Factor Series 5
- Darren Byfield, Footballer currently with Walsall
- Naomi Campbell, Supermodel, singer, author, actress, and fashion designer
- Sol Campbell, Football defender currently with Arsenal
- Jamal Campbell-Ryce, Footballer currently with Barnsley
- Capone, Rapper
- Natalia Cappuccini, Actress, songwriter, singer and rapper
- Chipmunk, Rapper
- Errol Christie, European champion boxer
- Linford Christie, Former athlete and the only British man to win Olympic, World, Commonwealth and European 100m gold medals
- Andrew Cole, Footballer currently with Nottingham Forest

- Des Coleman, Actor and TV presenter
- Elvis Comrie, Former footballer most notable in American teams
- Clova Court, Former heptathlete
- Norman Cowans, Former cricketer who played in 19 Tests and 23 ODIs
- Mikey Craig, Former DJ who became the bassist with Culture Club
- Doña Croll, TV and theatre actress
- Garth Crooks, Footballer turned journalist
- Laurie Cunningham, The first English footballer to play for Real Madrid
- Dan I, Disco recording artist
- William Davidson, Radical executed by the British government
- Kirk Dawes, Former Police Constable with West Midlands Police
- Alesha Dixon, Singer, MC, songwriter, model and television personality
- Desmond Douglas, Table tennis player
- Robbie Earle, Former footballer
- Alton Ellis, OD, Musician best known as one of the innovators of rocksteady music
- Jessica Ennis, Athlete, competing in the heptathlon
- Chris Eubank Jr., Boxer and television personality
- Chris Eubank, Former boxer and WBO Middleweight and Super Middleweight champion
- Jason Euell, Footballer currently with Southampton
- Jade Ewen, Singer and actress representing Britain in Eurovision 2009
- Nathan Fagan-Gayle, R&B singer and *Big Brother: Celebrity Hijack* contestant
- Craig Fagan, Footballer currently with Hull City
- Damien Francis, Former footballer
- Brian Gayle, Former football defender
- Marcus Gayle, Footballer and manager of AFC Wimbledon
- Mel Gaynor, Musician best known for being a member of Simple Minds
- Junior Giscombe, Singer, songwriter and one of the first British R&B artists to become successful in the United States
- Goldie, Electronic music artist, disc jockey, and actor
- Lynval Golding, Musician and member of The Specials
- Ben Gordon, Basketball player currently with the American side Chicago Bulls
- Stephen Graham, Television and film actor
- Joel Grant, Footballer currently with Crewe Alexandra
- Sandy Green, Singer, songwriter
- A Guy Called Gerald, Musician, record producer and DJ
- Andy Hamilton, MBE, Jazz saxophonist and composer
- Paul Hall, Footballer currently with Newport County
- Stuart Hall, Cultural theorist and sociologist
- Mona Hammond, Actress of Chinese Jamaican origin similar to Naomi Campbell
- Ainsley Harriott, Celebrity chef famous mfor his role on Ready Steady Cook
- Naomie Harris, Actress notable for her roles on 28 Days Later and the Pirates of the Caribbean series
- Lenny Henry, CBE writer, comedian and actor
- David Hinds, Rhythm guitarist and lead vocalist of Steel Pulse
- Kelly Holmes, DBE, MBE, two time Olympic champion athlete
- Micah Hyde, Footballer currently with Peterborough United
- Tippa Irie, Reggae singer and DJ
- Abu Izzadeen, Spokesman for terrorist group Al Ghurabaa

- Colin Jackson, Former sprint and hurdling athlete
- Jamelia, R&B singer, songwriter
- David James, Footballer currently with Portsmouth
- David Johnson, Former footballer
- Linton Kwesi Johnson, Dub poet aka LKJ
- Michael Johnson, Footballer currently with Notts County
- Darren Jordon, Journalist working for the channel Al Jazeera English
- Julius Soubise, Well known slave fop
- Kano, Rapper and former member of the N.A.S.T.Y. Crew
- Janet Kay, Singer considered a one-hit wonder
- Marlon King, Footballer currently with Wigan Athletic
- Beverley Knight, MBE, Soul and R&B singer, songwriter, and record producer
- Leon Knight, Footballer currently with Rushden & Diamonds
- Nathan Koo-Boothe, Under-21 Footballer currently with Aldershot Town
- Cleo Laine, Jazz singer and an actor, noted for her scat singing
- Richard Langley, Footballer currently with Luton Town
- David Lawrence, Former cricketer who played in five Tests and one ODI
- Doreen Lawrence, Human rights campaigner (mother of Stephen Lawrence)
- Jamie Lawrence, Footballer currently with Harrow Borough
- Stephen Lawrence, Murdered teenager
- Rustie Lee, Chef and actress
- Adrian Lester, Actor most notable for roles in Hustle and The Day After Tomorrow
- Don Letts, Film director and musician
- Andrea Levy, Author and winner of the 2004 Orange Prize for Fiction.
- Lennox Lewis, CM, CBE, Former boxing heavyweight champion
- Shaznay Lewis, Singer, songwriter and member of All Saints
- Delroy Lindo, Actor mainly working in the United States famed for roles in The Cider House Rules and Get Shorty
- Germaine Lindsay, One of four terrorists who detonated bombs during the 7 July 2005 London bombings
- Kevin Lisbie, Footballer currently with Ipswich Town
- Nigel Lord, photographer and publisher
- Omar Lye-Fook, Soul singer, songwriter and musician
- Danny Maddix, Former footballer
- Jobi McAnuff, Footballer currently with Watford
- Devon Malcolm, Former cricketer
- Roots Manuva, Rapper aka Roots Manuva
- Julian Marley, Reggae musician and son of Bob Marley
- Dwight Marshall, Former footballer
- Noël Martin, Prominent Neo-Nazi victim who was attacked by German Neo-Nazis in 1996
- Val McCalla, Founder of The Voice, a weekly newspaper
- Tyrone Mears, Footballer currently with Olympique de Marseille
- Lewis McGugan, Footballer currently with Nottingham Forest
- Winston McKenzie, Politician and former amateur boxer who came 10th in the London mayoral contest
- Bradley McIntosh, Singer and actor
- Count Prince Miller, Actor and musician
- Wentworth Miller, Actor most noted for his role in US TV series Prison Break
- Diane Modahl, Former middle distance runner

- Harold Moody, Physician who established the League of Coloured Peoples
- Darren Moore, Footballer currently with Barnsley
- Lisa Moorish, Singer, songwriter
- Bill Morris, OJ, Former general secretary of the Transport and General Workers' Union
- Clinton Morrison, Footballer currently with Coventry City
- Ms. Dynamite, Mercury Prize-winning R&B and hip hop singer-rapper
- Musical Youth, Pop/reggae band
- Nyron Nosworthy, Football defender currently with Sunderland
- Bruce Oldfield, OBE, fashion designer, best known for his couture occasionwear
- Marcus Patrick, Actor who has been based in the United States for several years
- Cass Pennant, Writer and former football hooligan
- Jermaine Pennant, Footballer currently with Liverpool
- Ranking Miss P, Radio presenter
- Darryl Powell, Former footballer
- Maxi Priest, Reggae singer, songwriter
- Richard Reid, Convicted terrorist serving a life sentence in the USA for attempting to blow up aircraft
- Tessa Sanderson, CBE, Javelin thrower and heptathlete
- Mary Seacole, Nurse best known for her involvement in the Crimean War
- Dennis Seaton, Grammy Award-nominated R&B/Reggae singer, songwriter
- Fitzroy Simpson, Footballer currently with Eastleigh
- Charmaine Sinclair, Glamour model and pornographic actress
- Frank Sinclair, Footballer currently with Lincoln City
- Neil Reidman, Film and TV actor
- Slick Rick, Grammy Award-nominated rapper, songwriter and actor
- Smiley Culture, Reggae singer and DJ
- Louis Smith, Artistic gymnast and Olympic bronze medalist
- Zadie Smith, Novelist and Winner of the 2006 Orange Prize for Fiction.
- Neville Staple, Roadie-turned-singer for the second-wave ska band, The Specials
- Cleveland Taylor, Footballer currently with Carlisle United
- Marsha Thomason, Actress most famous for her roles in Las Vegas, Lost and The Haunted Mansion
- Darius Vassell, Footballer currently with Manchester City
- Hugh Verity, Royal Air Force officer of the Second World War
- Terri Walker, R&B and soul singer, songwriter
- Theo Walcott, Footballer currently with Arsenal
- Robert Wedderburn, Political writer
- Francis Williams, Scholar and poet, also the first known person of African descent to be educated at Cambridge University
- Leo Williams, Bass guitarist
- Shaun Wright-Phillips, Footballer currently with Manchester City
- Ashley Young, Football midfielder currently with Watford
- Benjamin Zephaniah, Rastafarian writer and dub poet
- Tasha Danvers, Athlete

Gallery

Diane Abbott

Giles Barnes

Darren Bent

Downtown Julie Brown

Frank Bruno

Keisha Buchanan

Deon Burton

Naomi Campbell

Sol Campbell

Errol Christie

Chris Eubank

Goldie

Ben Gordon

Ainsley Harriott

Naomie Harris

Delroy Lindo

Michael Johnson

Julius Soubise

Beverley Knight

Cleo Laine

Rustie Lee

Shaznay Lewis

Jobi
McAnuff

Winston
McKenzie

Jermaine Pennant

Tessa Sanderson

Mary Seacole

Frank Sinclair

Neville Staple

Theo Walcott

Francis Williams

Shaun
Wright-Phillips

See also

- British Jamaican
- List of Jamaicans
- List of Jamaican Americans

Black British

Black British

Black Britons (From top left):

John Taylor, Baron Taylor of Warwick, Naomi Campbell, Olaudah Equiano, Diane Abbott, Adewale Akinnuoye-Agbaje, Chris Eubank, Chiwetel Ejiofor, Paul Ince, Naomie Harris, Shaznay Lewis, Estelle, Thandie Newton, Ignatius Sancho, Idris Elba, Francis Williams, Shaun Wright-Phillips

Total population
England 1,447,900 (2007)[1]
Black Caribbean – 599,700
Black African – 730,600
Other Black – 117,600
Scotland 8,025 (2001)[2]
Black Caribbean – 1,778
Black African – 5,118
Other Black – 1,129
Wales 7,069 (2001)[3]
Black Caribbean – 2,597
Black African – 3,727
Other Black – 745
Northern Ireland 1,136 (2001)[4]
Black Caribbean – 255
Black African – 494
Other Black – 387
(The figures above are the most recent available and include only Black British individuals, not individuals of partial sub-Saharan African ancestry. The next UK census is to be performed in 2011)

Regions with significant populations
London, West Midlands, Greater Manchester, Sheffield, West Yorkshire, Bristol, Cardiff, East Midlands, Leeds, Liverpool

Languages
English (British English, Black British English, Caribbean English, African English), African languages, others

Religion
Majority are Christian (71%), with minorities of Muslims (9%), Irreligious (8%) and others 2001 census[5]

Black British is a term that usually describes British people of Black African descent. The term, which has had different meanings and uses as a racial and political label, has been historically used to refer to any non-white British nationals. The term was first used at the end of the British Empire, when several major colonies formally gained independence and thereby created a new form of national identity. The term was used primarily from the 1950s to describe those from the former colonies of Africa, and the Caribbean, i.e. the New Commonwealth. In some circumstances the word 'Black' still signifies all ethnic minority populations.[6]

More recently it has come to define a British resident with specifically Sub-Saharan African ancestral origins, who self-identifies, or is identified, as "Black", African or Afro-Caribbean. Black British is used as a category in UK national statistics ethnicity classifications, where it is sub-divided into Caribbean, African and Other Black groups.

Terminology

Historically, the term has most commonly been used to refer to Black people of New Commonwealth origin. For example, Southall Black Sisters was established in 1979 "to meet the needs of black (Asian and Afro-Caribbean) women".[7] (Note that "Asian" in the British context means from South Asia only.) "Black" was used in this inclusive political sense[8] to mean "not white British" – the main groups in the 1970s were from the British West Indies and the Indian subcontinent, but solidarity against racism extended the term to the Irish population of Britain as well.[9] [10] Several organisations continue to use the term inclusively, such as the Black Arts Alliance,[11] [12] who extend their use of the term to Latin America and all refugees,[13] and the National Black Police Association.[14] This is unlike the official British Census definition which adheres to the clear distinction between "British South Asians" and "British Blacks".[15] Note that because of the Indian diaspora and especially Idi Amin's expulsion of Asians from Uganda in 1972, many British Asians come from families that have spent several generations in the British West Indies or East Africa, so not everyone born in, or with roots in, the Caribbean or Africa can be assumed to be "black" in the exclusive sense;[16] Lord Alli is a good example.

Historical usage

Black British was also an identity of Black people in Sierra Leone (known as the Krio) who considered themselves British.[17] They are generally the descendants of black people who lived in England in the 18th century and freed Black American slaves who fought for the Crown in the American Revolutionary War (see also Black Loyalists). In 1787, hundreds of London's Black poor (a category which included the East Indian seamen known as lascars) agreed to go to this West African country on the condition that they would retain the status of British subjects, to live in freedom under the protection of the British Crown and be defended by the Royal Navy. Making this fresh start with them were many white people, including girlfriends, wives and widows of the black men.[18]

History

16th century

Early in the 16th century Africans arrived in London when Catherine of Aragon travelled to London and brought a group of her African attendants with her. When trade lines began to open between London and West Africa, Africans slowly began to become part of the London population. The first record of an African in London was in 1593. His name was Cornelius. London's residents started to become fearful of the increased black population. At this time Elizabeth I declared that black "Negroes and black Moors" were to be arrested and expelled from her kingdom.[19]

17th–18th centuries

The slave trade

During this era there was a rise of black settlements in London. Britain was involved with the tri-continental slave trade between Europe, Africa and the Americas. Black slaves were attendants to sea captains and ex-colonial officials as well as traders, plantation owners and military personnel. This marked growing evidence of the black presence in the northern, eastern and southern areas of London. There were also small numbers of free slaves and seaman from West Africa and South Asia. Many of these people were forced into beggary due to the lack of jobs and racial discrimination.[20] [21]

Seven African slaves in chains alongside two sailors at the Port of Liverpool

The involvement of merchants from the British Isles in the transatlantic slave trade was the most important factor in the development of the Black British community. These communities flourished in port cities strongly involved in the slave trade, such as Liverpool (from 1730)[22] and Bristol. As a result, Liverpool is home to Britain's oldest Black community, dating to at least the 1730s, and some Black Liverpudlians are able to trace their ancestors in the city back ten generations.[23] Early Black settlers in the city included seamen, the children of traders sent to be educated, and freed slaves, since slaves entering the country after 1722 were deemed free men.[24]

The legality of slavery in England had been questioned following the Cartwright decision of 1569, when it was "resolved that England was too pure an air for a slave to breathe in." From the early 18th century, there are records of slave sales and various attempts to capture Africans described as escaped slaves. The issue was not legally contested until the Somerset case of 1772, which concerned James Somersett, a fugitive black slave from Virginia. Chief Justice Mansfield (whose own presumed great-niece Dido was of mixed race) concluded that Somersett could not be forced to leave England against his will. (See generally, Slavery at common law.)

William Hogarth's engraving *Four Times of the Day: Noon* (1738) shows a black London resident.

Around the 1750s London became the home of many of Blacks, Jews, Irish, Germans, and Huguenots. According to Gretchen Gerzina in her *Black London*, by the middle of the 18th century Blacks comprised somewhere between one and three percent of the London populace.[25]

[26] Evidence of the number of Black residents in London has been found through registered burials. The whites of London had widespread views that Black people in London were less than human; these views were expressed in slave sale advertisements. Some Black people in London resisted through escape. Leading Black activists of this era included Olaudah Equiano, Ignatius Sancho and Quobna Ottobah Cugoano.

With the support of other Britons these activists demanded that Blacks be freed from slavery. Supporters involved in this movements included workers and other nationalities of the urban poor. London Blacks vocally contested slavery and the slave trade. At this time the slavery of whites was forbidden, but the legal statuses of these practices were not clearly defined. Free black slaves could not be enslaved, but blacks who were bought as slaves to Britain were considered the property of their owners. During this era, Lord Mansfield declared that a slave who fled from his master could not be taken by force or sold abroad. This verdict fueled the numbers of Blacks that escaped slavery, and helped send slavery into decline. During this same period, many slave soldiers who had fought on the side of the British in the American Revolutionary War arrived in London. These soldiers were deprived of pensions and many of them became poverty-stricken and were reduced to begging on the streets. The Blacks in London lived among the whites in areas of Mile End, Stepney, Paddington and St Giles. The majority of these people did not live as slaves, but as servants to wealthy whites. Many became labeled as the "Black Poor" defined as former low wage soldiers, seafarers and plantation workers.[27]

During the late 18th century there were many publications and memoirs written about the "black poor". One example is the writings of Equiano, who became an unofficial spokesman for Britain's Black community. A memoir about his life and attributions in Black London is entitled, *The Interesting Narratives of the Life of Olaudah Equiano*.

The Black Londoners, encouraged by the Committee for the Relief of the Black Poor, decided to immigrate to Sierra Leone to found the first British colony in Africa. They demanded that their status as British subjects be recognized, along with the duty of the Royal Navy to defend them.

The number of people in the United Kingdom with Black African origins was relatively small. There were, however, significant communities of South Asians, especially East Indian seamen known as lascars. In short, the links established through the British Empire led to increased population movement and immigration.

In a famous case, an Indian Briton, Dadabhai Naoroji, stood for election to parliament for the Liberal Party in 1886. He was defeated, leading the leader of the Conservative Party, Lord Salisbury to remark that "however great the progress of mankind has been, and however far we have advanced in overcoming prejudice, I doubt if we have yet got to the point of view where a British constituency would elect a black man".[28] This led to much discussion about the applicability of the term "black" to South Asians. Naoroji was subsequently elected to parliament in 1892, becoming the first Member of Parliament (MP) of Indian descent.

19th century

Coming into the early 19th century, more groups of black soldiers and seaman were displaced after the Napoleonic wars and settled in London. These settlers suffered and faced many challenges as did many Black Londoners. In 1807 the British slave trade was abolished and the slave trade was abolished completely in the British empire by 1834. The number of blacks in London was steadily declining with these new laws. Fewer blacks were brought into London from the West Indies and parts of Africa.[27]

The 19th century was also a time when "scientific racism" flourished. Many white Londoners claimed that they were the superior race and that blacks were not as intelligent as whites. They tried to hold up their accounts with scientific evidence, for example the size of the brain. Such claims were later proven false, but this was just one more obstacle for the blacks in London to hurdle over. The late 19th century effectively ended the first period of large scale black immigration to London and Britain. This decline in immigration gave way to the gradual incorporation of blacks and their descendents into this predominantly white society.

During the mid-19th century there were restrictions on African immigration. In the later part of the 19th century there was a build up of small groups of black dockside communities in towns such as Canning Town,[29] Liverpool, and Cardiff. This was a direct effect of new shipping links that were established with the Caribbean and West Africa.

Early 20th century

Before the Second World War, the largest Black communities were to
be found in the United Kingdom's great port cities: London's East End,
Liverpool, Bristol and Cardiff's Tiger Bay, with other communities in
South Shields in Tyne & Wear and Glasgow. The South Shields
community (mostly South Asians and Yemenis) were victims of the
UK's first race riot in 1919.[30] Soon all the other towns with
significant non-white communities were also hit by race riots which
spread across the Anglo-Saxon world. At this time, on Australian
insistence, the British refused to accept the Racial Equality Proposal
put forward by the Japanese at the Paris Peace Conference, 1919.
Australian soldiers were reported to be the leaders of the attacks on the
Black community in Butetown, Cardiff.[31]

Members of the West India Regiment on the
Somme, September 1916. All of the men pictured
were African-Caribbeans who volunteered in the
UK to fight for the British Army

World War I

World War I was another growth period for blacks in London. Their
communities grew with the arrival of merchant seaman and soldiers. At
the same time there is also a continuous presence of small groups of
students from Africa and the Caribbean slowly immigrating into
London. These first communities which housed London's first black
immigrants survive and now are among the oldest black communities
of London.

The Empire Windrush is extremely important
within Black British history, as aboard the ship in
1948 was the first large wave of Jamaican
immigrant to the UK

World War II

World War II marked another growth period for the black communities
into London, Liverpool and elsewhere in Britain. Many blacks from the Caribbean and West Africa arrive in small
groups as wartime workers, merchant seaman, and servicemen from the army, navy, and air forces. For example in
February 1941 345 West Indians came to work in factories in and around Liverpool, making munitions.[32] By the
end of 1943 there were a further 3,312 African American soldiers based at Maghull and Huyton, near Liverpool.[33]
It is estimated that approximately twenty thousand black Londoners lived in communities concentrated in the dock
side areas of London, Liverpool and Cardiff. One of these black Londoners, Learie Constantine, who was a welfare
officer in the RAF, was refused service at a London hotel. He stood up for his rights and later was awarded damages.
This particular example is used by some to illustrate the slow change from racism towards acceptance and equality
of all citizens in London.[34]

Post War

It was in the period after the Second World War, however, that the largest influx of Black people occurred, mostly
from the British West Indies.Over a quarter of a million West Indians, the overwhelming majority of them from
Jamaica, settled in Britain in less than a decade. In the mid-1960s Britain had become the centre of the largest
overseas population of West Indians.[35] This migration event is often labeled "Windrush", a reference to the Empire
Windrush, the ship that carried the first major group of Caribbean migrants to the United Kingdom in 1948.[36]
"Caribbean" is itself not one ethnic or political identity; for example, some of this wave of immigrants were
Indo-Caribbean. The most widely used term then used was "West Indian" (or sometimes "coloured"). "Black British"
did not come into widespread use until the second generation were born to these post-war immigrants to the country.
Although British by nationality, due to friction between them and the white majority, they were often being born into
communities that were relatively closed, creating the roots of what would become a distinct Black British identity.

By the 1950s, there was a consciousness of black people as a separate people that was not there between 1932 and 1938.[37]

Late 20th century

In 1962 the Commonwealth Immigrants Act was passed in Britain along with a succession of other laws in 1968, 1971, and 1981 that severely restricted the entry of Black immigrants into Britain. During this period it is widely argued that emergent blacks and Asians struggled in Britain against racism and prejudice.During the 1970s – and partly in response to both the rise in racial intolerance and the rise of the Black Power movement abroad – 'black' became detached from its negative connotations, and was reclaimed as a marker of pride: black is beautiful.[37] In 1975 a new voice emerged for the black London population; his name was David Pitt and he brought a new voice to the House of Lords. He spoke against racism and for equality in regards to all residents of Britain. With this new tone also came the opportunity for the black population to elect four Black members into Parliament.

A scene during the 1980 St. Pauls riot

Since the 1980s, the majority of black immigrants into the country have come directly from Africa, in particular, Nigeria and Ghana in West Africa, Kenya in East Africa, and Zimbabwe and South Africa in Southern Africa. Nigerians and Ghanaians have been especially quick to accustom themselves to British life, with young Nigerians and

One of the few recent race riots occurred in Leeds in 2001

Ghanaians achieving some of the best results at GCSE and A-Level, often on a par or above the performance of Caucasian pupils.[38] The rate of inter-racial marriage between British citizens born in Africa and native Britons is still fairly low, compared to those from the Caribbean. This might change over time as Africans become more part of mainstream British culture as second and third generation African communities become established.

By the end of the 20th century the number of black Londoners numbered half a million, according to the 1991 census. An increasing number of these black Londoners were London- or British-born. Even with this growing population and the first blacks elected to Parliament, many argue that there was still discrimination and a socio-economic imbalance in London among the Blacks. In 1992 the number of blacks in Parliament increased to six and in 1997 they increased their numbers to nine. There are still many problems that Black Londoners face; the new global and high tech information revolution is changing the urban economy and some argue that it is driving unemployment rates among blacks up relative to non-blacks, something which, it is argued, threatens to erode the progress made thus far.[27]

Race and Anti-Police riots

The late 1950s through to the late 1980s saw some of the most violent riots in recent British history, a large number of these were in large British cities as a result of mounting tensions between the local black and white communities. The first major incident occurred in 1958 in Notting Hill and was thought to have been fuelled by a group of white youth's dislike of an interracial couple. A mob of 300 to 400 white people descended on a primarily Afro-Caribbean area and attacked houses across the neighbourhood. The 1980 St. Pauls riot in Bristol was also equally as violent resulting in numerous casualties, this incident was fuelled by the local Afro-Caribbean community believing they were being specifically targeted by the Sus law because of their race. 1981 brought another spate of riots, in Brixton 5,000 people were involved in a riot between the Metropolitan Police and local Afro-Caribbean community, the same happened further north in Toxteth, Liverpool. There was a nationwide wave of uprisings in the wake of the

Brixton riots and riots occurred in Handsworth, Birmingham in 1981 and 1985 the local South Asian community also became involved in the former. Riots occurred elsewhere in Moss Side, Manchester and again in numerous places within Inner London. Surprisingly there was only one fatal riot (being the Broadwater Farm riot), and as deprivation and unemployment decreased, order was maintained and the frequency of race riots in the UK has decreased dramatically since. Despite this some members of the Black British community were involved in the 2001 Harehills race riot and 2005 Birmingham race riots.

Demographics

Population

In the 2001 UK Census, 565,876 people stated their ethnicity as Black Caribbean, 485,277 as Black African and 97,585 as Black Other, making a total of 1,148,738 in the census's Black or Black British category. This was equivalent to 2 per cent of the UK population at the time.[39]

Mid-2007 estimates for England only put the Black British population there at 1,448,000 compared to 1,158,000 in mid-2001.[40]

Population distribution

Most Black Britons can be found in the large cities and metropolitan areas of the country, there are almost 1 million Black Britons in London. According to 2005 estimates, cities with large and significant Black communities are as follows (London boroughs included).[41]

Large Black British Communities	
Greater London	1,100,000
Birmingham Metro Area	176,700
Hackney, East London	67,104
Lambeth, South London	65,800
Southwark, South London	64,400
Lewisham, South London	63,700
Croydon, South London	55,900
Newham, East London	55,400
Brent, North West London	54,300
Haringey, North London	47,200
Waltham Forest, East London	39,300
Waltham Forest, East London	50,400
Greater Manchester	38,300
Redbridge, North East London	98,400
Leeds	21,000
Sheffield	18,300
Bristol	16,100
Wolverhampton	16,000
Hillingdon, West London	15,000
Liverpool	12,200
Coventry	11,800

| Bradford | 11,000 |
| Sandwell | 14,769 |

Areas with pop. over 7 million

- London 15.7%

Over 1 million

- Birmingham 7.8%

Over 700,000

- Leeds 2.9%

Over 500,000

- Sheffield 3.4%

Over 400,000

- Manchester 7.1%
- Bristol 4.0%
- Liverpool 1.8%

Over 300,000

- Croydon 16.6%
- Coventry 7.8%
- Cardiff 2.7%
- Dudley 2.2%
- Bradford 2.2%

- Wolverhampton 6.7%
- Hillingdon 6.0%
- Leicester 5.6%
- Milton Keynes 4.5%
- Southampton 2.6%
- Derby 2.4%
- Brighton 2.3%
- Medway 1.9%
- Newcastle-upon-Tyne 1.5%
- Kingston-upon-Hull 1.4%
- Stoke-on-Trent 1.4%
- Plymouth 0.3%

- Colchester 1.6%
- Newport 1.5%
- Tunbridge Wells 1.5%
- Basingstoke 1.5%
- Bournemouth 1.4%
- Norwich 1.4%
- Bath 1.4%

Over 50,000

- Watford 4.5%
- Stevenage 2.7%
- Crawley 2.5%
- Epsom and Ewell 2.4%
- Hastings 2.2%
- Redditch 2.0%
- Woking 1.6%
- Eastbourne 1.5%
- Loughborough 1.5%

Over 10,000

- Chapeltown 61.6%
- Moss Side 31.8%
- Aston 24.8%
- Lozells 21.0%
- Hulme 18.97%
- Butetown 18.81%

Over 200,000

- Hackney 29.9%
- Lewisham 24.9%
- Lambeth 24.2%
- Southwark 23.9%
- Newham 22.3%
- Haringey 20.9%
- Brent 20.0%
- Waltham Forest 17.7%
- Greenwich 12.4%
- Redbridge 10.4%
- Merton 8.1%
- Nottingham 6.8%

Over 100,000

- Luton 9.5%
- Slough 6.5%
- Reading 5.7%
- Oxford 4.2%
- Bedford 4.1%
- Northampton 3.9%
- Thurrock 3.2%
- Cambridge 2.9%
- Peterborough 2.8%
- Huddersfield 2.5%
- Basildon 2.1%
- Preston 2.0%
- Chelmsford 1.9%
- Ipswich 1.9%
- Canterbury 1.9%
- Ashford 1.8%
- Guildford 1.8%
- Maidenhead 1.7%
- Richmond 1.7%
- Swindon 1.7%
- Portsmouth 1.6%
- Southend-on-Sea 1.6%

Culture and community

Dialect

British Black English is a variety of the English language spoken by a large number of the Black British population of Afro-Caribbean ancestry.[42] The British Black dialect is heavily influenced by Jamaican English owing to the large number of British immigrants from Jamaica, but it is also spoken by those of different ancestry.

British Black speech is also heavily influenced by social class and the regional dialect (Cockney, Mancunian, Brummie, Scouse, etc.).

Music

Black British music is a long-established and influential part of British music. Its presence in the United Kingdom stretches from concert performers like George Bridgetower in the 18th century to street musicians like Billy Waters.

In the late 1970s and 1980s, 2 Tone became popular with the British youth, especially in the West Midlands. A blend of punk, ska and pop made it popular with both white and black audiences. Famous bands include The Selecter, The Specials, The Beat and The Bodysnatchers.

Jungle, Dubstep, Drum and Bass and Grime music were invented in London and involve a number of artists from Black African and Caribbean communities, most notably Jamaican, Ghanaian and Nigerian. Famous grime artists include Dizzee Rascal, Kano (rapper), Wiley, Lethal Bizzle, Tinchy Stryder and Chipmunk. It is now common to hear British MCs rapping in a strong London Accent. Niche, with its origin in Sheffield and Leeds, has a much faster bassline and is often sung in a northern accent. Famous Niche artists include producer T2.

Social issues

There is much controversy surrounding the politics of integrating the United Kingdom's black community, particularly concerning crime, discrimination in basic services, employment and education.

The poverty rate for the United Kingdom's minority ethnic groups stands at 40%, double the 20% found amongst white British people, according to new research published in 2007 (30 April) by the Joseph Rowntree Foundation (JRF). Minority ethnic groups are also being paid lower wages, despite improvements in education and qualifications. The research highlights the differences between minority ethnic groups with 45% of Black Africans and 30% of Black Caribbeans living in poverty. Over half of Black African children in the UK are growing up in poverty. The research shows that people from minority ethnic groups who have higher educational achievements do not receive the same rewards as those from white British backgrounds with similar qualifications. A wide range of factors are shown to affect different groups and the research highlights how the Government needs to consider and implement more targeted policies.

Diane Abbott ran for Labour Party (UK)
leadership election, 2010

According to the TUC report *Black workers, jobs and poverty*,[43] people from black and Asian groups are far more likely to be unemployed than the white population, despite having the required skills and qualifications. The rate of unemployment among the white population is only 11%, but among black groups it is 13%, mixed-race 15%, Indian 7%, Pakistani 15% and Bangladeshi 17%. The usual argument to counter high unemployment rates among black and Asian people — namely that they lack the necessary skills and qualifications — does not bear merit, the report states. For example, 81.4% of black and Asian people with degrees are employed, compared with 87.4% of white people. This statistic however does not take account of the qualitative distinction of these degrees, since degrees vary greatly in their employability. Furthermore, a white person whose highest qualification is GCSE's at grades A-C is more likely to have a job than a black or Asian person with A-levels.

Both racist crime and black on black gang-related crime continues to affect black communities. Numerous deaths in police custody of black men have grown a general distrust of police amongst urban blacks in the UK. According to the Metropolitan Police Authority in 2002–2003 of the 17 deaths in police custody, 10 were black or Asian. The government reports[44] the overall number of racist incidents recorded by the police rose by 7% from 49,078 in 2002/3 to 52,694 in 2003/4.

The media has highlighted black gangs and black on black violence. According to a Home Office report,[44] 10% of all homicide victims between 2000 and 2004 were black. Of these, 56% were murdered by other blacks. Given that blacks represent approximately 3% of the British population, black on black violence is a significant problem.

Black people, who according to government statistics[45] make up 2% of the population, are the principal suspects in 11.7% of homicides, i.e. in 252 out of 2163 homicides committed 2001/2, 2002/3, and 2003/4.[46] It should be noted that, judging on the basis of prison population, a substantial minority (about 35%) of black criminals in the UK are not British citizens but foreign nationals.[47] In November 2009, the Home Office published a study that showed that, once other variables had been accounted for, ethnicity was not a significant predictor of offending, anti-social behaviour or drug abuse amongst young people.[48]

After several high-profile investigations such as that of the murder of Stephen Lawrence, the police have often been accused of racism, from both within and outside the service. Cressida Dick, head of the Metropolitan Police's anti-racism unit in 2003, remarked that it was 'difficult to imagine a situation where we will say we are no longer institutionally racist'.[49]

Notable Black Britons

Well-known Black Britons living before the 20th century include the Chartist William Cuffay; William Davidson, executed as a Cato Street conspirator; Olaudah Equiano (also called Gustavus Vassa), a former slave who bought his freedom, moved to England, and settled in Soham, Cambridgeshire, where he married and wrote an autobiography, dying in 1797; Ukawsaw Gronniosaw, pioneer of the slave narrative; and Ignatius Sancho, a grocer who also acquired a reputation as a man of letters. In 2004, a poll found that people considered the Crimean War heroine Mary Seacole to be the greatest Black Briton.[50] Seacole was born in Jamaica in 1805 to a white father and black mother.[51] A statue of her is planned for the grounds of St. Thomas' Hospital in London.[50]

Crimean War nurse, Mary Seacole is dubbed as the Greatest Black Briton

More recently, a large number of Black British people have achieved prominence in public life. An example from television is reporter and newsreader Sir Trevor McDonald, born in Trinidad, who was knighted in 1999. McDonald is now seen as a part of the broadcasting establishment. His clear, confident delivery and serious attitude have made him one of British television's most trusted presenters, winning more awards than any other British broadcaster. Other examples from television are entertainer Lenny Henry and chef Ainsley Harriott.

In art and film, Steve McQueen won the Turner prize in 1999, he has since directed his first feature Hunger. The film earned him the Caméra d'Or at the 2008 Cannes Film Festival.

Michael Fuller, after a successful career in the Metropolitan Police, has been Chief Constable of Kent since 2004. He is the son of Jamaican immigrants who came to the United Kingdom in the 1950s. Fuller was brought up in Sussex, where his interest in the police force was encouraged by an officer attached to his school. He is a graduate in social psychology.[52]

In business, Damon Buffini heads Permira, one of the world's largest private equity firms. Buffini topped the 07 'power list' as the most powerful Black male in the United Kingdom by New Nation magazine and was recently appointed to Prime Minister Gordon Brown's business advisory panel.

Olaudah Equiano, a significant figure involved with he abolition of the Atlantic Slave Trade

René Carayol is a successful broadcaster, broadsheet columnist, business & leadership speaker and author, best known for presenting the BBC series Did They Pay Off Their Mortgage in Two Years?. He has also served as an executive main board director for blue-chip companies as well as the public sector.

Wol Kolade is council member and Chairman of the BVCA (British Venture Capital Association) and a Governor and council member of the London School of Economics and Political Science, chairing its Audit Committee.

Adam Afriyie, is a politician, and Conservative Member of Parliament for Windsor. He is also the founding director of Connect Support Services, an IT services company pioneering fixed-price support. He was also Chairman of DeHavilland Information Services plc, a news and information services company, and was a regional finalist in the 2003 Ernst and Young Entrepreneur of the year awards.

Alexander Amosu is an entrepreneur and one of the first people in the UK to create high-end customised mobile phones in gold, white gold and various colours of diamonds, selling to wealthy clients worldwide.

Finally, Wilfred Emmanuel-Jones is a businessman, farmer and founder of the popular Black Farmer range of food products. In addition, he is also a prospective Conservative Party candidate for the Chippenham constituency for the next general election.

In 2005, soldier Johnson Beharry, born in Grenada of mixed Black African and East Indian roots, became the first man to win the Victoria Cross, the United Kingdom's foremost military award for bravery, since the Falklands War of 1982. He was awarded the medal for service in Iraq in 2004.

Shirley Bassey is the UK's most successful female artist of all time

In sport, prominent examples of success include boxing champion Frank Bruno, whose career highlight was winning the WBC world heavyweight championship in 1995. Altogether, he has won 40 of his 45 contests. He is also well known for acting in pantomime.

Lennox Lewis, born in east London, is another successful Black British boxer and former undisputed heavyweight champion of the world.

Recently, Lewis Hamilton, who is mixed-race, has created a major impact in the world of Formula One racing, with his most notable achievement being the winner (and first Black person) of the 2008 formula 1 world championship.

Kelly Holmes, who won two gold medals in the 2004 Athens Olympics, is also mixed-race: her black father was born in Jamaica, while her white mother is English.

People of black ancestry such as Bernie Grant, Baroness Amos and Diane Abbott, as well as Oona King and Paul Boateng who are of mixed race, have made significant contributions to politics and trade unionism.

Paul Boateng became the UK's first black biracial cabinet minister in 2002 when he was appointed as Chief Secretary to the Treasury.

Bill Morris was elected general secretary of the Transport and General Workers' Union in 1992. He was knighted in 2003, and in 2006 he took a seat in the House of Lords as a working life peer, Baron Morris of Handsworth.

Diane Abbott became the first black woman Member of Parliament when she was elected to the House of Commons in the 1987 general election.

There have also been several unsuccessful black and mixed race parliamentary candidates in recent elections (particularly those since 1997). Musician and community activist Richard Bilcliffe achieved local fame (which regretably did not lead to many votes) in the Petch-Waters Valley district by-election of 1999; his older sister Melody (of entirely white origin) had stood for the same seat in 1987.

Valerie Amos became the first black woman cabinet minister and the first black woman to become leader of the House of Lords.

Numerous Black British actors have become successful in US television, such as Adewale Akinnuoye-Agbaje, Idris Elba, Lennie James, Marsha Thomason and Marianne Jean-Baptiste. Black British actors are also increasingly found starring in major Hollywood movies, notable examples include Adrian Lester, Ashley Walters, Chiwetel Ejiofor,

Colin Salmon, David Harewood, Eamonn Walker, Hugh Quarshie, Naomie Harris, Sophie Okonedo and Thandie Newton.

See also

- 100 Great Black Britons
- British Black English
- Black and Asian Studies Association
- Black Scottish
- British African-Caribbean community
- Other Black
- British Mixed-Race
- Ethnic groups of the United Kingdom
- List of black Britons

References

[1] http://www.neighbourhood.statistics.gov.uk/dissemination/LeadTableView.do?adminCompAndTimeId=25403%3A280&a=7& b=276743&c=london&d=13&r=1&e=13&f=24438&o=254&g=325264&i=1001x1003x1004x1005&l=1809&m=0& s=1254850916322&enc=1

[2] http://83.137.212.42/sitearchive/cre/diversity/map/scotland/index.html

[3] http://83.137.212.42/sitearchive/cre/diversity/map/wales/index.html

[4] http://www.nisranew.nisra.gov.uk/census/start.html

[5] Religion by ethnic groups (http://www.statistics.gov.uk/STATBASE/ssdataset.asp?vlnk=8288) 2001 census. Retrieved on 2009-10-23.

[6] Glossary of terms relating to ethnicity and race: for reflection and debate (http://jech.bmjjournals.com/cgi/content/full/58/6/441) R Bhopal. Journal of Epidemiology and Community Health. Accessed 6 October 2006

[7] Southall Black Sisters website (http://www.southallblacksisters.org.uk/)

[8] [[The Guardian (http://www.guardian.co.uk/g2/story/0,,2238188,00.html)] "What the migrant saw" by Jatinder Verma, founder in 1977 of Tara Arts, the first Asian theatre company in Britain – "Everywhere my friends and I looked, it seemed black people, as we identified ourselves, were victims of white oppression."]

[9] What is meant by Black and Asian? (http://www.branching-out.net/branching-out/page2.asp?idno=453) "In the 1970s Black was used as a political term to encompass many groups who shared a common experience of oppression – this could include Asian but also Irish, for example"

[10] The term Black and Asian – a Short History (http://www.designfordiversity.eu/blog/2006/03/term-black-and-asian-short-history.html) "In the late 1960's through to the mid 1980's, we progressives called ourselves Black. This was not only because the word was reclaimed as a positive, but we also knew that we shared a common experience of racism because of our skin colour."

[11] http://www.blackartists.org.uk/

[12] The Black Arts Alliance (http://www.actsofachievement.org.uk/) encourages "a coming together of Black people from Africa, Asia and the Caribbean because our histories have parallels of oppression"

[13] Their website intro states "Black Arts Alliance is 21 years old. Formed in 1985 it is the longest surviving network of Black artists representing the arts and culture drawn from ancestral heritages of South Asia, Africa, South America, and the Caribbean and, in more recent times, due to global conflict, our newly arrived compatriots known collectively as refugees." the Black Arts Alliance (http://www. blackartists.org.uk/)

[14] National Black Police Association (http://www.nbpa.co.uk/index.php?option=com_content&task=view&id=17&Itemid=31) states that their "emphasis is on the common experience and determination of the people of African, African-Caribbean and Asian origin to oppose the effects of racism."

[15] Census classifications (http://www.statistics.gov.uk/about/Classifications/ns_ethnic_classification.asp)

[16] (http://news.bbc.co.uk/1/hi/uk/4223322.stm) BBC article on "Multiculturalism the Wembley way"

[17] (http://www.britishempire.co.uk/maproom/sierraleone.htm)

[18] National Archives (http://www.nationalarchives.gov.uk/pathways/blackhistory/work_community/poor.htm)

[19] Bartels, Emily (22 March 2006). "Too many Blackamoors: deportation, discrimination, and Elizabeth I" (http://www.accessmylibrary. com/coms2/summary_0286-15698891_ITM). Studies in English Literature, 1500–1900. . Retrieved January 2008.

[20] Banton, Michael (1955), The Coloured Quarter. Jonathan Cape. London.

[21] Shyllon, Folarin, "The Black Presence and Experience in Britain: An Analytical Overview", in Gundara and Duffield eds. (1992), Essays on the History of Blacks in Britain. Avebury, Aldershot.http://www.chronicleworld.org

[22] Black liverpool: the early history of Britain's Oldest Black Community 1730–1918 by Ray Costello, Picton Press, Liverpool 2001

[23] Costello, Ray (2001). *Black Liverpool: The Early History of Britain's Oldest Black Community 1730–1918*. Liverpool: Picton Press. ISBN 1873245076.

[24] McIntyre-Brown, Arabella; Woodland, Guy (2001). *Liverpool: The First 1,000 Years*. Liverpool: Garlic Press. p. 57. ISBN 1904099009.

[25] Gerzina, Gretchen (1995). *Black London: Life before Emancipation*. New Brunswick: Rutgers University Press. p. 5. ISBN 0813522595.

[26] Bartels, Emily C. (2006). "Too Many Blackamoors: Deportation, Discrimination, and Elizabeth I" (http://www.press.jhu.edu/timeline/sel/Bartels_2006.pdf). *Studies in English Literature* **46** (2): 305–322. doi:10.1353/sel.2006.0012. .

[27] File, Nigel and Chris Power (1981), *Black Settlers in Britain 1555–1958*. Heinemann Educational. http://www.chronicleworld.org

[28] The Capital's history uncovered (http://www.stringofpearls.org.uk/obv/portrait.htm)

[29] Geoffrey Bell, *The other Eastenders : Kamal Chunchie and West Ham's early black community* (Stratford: Eastside Community Heritage, 2002)

[30] Tyne Roots (http://www.bbc.co.uk/tyne/roots/2003/10/arabontyne.shtml)

[31] Tristram Hunt, "Lest we forget", section entitled "Cardiff race riots, 1919 Scene of the first credible declaration of black British identity", *The Guardian*, July 24th, 2006, http://www.guardian.co.uk/politics/2006/jul/24/past.britishidentity

[32] 'Liverpool's Black Population During World War II', *Black and Asian Studies Association Newsletter* No. 20, January 1998, p6

[33] 'Liverpool's Black Population During World War II', *Black and Asian Studies Association Newsletter* No. 20, January 1998, p10

[34] Rose, Sonya (May 2001). "Race, empire and British wartime national identity, 1939–45" (http://www.blackwell-synergy.com/action/showPdf?submitPDF=Full+Text+PDF+(247+KB)&doi=10.1111/1468-2281.00125&cookieSet=1). *Historical Research* **74** (184): 224. doi:10.1111/1468-2281.00125. .

[35] Writing black Britain 1948–1998. James Procter.(Manchester)

[36] http://www.icons.org.uk/theicons/collection/ss-windrush icons: a portrait of England: SS Empire Windrush

[37] Writing black Britain 1948–1998. James Procter. (Manchester)

[38] Ethnicity and Education: The Evidence on Minority Ethnic Pupils aged 5–16 http://www.dcsf.gov.uk/research/data/uploadfiles/DFES-0208-2006.pdf The Department for Education and Skills 2006

[39] "Population size: 7.9% from a minority ethnic group" (http://www.statistics.gov.uk/CCI/nugget.asp?ID=273). Office for National Statistics. 2003-02-13. . Retrieved 2009-06-20.

[40] "Population estimates by ethnic group: 2001 to 2007 commentary" (http://www.statistics.gov.uk/downloads/theme_population/PEEGCommentary.pdf). Office for National Statistics. September 2009. p. 5. . Retrieved 2009-10-03.

[41] Neighbourhood Statistics Home Page (http://neighbourhood.statistics.gov.uk/dissemination/)

[42] Mark Sebba, "Caribbean creoles and Black English", chap. 16 of *Language in the British Isles*, ed. David Britain (Cambridge: Cambridge University Press, 2007; ISBN 0-521-79488-9).

[43] www.tuc.org.uk/welfare/tuc-10172-f0.pdf

[44] http://www.homeoffice.gov.uk/rds/pdfs05/s95race04.pdf.

[45] http://www.statistics.gov.uk/cci/nugget.asp?id=273; accessed 21 May

[46] Table 3.6 of Home Office publication "Statistics on Race and the Criminal Justice System 2004"

[47] Chapter 9, tables 9.1 – 9.4, of Home Office publication "Statistics on Race and the Criminal Justice System 2004"

[48] Hales, Jon; Nevill, Camilla; Pudney, Steve; Tipping, Sarah (November 2009). "Longitudinal analysis of the Offending, Crime and Justice Survey 2003–06" (http://rds.homeoffice.gov.uk/rds/pdfs09/horr19c.pdf). *Research Report* (London: Home Office) **19**: 23. . Retrieved 7 October 2010.

[49] 'Metropolitan police still institutionally racist' I Special reports I Guardian Unlimited (http://www.guardian.co.uk/lawrence/Story/0,,941167,00.html)

[50] "Seacole sculpture design revealed" (http://news.bbc.co.uk/1/hi/england/london/8106416.stm). BBC News. 2009-06-18. . Retrieved 2009-06-19.

[51] "Historical figures: Mary Seacole (1805–1881)" (http://www.bbc.co.uk/history/historic_figures/seacole_mary.shtml). BBC History. . Retrieved 2009-06-19.

[52] Alumni and friends I Notable Alumni I Michael Fuller (http://www.sussex.ac.uk/Units/alumni/notable_alumni/interviews/Fuller_interview.html)

External links

- The Black Presence in Britain – Black British History (http://www.blackpresence.co.uk)
- The Scarman Report into the Brixton Riots of 1981.
- The Macpherson Report into the death of Stephen Lawrence.
- Brixton Overcoat (http://www.searchwell.co.uk), ISBN 978-0-9552841-0-6
- Reassessing what we collect website – The African Community in London (http://www.museumoflondon.org.uk/English/Collections/OnlineResources/RWWC/Themes/1078/) History of African London with objects and images
- Reassessing what we collect website – Caribbean London (http://www.museumoflondon.org.uk/English/Collections/OnlineResources/RWWC/Themes/1102/) History of Caribbean London with objects and images
- "The Contestation of Britishness" by Ronald Elly Wanda (http://libr.org/isc/issues/ISC24/A32-Wanda.pdf)

Mixed (United Kingdom ethnicity category)

Mixed (United Kingdom ethnicity category)

Top row: Corinne Bailey Rae, Myleene Klass, Rio Ferdinand
Bottom row: Lewis Hamilton, Ben Kingsley, Leona Lewis, Michael Chopra

Total population

✚ England 870,000 (2007)[1]
White and Black Caribbean – 282,900
White and Black African – 114,300
White and Asian – 260,900
Other Mixed – 212,000
Wales 17,661 (2001)
Scotland 12,764 (2001)
Northern Ireland 3,319 (2001)

Mixed is an ethnicity category included in the 2001 United Kingdom Census. Colloquially it refers to British citizens or residents whose parents are of two or more different races or ethnic backgrounds. Mixed-race people are the fastest growing ethnic group in the UK.

Statistics

In the 2001 census, 677,177 classified themselves as of mixed race, making up 1.2 per cent of the UK population.[2] Office for National Statistics estimates suggest that 870,000 mixed race people were resident in England (as opposed to the whole of the UK) as of mid-2007, compared to 654,000 at mid-2001.[3] It has been estimated that, by 2020, 1.24 million people in the UK will be of mixed race.[4]

3.5 per cent of all births in England and Wales in 2005 were mixed race babies, with 0.9 per cent being Mixed White and Black Caribbean, 0.5 per cent White and Black African, 0.8 per cent White and Asian, and 1.3 per cent any other mixed background.[5]

Mixed-race people are the fastest growing ethnic minority group (defined according to the National Statistics classification) in the UK and are predicted to be the largest minority group by 2020.[6]

Subgroups

In England and Wales, the 2001 census included four sub-categories of mixed ethnic combinations: "White and Black Caribbean", "Mixed White and Black African", "Mixed White and Asian" and "Any other Mixed background", with the latter allowing people to write in their ethnicity. Analysis of census results shows that, in England and Wales only, 237,000 people stated their ethnicity as Mixed White and Black Caribbean, 189,000 as Mixed White and Asian, 156,000 as Other Mixed, and 79,000 Mixed White and Black African.[7]

The estimates for mid-2007 for England only suggest that there are 283,000 people in the Mixed White and Black Caribbean category, 114,000 Mixed White and Black African, 261,000 Mixed White and Asian, and 212,000 Other Mixed.[3] The White and Black African group grew fastest in percentage terms from 2001 to 2007, followed by White and Asian, Other Mixed and then White and Black Caribbean.[3]

The census forms in Scotland and Northern Ireland did not include sub-groups, but rather single categories: "Any Mixed Background" in Scotland and simply "Mixed" in Northern Ireland.[8]

Associations

Associations in the UK that help promote mixed-race hertiage and raise awareness of issues relating to mixed ethnicity include the Turquoise Association.[9]

See also

• Multiracial

References

[1] "Neighbourhood statistics: Resident population estimates by ethnic group, all persons" (http://www.neighbourhood.statistics.gov.uk/ dissemination/LeadTableView.do?adminCompAndTimeId=25403:280&a=7&b=276743&c=london&d=13&r=1&e=13&f=24438& o=254&g=325264&i=1001x1003x1004x1005&l=1809&m=0&s=1254850916322&enc=1). Office for National Statistics. 14 September 2009. . Retrieved 21 August 2010.

[2] "Population size: 7.9% from a minority ethnic group" (http://www.statistics.gov.uk/CCI/nugget.asp?ID=273). Office for National Statistics. 13 February 2003. . Retrieved 3 October 2009.

[3] "Population estimates by ethnic group: 2001 to 2007 commentary" (http://www.statistics.gov.uk/downloads/theme_population/ PEEGCommentary.pdf). Office for National Statistics. September 2009. p. 5. . Retrieved 3 October 2009.

[4] Smith, Laura (23 January 2007). "Mixed messages" (http://www.guardian.co.uk/commentisfree/2007/jan/23/post975). The Guardian. . Retrieved 3 October 2009.

[5] Moser, Kath; Stanfield, Kristina M. and Leon, David A. (2008). "Birthweight and gestational age by ethnic group, England and Wales 2005: Introducing new data on births" (http://www.statistics.gov.uk/articles/hsq/HSQ39Birthwt&Gest_ethnicity.pdf). Health Statistics Quarterly 39: 22–31. .

[6] Pinnock, Karlene (12 August 2009). "Mixed race 'fastest growing minority'" (http://news.bbc.co.uk/newsbeat/hi/the_p_word/ newsid_10000000/newsid_10000900/10000910.stm). BBC 1Xtra. . Retrieved 4 October 2009.

[7] Bradford, Ben (May 2006). "Who are the 'Mixed' ethnic group?" (http://www.statistics.gov.uk/articles/nojournal/ Mixed_ethnic_groups_pdf.pdf). Office for National Statistics. pp. 4, 8. . Retrieved 21 August 2010.

[8] "Harmonised Concepts and Questions for Social Data Sources: Primary Standards – Ethnic Group" (http://www.statistics.gov.uk/about/ data/harmonisation/downloads/P3.pdf). Office for National Statistics. April 2008. . Retrieved 21 August 2010.

[9] "21st-century Britons are no longer either black or white" (http://www.guardian.co.uk/uk/2009/jan/18/race-integration-study). The Observer. 18 January 2009. . Retrieved 21 August 2010.

British Indo-Caribbean community

British Indo-Caribbean

Notable Bristish people of Indo-Caribbean descent: Raj Persaud • Shakira Caine Mark Ramprakash • Waheed Alli, Baron Alli
Total population
Indo-Guyanese - *Unknown* Indo-Jamaican - *Unknown* Indo-Trinidadians - *Approx 25,000*[1]
Regions with significant populations
United Kingdom In particular London, Birmingham, Manchester, Leicester, Leeds, Glasgow, Preston, Sheffield, Liverpool, Nottingham, Southampton, Bristol, Newcastle upon Tyne, Slough, Edinburgh, Cardiff, Stoke on Trent, Coventry
Languages
British English · Caribbean English · Various Languages of India
Religion
Hinduism · Sikhism · Islam · Christianity · Amongst others
Related ethnic groups
British Indian · Indian diaspora · Indo-Caribbean · British African-Caribbean community

The **British Indo-Caribbean community** consists of residents of the United Kingdom who are of Caribbean origin and whose ancestors were indigenous to India. The UK (along with Canada and the United States), is a non-Caribbean nation with a significant population of Indo-Caribbean residents.[2]

Background

Indian people were first introduced to the Caribbean by the British government in the 1800s after the abolition of slavery and when cheap labour was needed. The majority settled in Guyana, Trinidad and Tobago and Jamaica, the Indian communities in these countries have now become extremely well established and currently have a very successful diaspora. With the strong links between the Caribbean and the UK, as well as the large Indian community in the UK, it has proven a popular destination for Indo-Caribbean emigrants. In 1990 between 22,800 and 30,400 Indo-Caribbeans were estimated to be living in the UK, it is unknown how many of the 1.6 million Britons of Indian origin are also linked to the Caribbean.[3]

Sub-groups

Indo-Guyanese

Notable Britons of Indo-Guyanese descent include Waheed Alli, Baron Alli, Shakira Caine, David Dabydeen and Mark Ramprakash.

Indo-Jamaican

Notable Britons of Indo-Jamaican descent include Omar Lye-Fook.

Indo-Trinidadians

Indo-Trinidadian people are thought to number well over 25,000, which is even more than the number of people born in Trinidad and Tobago living in the UK according to the 2001 Census.[1] Notable Britons of Indo-Trinidadian descent include Waheed Alli, Baron Alli, Chris Bisson, Vahni Capildeo, Krishna Maharaj, Shiva Naipaul, V. S. Naipaul, Lakshmi Persaud, Raj Persaud and Ron Ramdin.

See also

- Indo-Caribbean
- British Indian
- British African-Caribbean community
- British Asian
- Indo-Caribbean American

References

[1] (http://www.scribd.com/doc/7099691/IndoCaribbean-Times-December-2007)

[2] (http://www.smallislandread.com/read_more/indo_carribean.htm)

[3] Indo-Caribbean British history (http://www.movinghere.org.uk/galleries/histories/caribbean/settling/indo_caribbean2.htm#)

Classification of ethnicity in the United Kingdom

The **classification of ethnicity in the United Kingdom** has attracted controversy in the past: particularly at the time of the 2001 Census where the existence and nature of such a classification, which appeared on the Census form, became more widely known than general.

Different classifications, both formal and informal, are used in the UK.

National statistics

The ethnicity data used in UK national statistics relies on individuals' self-definition. The Office for National Statistics explain this as follows:

> Is a person's ethnic group self-defined? Yes. Membership of an ethnic group is something that is subjectively meaningful to the person concerned, and this is the principal basis for ethnic categorisation in the United Kingdom. So, in ethnic group questions, we are unable to base ethnic identification upon objective, quantifiable information as we would, say, for age or gender. And this means that we should rather ask people which group they see themselves as belonging to.[1]

The current ONS classification, which was also used for classifying ethnicity in the 2001 UK Census, is given below.[2] Slightly different categories were employed in Scotland and Northern Ireland, as compared with England and Wales, "to reflect local differences in the requirement for information".[3] However, the data collected still allow for comparison across the UK.[3] Different classifications were used in the 1991 Census, which was the first to include a question on ethnicity.[4]

England and Wales	Scotland	Northern Ireland
White	**White**	White
British	White Scottish	Irish Traveller
Irish	Other White British	Mixed
Any other White background	White Irish	Indian
Mixed	Other White	Pakistani
White and Black Caribbean	**Indian**	Bangladeshi
White and Black African	**Pakistani and other South Asian**	Other Asian
White and Asian	Pakistani	Black Caribbean
Any other Mixed background	Bangladeshi	Black African
Asian or Asian British	Other (South) Asian	Other Black
Indian	**Chinese**	Chinese
Pakistani	**Other ethnic group**	Other ethnic group
Bangladeshi	Caribbean	**Not stated**
Any other Asian background	African	
Black or Black British	Black Scottish and other Black	
Caribbean	Any Mixed Background	
African	Other Ethnic Group	
Any other Black background	**Not stated**	
Chinese or other ethnic group		
Chinese		

Any other ethnic group		
Not stated		

More detail on this classification is available on the National Statistics website.[5]

Proposed changes to the 2011 Census regarding ethnicity

There have been calls for the 2011 national census in England and Wales to include extra tick boxes so people can identify their ethnic group in category A as Welsh, English and Cornish[6] [7] (at present, the tick boxes only include British, Irish or any other).

Some experts, community and special interest group respondents also pointed out that the 'Black African' category is too broad. They remarked that the category does not provide enough information on the considerable diversity that exists within the various populations currently classified under this heading. This concealed heterogeneity ultimately makes the gathered data of limited use analytically. To remedy this, the Muslim Council of Britain proposes that this census category be broken down instead into specific ethnic groups:[8]

The National Association of British Arabs and other Arab organizations have also lobbied for the inclusion of a separate "Arab" entry, which would include under-reported groups from the Arab world such as Syrians, Somalis and Yemenis.[9]

The specimen 2011 Census questions were published in 2009 and included new "Gypsy or Irish Traveller" and "Arab" categories.[10]

Police

The police services of the UK began to classify arrests in racial groups in 1975, but later replaced the race code with an *Identity Code (IC)* system.[11]

- IC1 White person
- IC2 Mediterranean person
- IC3 African/Caribbean person
- IC4 Indian, Nepalese, Maldivian, Sri Lankan, Bangladeshi, or any other (South) Asian person
- IC5 Chinese, Japanese, or South-East Asian person
- IC6 Arabic, Egyptian or Maghreb person
- IC0 Origin unknown

This classification is still referred to on some police websites and police chase TV shows, e.g. "Driver is IC1 male, passenger is IC3 male".[12]

From 1 April 2003, police forces were required to use the new system described above. Police forces and civil and emergency services, the NHS and local authorities in England and Wales may refer to this as the "16+1" system, named for the 16 classifications of ethnicity plus one category for "not stated". The IC classification is still used for descriptions of suspects by police officers amongst themselves, but does risk incorrectly identifying a victim a witness or a suspect compared to that person's own description of their ethnicity. When a person is stopped by a police officer exercising statutory powers and asked to provide information under the Police and Criminal Evidence Act, they are asked to select one of the five main categories representing broad ethnic groups and then a more specific cultural background from within this group.[13] Officers must record the respondent's answer, not their own opinion.

Notes

[1] "Ethnic group statistics: A guide for the collection and classification of ethnicity data" (http://www.ons.gov.uk/about-statistics/ measuring-equality/equality/ethnic-group-statistics/ethnic-group-statistics--a-guide-for-the-collection-and-classification-of-ethnicity-data. pdf). Office for National Statistics. 2003. p. 9. . Retrieved 20 October 2009.

[2] "Harmonised Concepts and Questions for Social Data Sources: Primary Standards − Ethnic Group" (http://www.statistics.gov.uk/about/ data/harmonisation/downloads/P3.pdf). Office for National Statistics. April 2008. . Retrieved 2009-10-21.

[3] "Population size: 7.9% from a non-White ethnic group" (http://www.statistics.gov.uk/cci/nugget.asp?id=455). Office for National Statistics. 2004-01-08. . Retrieved 2009-10-21.

[4] Sillitoe, K.; White, P.H. (1992). "Ethnic group and the British census: The search for a question" (http://www.jstor.org/stable/2982673). *Journal of the Royal Statistical Society. Series A (Statistics in Society)* **155** (1): 141-163. . Retrieved 29 September 2010.

[5] "The Classification of Ethnic Groups" (http://web.archive.org/web/20070406195623/http://www.statistics.gov.uk/about/ Classifications/ns_ethnic_classification.asp). National Statistics. 2001-02-16. Archived from the original (http://www.statistics.gov.uk/ about/Classifications/ns_ethnic_classification.asp) on 2007-04-06. . Retrieved 2007-04-20.

[6] Fight goes on to include Cornish ethnicity and language in Census 2011 options (http://www.thisiscornwall.co.uk/displayNode. jsp?nodeId=144143&command=displayContent&sourceNode=144131&contentPK=16421143&moduleName=InternalSearch& formname=sidebarsearch)

[7] Cornish ethnicity data from the 2001 Census (http://www.lse.ac.uk/collections/BSPS/annualConference/2006_localgov. htm#generated-subheading3)

[8] Summary report: experts, community and special interest groups (http://www.ons.gov.uk/census/2011-census/consultations/ eth-group-nat-iden/sum-rep-exp-com-grp.pdf)

[9] Arab Population in the UK - Study for consideration of inclusion of 'Arab' as an ethnic group on future census returns (http://www.naba. org.uk/content/theassociation/Reports/arabPopUK_04.htm)

[10] "2011 census questions published" (http://news.bbc.co.uk/1/hi/uk_politics/8318637.stm). BBC News. 21 October 2009. . Retrieved 4 April 2010.

[11] Mackie, Lindsay (1978-06-14). "Race causes an initial confusion" (http://century.guardian.co.uk/1970-1979/Story/0,,106880,00.html). *The Guardian*. . Retrieved 2007-04-20.

[12] "Abbreviations Used" (http://www.sussex.police.uk/foi/abbreviation.asp#I). *Freedom of Information Act* (Sussex Police Online). . Retrieved 2007-04-20.

[13] "Code of Practice for the Exercise by Police Officers of Statutory Powers of Stop and Search; Police Officers and Police Staff of Requirements to Record Public Encounters" (http://www.icva.org.uk/site/downloads/PACE05/PACE_Chapter_A.pdf). *Police and Criminal Evidence Act 1984 CODE A* (HMSO). .

External links

• Ethnic group classification at ONS (PDF) (http://www.ons.gov.uk/about-statistics/harmonisation/ primary-concepts-and-questions/P3.pdf)

Jamaicans of African ancestry

Jamaicans of African ancestry

Jamaicans of African ancestry
Notable Jamaicans of African ancestry: Bob Marley Marcus Garvey
Total population
Approx. **2.5 million** 91.2% of the Jamaican population[1]
Languages
Jamaican Patois, Jamaican English
Religion
Christianity, Rastafari, Minorities Practicing Atheism, Judaism or Islam
Related ethnic groups
African American, Black British, Black Canadians

Jamaicans of African ancestry, or **Afro-Jamaicans**, are citizens of Jamaica whose ancestry lies in the continent of Africa, specifically West Africa. Up until the early 1690s Jamaica's population was relatively equally mixed between white and black people. The first Africans to arrive came in 1513 from the Iberian Peninsula after having been taken from West Africa by the Spanish and the Portuguese. They were servants, cowboys, herders of cattle, pigs and horses, as well as hunters. When the English captured Jamaica in 1655, many of them fought with the Spanish who gave them their freedom and then fled to the mountains resisting the British for many years to maintain their freedom, becoming known as Maroons.

Origin

Between 1500 and 1800, some eleven million Africans were moved to the Caribbean. They were captured by war, as retribution for crimes committed, or by abduction, and marched to the coast in "coffles" with their necks yoked to each other. They were placed in trading posts or forts to await the horrifying six to twelve week Middle Passage voyage between Africa and the Americas during which they were chained together, underfed, kept in the ship's hold in the thousands packed more like sardines than humans. Those who survived were fattened up and oiled to look healthy prior to being auctioned in public squares to the highest bidders.

Ethnicities

Enslaved Jamaicans tended to come from the Akan, Bantu, Igbo, Fon and other Kongo people. There were also the Yoruba, Efik and "Moko" people. Field slaves fetched £25- £75 while skilled slaves such as carpenters fetched prices as high as £300. On reaching the plantation, they underwent a 'seasoning' process in which they were placed with an experienced slave who taught them the ways of the estate. Although the initial slave traders were the Portuguese and the Dutch, between 1750 and 1807 (the year in which the British Empire abolished the slave trade), Britain "dominated the buying and selling of slaves to the Americas". Shipbuilding flourished and manufacturing expanded: the "process of industrialization in England from the second quarter of the eighteenth century as to an important extent a response to colonial demands for rails, axes, buckets, coaches, clocks, saddles...and a thousand other things"

History

Atlantic slave trade

Region of Embarkment, 1701—1800	Amount %
Senegambia (Mandinka, Fula, Wolof)	1.8
Sierra Leone (Mende, Temne)	3.5
Windward Coast (Mandé, Kru)	5.2
Gold Coast (Akan, Fon)	28.9
Bight of Benin (Yoruba, Ewe, Fon, Allada and Mahi)	11.2
Bight of Biafra (Igbo, Ibibio)	34.5
West-central Africa (Kongo, Mbundu)	14.5
Southeast Africa (Macua, Malagasy)	0.1
(Unknown)	**31.0**[2]

The Atlantic Slave Trade began in the 15th century when the Portuguese took hold of land near Gibraltar and soon encountered Africans. Devout Catholics, they quickly took these "heathens" prisoner, and by mid-century, the first public sale of these prisoners was held. By 1455 Portugal was importing close to 800 African slaves a year bartering for them peacefully instead of capturing them through warfare. Sugar cultivation began in the Azores islands, and as the demand for sugar grew, so did the demand for slaves to work the fields of sugar cane. By the 16th century, other countries wanted a piece of this action and the competition for the sugar and slave trades began.

By 1700 Jamaica was awash with sugar plantations and Jamaica's population consisted of 7,000 English to 40,000 slaves. The sugar industry grew quickly in Jamaica—in 1672 there were 70 plantations producing 772 tonnes of sugar per annum—growing in the 1770s to over 680 plantations. By 1800, it was 21,000 English to 300,000 slaves, which increased to some 500,000 slaves by the 18th century. In 1820 there were 5,349 properties in Jamaica of which 1,189 contained over 100 slaves. Each estate was its own small world, complete with an entire labour force of field workers and skilled artisans, a hospital, water supply, cattle, mules and horses as well as its own fuel source. Each plantation fueled the wheels of British mercantilism. Sugar, molasses and rum were exported to England for sale and ships were financed to return to Africa and collect more slaves in exchange for trinkets and transport them to the West Indies as a labour source. This became known as The Triangular Trade. Money was not left in England's colonies, the financing came from Mother England, and to Mother England the profits returned.

Sugar Estates

A typical sugar estate was 900 acres. This included a Great House where the owner or overseer and the domestic slaves lived, and nearby accommodation for the bookkeeper, distiller, mason, carpenter, blacksmith, cooper and wheelwright. With the exception of the bookkeeper, by the middle of the eighteenth century, skilled black slaves had replaced white indentured servants in these posts. The field slaves' quarters were usually about a half mile away, closer to the industrial sugar mill, distillery and the boiling and curing houses, as well as the blacksmiths' and carpenters' sheds and thrash houses. In addition, there was a poultry pen and a cattle yard along with a Negro hospital. Some estates, if large enough, had accommodation for an estate doctor. Estates had estate gardens and the slaves had their own kitchen gardens as well as polnicks provision grounds found in the hills, which were required by law from as early as 1678. During slavery, however, slaves kept pigs and poultry and grew mangoes, plantain, ackee, okra, yam and other ground provisions. . The cultivation of these lands took on greater proportions as plantations were abandoned when the island faced increasing competition from Brazil, Cuba and beet sugar, a loss in labour after emancipation in the 1830s as well as the loss of protective trade duties after the passage of the 1846 Sugar Equalization Act in England.

The workforce on each plantation was divided into gangs determined by age and fitness. On average most estates had three main field gangs. The first was made up of the strongest and most able men and women. The second, of those no longer able to serve in the first, and the third, of older slaves and older children. Some estates had four gangs, depending on the number of children living on the estate. Children started working as young as 3 or 4 years old.

Significance of sugar

To a large extent, Jamaican customs and culture were fashioned by sugar. According to John Hearne (1965), for two hundred years sugar was the only reason behind Jamaica's existence as a centre for human habitation. For centuries, sugar was Jamaica's most important crop. Jamaica was once considered the 'jewel' in Britain's crown. In 1805, the island's peak of sugar production, it produced 101,600 tonnes of sugar. It was the world's leading individual sugar producer.

The cultivation of sugar was intricately intertwined with the system of slavery. This connection has set the course of the nation's demographics since the 18th century when slaves vastly outnumbered any other population group. The descendants of these slaves comprise the majority of Jamaica's population. They have influenced every sphere of Jamaican life and their contributions are immeasurable.

Culture

As Jamaican slaves came from Eastern, Central, and Western Africa, many of their customs survived based on memory and myths. They encompassed the life cycle, i.e. a newborn was not regarded as being of this world until nine days had passed and burial often involved libations at the graveside, and the belief that the dead body's spirit would not be at rest for some 40 days. They included forms of religion in which healing was considered an act of faith completed by obeahmen and communication with the spirits involved possession often induced by dancing and drumming. African-based religions include Kumina, Myal and Revival. Many involved recreational, ceremonial and functional use of music and dance. "Slaves," Brathwaite explains, "danced and sang at work, at play, at worship, from fear, from sorrow from joy". They recreated African musical instruments from materials found in Jamaica (calabash, conch, bamboo, etc.) and featured improvisation in song and dance. All of these customs and many more such as the Christmas street parades of Jonkonnu, were misunderstood and undervalued by Europeans with the exception of the political use of drumming to send coded messages from plantation to plantation.

Drumming of any kind was therefore often banned. Jamaican music today has emerged from the traditional musical forms of work songs sung by slaves, the ceremonial music used in religious services and the social and recreational music played on holidays and during leisure time. The cramped housing space provided to the slaves, which limited their dwellings (often made of wattle and daub) to one window and one door, meant that very little other than sleeping took place indoors. Life, as in Africa, was lived communally, outside. Similarly language, as in Africa, is considered powerful particularly naming. Brathwaie (1971) gives an example of a woman whose child falls ill and wants her name to be changed, believing that this would allow her to be cured. Language is certainly an area where African retention is strongest. Jamaicans today move between Patois a creolised English and standard English. Jamaican patois was born from the intermixing of African slaves and English, Irish, Welsh, Scottish sailors, slaves, servants, soldiers and merchants. The African slaves spoke many dialects, and given the need for a common tongue, Jamaican patois was born. It has been in use since the end of the 17th century by Jamaicans of all ethnicities and has been added to by the Jews, Chinese, Indians, Lebanese, Germans, and French Creoles who also settled on the island.

Some words also indicate Spanish and Taino presence in Jamaican history. Many of these traditions survive to this day, testament to the strength of West African culture despite the process of creolisation (the intermingling of peoples adjusting to a new environment) it encountered.

Jamaican Patois

Jamaican Patois, known locally as (Patwa, is an English–African creole language spoken primarily in Jamaica and the Jamaican diaspora. It is not to be confused with Jamaican English nor with the Rastafarian use of English. The language developed in the 17th century, when slaves from West and Central Africa were exposed to, learned and nativized the vernacular and dialectal forms of English spoken by their masters: British Englishes (including significant exposure to Scottish English) and Hiberno English. Jamaican Patwa is a *post-creole speech continuum* (a *linguistic continuum*) meaning that the variety of the language closest to the lexifier language (the acrolect) cannot be distinguished systematically from intermediate varieties (collectively referred to as the mesolect) nor even from the most divergent rural varieties (collectively referred to as the basilect). Jamaicans themselves usually refer to their use of English as patwa, a term without a precise linguistic definition.

Notable Jamaicans of African descent

• Bob Marley	• Sean Paul
• Lee "Scratch" Perry	• I Wayne
• Peter Tosh	• Capleton
• Bunny Wailer	• Bounty Killer
• Big Youth	• Black Uhuru
• Jimmy Cliff	• Third World Band
• Dennis Brown	• Inner Circle
• Desmond Dekker	• Chalice Reggae Band
• Beres Hammond	• Morgan Heritage
• Beenie Man	• Marcus Garvey
• Shaggy	• Ricardo Gardner
• Grace Jones	• Super Cat
• Shabba Ranks	• Usain Bolt
• Buju Banton	

Mavado Vybz Kartel Gyptian Jah Cure

See also

- Jonkanoo
- Dancehall
- Dub music
- Reggae
- Rocksteady
- Ska
- Mento
- Jungle
- Passa Passa
- Punk Rock
- Metal
- Michael Manley
- Rex Nettleford

- Louise Bennett
- Donald Quarrie

References

[1] The CIA World Factbook - Jamaica (https://www.cia.gov/library/publications/the-world-factbook/geos/jm.html)

[2] Rucker, Walter C. (2006). *The river flows on: Black resistance, culture, and identity formation in early America* (http://books.google.com/books?id=c2XlG4rRK4QC&pg=PA126). LSU Press. p. 126. ISBN 0-807-13109-1. .

Article Sources and Contributors

British Jamaican *Source*: http://en.wikipedia.org/w/index.php?oldid=389291084 *Contributors*: 159753, A8UDI, Ageekgal, AndrewHowse, Bearcat, BigBossBlues, BilCat, Billinghurst, Blackable2323, Blackjays1, Bobblehead, Bunnyhop11, Carl.bunderson, Cbtty, CoCoLumps, Contributor777, Cop 663, Cordless Larry, Cup22, DHN, DisillusionedBitterAndKnackered, Ezeu, Fingerpuppet, Futurebird, Garion96, Hashmi, Usman, Hmains, Ian Pitchford, Indisciplined, Indo hindu, Iridescent, Jagged 85, Jeffro77, John of Reading, Johnnymurda, JonHarder, Josh477, Kbdank71, Kerrisene, Kman543210, Koavf, Koolboy111111, LilHelpa, Malik Shabazz, Mayumashu, Mild Bill Hiccup, Neropolis, One Night In Hackney, Rannpháirtí anaithnid (old), Rich Farmbrough, Sardanaphalus, Sicar, SkanterBrazil, SnapSnap, Stayer08, Steps1000, Stevvvv4444, Tabletop, Tassedethe, TheTruthIsComing, Tide rolls, Troy86, Versus22, WereSpielChequers, Woohookitty, 160 anonymous edits

Jamaican diaspora *Source*: http://en.wikipedia.org/w/index.php?oldid=386778937 *Contributors*: Acesar, Aoa8212, Awiseman, BilCat, Blackjays1, Blackmoon33, Burtonpe, CoCoLumps, Dominictimms, Dricherby, Duhon, Jamaicanbwoy, Jeodesic, Jwillbur, Keilana, Krallja, MRSC, Rebelronni, SalineBrain, Smooth0707, Startstop123, Stevvvv4444, Telsys, Thumperward, Vgmaster, VirtualDelight, YUL89YYZ, 57 anonymous edits

Office for National Statistics *Source*: http://en.wikipedia.org/w/index.php?oldid=387693012 *Contributors*: (, Alai, Alansohn, Andycjp, Anenglishmaninnewport, Anwar saadat, Bhoeble, Caesura, Carboli, CarolGray, Ceyockey, Chill doubt, Cnyborg, Coolhawks88, Cordless Larry, CottrellS, David Newton, DinosaursLoveExistence, ESkog, Edward, Farsee50, GabrielRozenberg, Gaius Cornelius, Guineveretoo, JaT, Jasca Ducato, Jimfbleak, Johnmarkh, Jolly Janner, Jza84, Keith Edkins, Kingturtle, KitMoyles, Lambiam, Londoneye, Mais oui!, Malcolmxl5, Marky-Son, Matt Clacher, Mauls, Millstream3, Moviedefender, Necrothesp, Newport, Ninetyone, Owain, Pcpcpc, Picapica, RHaworth, RachelBrown, Robert K S, Rubena, Runcorn, SemperBlotto, SimonP, Snoyes, Splash, Str1977, Tagishsimon, TreasuryTag, Van helsing, Wingman555, 49 anonymous edits

History of Jamaica *Source*: http://en.wikipedia.org/w/index.php?oldid=385219148 *Contributors*: A More Perfect Onion, Abbyandtam, Addshore, Afv2006, Ahoerstemeier, Alai, Alansohn, Alchemist Jack, Alister, Altaar, Andre Engels, Apparition11, Arthena, AtheWeatherman, Atif.t2, Basketball110, Bastin, Belle9, Biruitorul, Blackable2323, Bobo192, Bobrayner, Boothy443, Brams24, Burgher, Byzanz, CanadianLinuxUser, CaribDigita, Catgut, Cfailde, Chadloder, ChaosMaster16, Chill doubt, Chris Edgemon, Cjthellama, ClamDip, Closedmouth, Conversion script, Courcelles, Crackedman79, D6, DaL33T, Damifb, Darwinek, Dave souza, Dentren, Diagonalfish, Discospinster, Dmitrove, Dodobrown18, Drutt, Durova, Edivorce, Edward, Ekologkonsult, Elagatis, English Bobby, EoGuy, Epbr123, Excirial, Fastily, Finnrind, Fledgist, FreplySpang, Funnyfarmofdoom, Gadfium, Gadig, Gail, GavinSimmons, Gilliam, Green Giant, Gurch, Gökhan, Harrypotter, Heathersnathan, Hmains, Hu, I dream of horses, IRP, Iahmedia, Ian Pitchford, Ignacio Icke, Ingsoc, Insanity Incarnate, Iridescent, J.J., J.delanoy, Jake Wartenberg, Jamesday, Japanese Searobin, Jasmith, Jman943, Jmcc150, JoanneB, John Hill, JohnCD, Jon kare, Joyous!, Joyousjam, Jrt989, Jwillbur, KGBarnett, Kevin B12, Kingpin13, KoyaanisQatsi, Landon1980, Legis, Lofty, Lord Cornwallis, Lradrama, Luna Santin, Luren Marsh, Luwilt, MER-C, Mav, Mentifisto, Miquonranger03, NawlinWiki, Neptune5000, Normalbuddy1, OllieFury, Omicronpersei8, Op. Deo, Patrickthompson07, Pedro Lassouras, Ph89, PhilKnight, Piano non troppo, Piattrocks, Piotrus, Piratedan, Polly, Possum, Prodego, Quantumobserver, QueenCake, RSM, RTC, Radon210, Rbeharrie, Rentir, Retired user 0001, Rich Farmbrough, Ronhjones, RoyBoy, Rror, Rrostrom, Salvio giuliano, Sam Korn, Sannse, Seaphoto, Seth ze, Shanes, Shoemaker's Holiday, Sicar, Sidonuke, Simeon24601, Skoosh, Slartibartfast1992, Sligocki, Sluzzelin, SqueakBox, Stephen Bain, TarquiniusWikipedius, The Thing That Should Not Be, TheOuthouseMouse, Tommy2010, Topbanana, Topmanforever, Toscaesque, Triona, TwoOneTwo, Ulric1313, UnHoly, Uncle Dick, Versus22, Vervin, Vincent pearse, Warofdreams, WikiLaurent, Wimt, Wolmadrian, XPTO, Yamamoto Ichiro, 353 anonymous edits

British African-Caribbean community *Source*: http://en.wikipedia.org/w/index.php?oldid=386206868 *Contributors*: 215315.55t, 23prootie, A Fantasy, A bit iffy, Ackees, Ahoerstemeier, Alexmcfire, Altenmann, Anchoress, Andonic, Andrewlp1991, Andrij Kursetsky, Antaeus Feldspar, Antandrus, Asdfghjklolkjh, Avram, AyeWright, Babbage, Beetstra, Big Adamsky, Bobo192, BrainyBabe, Brian0918, Brighterorange, Bwhack, Bwithh, C777, Calorus, CaribDigita, CaribbeanOne, Catagraph, Ceoil, Ceyockey, Chairman S., Chris the speller, Christopher Connor, Claireros, Cocytus, Colin Keigher, Colonies Chris, Cordless Larry, Crystalclearchanges, D-Notice, DanielleZP, David.padgett, DavidFarmbrough, DeansFA, Derek R Bullamore, Domakpet, Doublederderp, DumebiRapu, Dw1a, Edward vortman, Epolk, Erebus555, Excalibur, Fayenatic london, Firsfron, Francis Tyers, FredFix, Funnyhat, Futurebird, Gammondog, Gerry Lynch, Gisgay, Godefroy, Gringo300, Guettarda, Gusworld, Gzkn, Harrypotter, IJA, Itsnoprob, J Milburn, J.P.Lon, Jasmine211, Jimal7, Jimfbleak, Jmax-, Joelr31, John, John Barley, John of Reading, Joy, Jrleighton, Jrockley, Jsferreira, Jwillbur, K1Bond007, Kad202@gmail.com, Karada, Karukera, Kbdank71, Keristrasza, Kingjamie, Kingturtle, Kurt Shaped Box, Leithp, Lightmouse, Ling.Nut, Luckystars, MBisanz, Marky-Son, Mattg82, Mboverload, Menzer, Michael Devore, Mikeblas, Million Little Gods, MisfitToys, Mkimemia, Molchar, Neropolis, Nikai, Niteowlneils, Nummer29, Paine Ellsworth, Parkwells, PatGallacher, Pcpcpc, Philgreg, Philip Baird Shearer, Piersmasterson, Postdlf, Prodego, Qophee, Quantpole, Quercusrobur, Quimbaraquimba, Qwghlm, R'n'B, RandomP, Rannpháirtí anaithnid (old), Raul654, RepublicanJacobite, RevRagnarok, Rich Farmbrough, Rmhermen, Rmky87, Robert of Ramsor, Robth, Rodhullandemu, SMasters, Saga City, SandyGeorgia, SantaMonicaMax, Sardanaphalus, SarekOfVulcan, Scoterican, Sd31415, Sean William, Sicar, Simmo676, Simple Bob, SkanterBrazil, Skarpl, Smeddlesboy, Sosa-hudds, Southbeachlegal, Spylab, SqueakBox, SteveSims, Stevvvv4444, StoptheDatabaseState, Str1977, SupaStarGirl, Suruena, Tassedethe, Tevildo, Thegreenj, Thusnelda, Tivedshambo, Tpbradbury, Treyt021, True Steppa, Tukes, Ulric1313, Vgmaster, Vivenot, Voyagerfan5761, WJBscribe, Wayland, Wik, Wiki alf, Wikipedister, Woohookitty, Xezbeth, Yannismarou, Yellowfiver, YeshuaDavid, Yunchy, Yusuf yearwood, Zagalejo, Zagubov, Zleitzen, Ἀλήθεια, 311 anonymous edits

Arrival of black immigrants in London *Source*: http://en.wikipedia.org/w/index.php?oldid=384285227 *Contributors*: Black Velveteen, Colonies Chris, Dr Gangrene, Firsfron, GJR, Harami2000, Harrypotter, Hmains, Huey Newton and the News, Iridescent, Jagged 85, John, Kbthompson, Lopakhin, MRSC, Paulbrock, Plasticup, Rjwilmsi, Rziesme2, SilasW, Stevvvv4444, Walton One, WereSpielChequers, WhisperToMe, 19 anonymous edits

Demographics of Jamaica *Source*: http://en.wikipedia.org/w/index.php?oldid=387017532 *Contributors*: AlbertR, Anandks007, Arb, ArielGold, Asdf01, Ben MacDui, BilCat, Blackjays1, CalJW, Conversion script, Cst17, Discospinster, Eastlaw, FargomeD, HaeB, Hmains, Jiang, Jmack8080, Jusdafax, Jwillbur, KGBarnett, Kazak, LizardWizard, Lordvaluemart, Lusitana, Mareino, Mausy5043, Natural Cut, Neelix, No Account, NoAccount, NoIdeaNick, Otterfan, Oxymoron83, Paul foord, Quill, Raymond Cruise, Rbeharrie, Rlvaughn, SLK, SimonP, Soulja nyn3, Static Sleepstorm, Swerdnaneb, TUF-KAT, The Transhumanist, Thehelpfulone, Thv, Timc, Tkynerd, 74 anonymous edits

Lists of UK locations with large ethnic minority populations *Source*: http://en.wikipedia.org/w/index.php?oldid=388176850 *Contributors*: A Fantasy, Angelo De La Paz, Billinghurst, BrownHairedGirl, Caulde, Cls14, Colonies Chris, CommonsDelinker, Cop 663, D-Notice, D.de.loinsigh, Dbachmann, Elitejcx, Fingerpuppet, Gasta220, JimmyGuano, Kazuko100, Kbthompson, Lozzaboy, Mahahahaneapneap, Man vyi, Mannerheim, MartinRobinson, Middayexpress, Mkimemia, Munci, Packardstown, Pondle, R'n'B, Rogwan, Sardanaphalus, Sassf, Stevvvv4444, The Grounded Dutchmen, Timrollpickering, Ulric1313, Una Smith, VEO15, WOSlinker, Warofdreams, Woohookitty, 68 anonymous edits

Jamaican cuisine *Source*: http://en.wikipedia.org/w/index.php?oldid=389491637 *Contributors*: Alexthe5th, Andycjp, Apparition11, ArchonMagnus, Avocado, Aymatth2, Badagnani, Banana04131, Barek, Beantwo, Biggstuu, Bob f it, Bunchofgrapes, Burschik, Calliopejen1, ChildofMidnight, Closedmouth, Coemgenus, Coffee, Colchester121891, Collabi, CommonsDelinker, Davewild, Dicerdaman, Dr.frog, Drewnami, Drmies, Dthomsen8, DubCrazy, Edgar181, Edward321, Empiresj1, Euchiasmus, Excirial, Fuzzy510, Galger, GarryMann, Girlyactress117, Guettarda, Gwellesley, HeartofaDog, Hmains, Icseaturtles, Islareina, J04n, Jamaicamix, Jamesontai, JeffyJeffyMan2004, Jerem43, Jooler, Joy, Jrepoman73, Jrgilmore, King of the Dancehall, Kintetsubuffalo, KnightLago, KoshVorlon, Larry V, Leithp, MLA, Masterswordmaster, Melaen, Mikeo, Nayak52, Neelix, Neier, Ntse, Ojay123, Open2universe, Papilgee4evaeva, Patrickklida, Paul Bowes, Paulewy1, Pekinensis, Persian Poet Gal, Phildm, Philip Trueman, Phonemonkey, Quena@sympatico.ca, R'n'B, Rakista, Rich Farmbrough, Robsavoie, Scepia, Secretlondon, Shattered Gnome, Sicar, SpookyX31, Taejo, Tanner-Christopher, Tehw1k1, Terrillja, Themightyquill, Thingg, ThirstyEar2, Tkynerd, Veren, Versageek, Vgmaster, W guice, WOSlinker, WhisperToMe, Wimsyp, WisTex, Wmahan, Woohookitty, X96lee15, Zahakiel, Zleitzen, 176 anonymous edits

Caribbean music in the United Kingdom *Source*: http://en.wikipedia.org/w/index.php?oldid=378117136 *Contributors*: AndrewHowse, CalJW, CaribDigita, DavidFarmbrough, Derek R Bullamore, Druiloor, Ebz123, GIRO61, Globalspy, Guettarda, Handicapper, Hughcharlesparker, JIP, JLaTondre, Jetson66, John Eden, Kabebz, Lightmouse, Lph, MartinUK, Michig, Moulinette, Neelix, Nick, Nummer29, Ogg, Organization13leader, RepublicanJacobite, Sardanaphalus, Secretlondon, Sicar, Spylab, Stevvvv4444, Str1977, TV Genius, Tabletop, Tassedethe, Teklund, TheAllSeeingEye, Ulric1313, Wunderful digby, ZhaoHong, 42 anonymous edits

Music of Jamaica *Source*: http://en.wikipedia.org/w/index.php?oldid=388412664 *Contributors*: (aeropagitica), AK Auto, Afv2006, Alansohn, AlexiusHoratius, Alister, AndrewHowse, Archivist, Area61, Babygurl 4u, Benwildeboer, Blackjays1, Bobblehead, Bustter, Capricorn42, Catapult, Cfailde, Chasingsol, Circeus, Cje, Clark Kimberling, Closedmouth, Cmdrjameson, Colonies Chris, Cronium, Cst17, DO'Neil, Dale Arnett, Derek R Bullamore, Dingoman2, DirEnGrey100666, Drbreznjev, Druiloor, Dv82matt, Dysprosia, Earle Martin, Efghij, Empiresj1, Epbr123, Epolk, Ezeu, Falcon8765, Farosdaughter, Fearlesslyhappy, GTBacchus, Gbeeker, Gggh, Globalspy, Greatestrowerever, Gsmgm, Guyinredsuit, Halmstad, Haxoanglemark, Heidimo, Heron, HexaChord, Htaccess, Hu12, Innotata, J.delanoy, Jaberwocky6669, Jackaranga, Jaimewinksta1, Jake Wartenberg, Jasmith, JayFox161, Jellyman, Jildez, John Eden, Jusdafax, Jwillbur, Keilana, Kingpin13, Kisholi, Kyle1278, Leesah71, Lyght, MBisanz, Mav, Maxamegalon2000, Michig, Mitchoyoshitaka, Mjb, Mjquinn id, Moulinette, Mwinog2777, Neelix, Nickydread, Nlu, No Account, Nummer29, Panmaker, R. fiend, Raprat0, Rbmcotterrell, Reinoutr, Rjwilmsi, RtnlSltn, Sam Hocevar, Sanjay Lewis, Sfan00 IMG, Silsor, Sixpacz, Slysplace, Snigbrook, Spitfire, Spylab, SqueakBox, Steelhead522, Student'scontribution, Sun King, SunCreator, TUF-KAT, TeaDrinker, Teklund, Template namespace initialisation script, TheBeaver, Themindset, Tristanb, Uncle Dick, Vgmaster, Wik, Wwwhatsup, Xchrisblackx, Zambaccian, 246 anonymous edits

List of Jamaican British people *Source*: http://en.wikipedia.org/w/index.php?oldid=389548360 *Contributors*: Ackees, Akerans, Anthony Appleyard, Apoc2400, BigBossBlues, Bonadea, C.Fred, Cbtty, CelebWiki, Cordless Larry, Darth Panda, Discospinster, Esradekan, Grondemar, Ground Zero, Islavuelta, Jamesb1996, LilHelpa, Mayumashu, Redrose64, Salavat, ShelfSkewed, Skier Dude, Stevvvv4444, Tassedethe, Zulaikha el, 16 anonymous edits

Black British *Source*: http://en.wikipedia.org/w/index.php?oldid=389908967 *Contributors*: 23prootie, Alexr2007, Aliwalla, Amitch, Andareed, Andreas Kaganov, AndrewHowse, Andrij Kursetsky, Anetode, Angelo De La Paz, Arctic Night, Avram, Bcorr, Bearcat, Beardo, Beckford10, Beetstra, Behemoth, Bensonby, Berolina, BillMasen, Binboy69, Blackable2323, Blackjays1, Boguslavmandzyuk, Bongwarrior, BrainyBabe, Bringmetehverizon, BritishWatcher, BrixtonOvercoat, Bsrboy, Bunnyhop11, C777, CPMcE, Can't sleep, clown will eat me, CanuckAnthropologist, Capricorn42, Causteau, Cfrydj, Christopher Connor, Coffee, Coralmizu, Cordless Larry, Crystalclearchanges, Cuchullain, D3av, DJ Clayworth, Danlyndon, Dark Tea, Dark Tichondrias, DarkFalls, Darth Panda, Dbachmann, Deon, DontWorryPlease, Dubs69, DumebiRapu, DuncanHill, EchetusXe, Edgar181, Editingoprah, ElijahTM, ElinorD, Elitism, Energyfreezer, Epa101, Erebus555, Ezenden, Fayenatic london, Fclass, Fieldday-sunday, Fishiehelper2, FrederickBM, FreeMorpheme, Freedomcomeup, Freize1, Funnyhat, Futurebird, Gaius Cornelius, Galati, Gepetto10, Guettarda, HSDR, Halmstad, Hammer Raccoon, Harrypotter, Hmains, Huey Newton and the News, I'mDown, II MusLiM HyBRiD II, Imperial Monarch, Indisciplined, Invertedzero, Iridescent, JNW, JaGa, Jagged 85, JameiLei, JamesAM, Jeanne boleyn, John Barley, Johnbod, Joshii, Jrleighton, JumboJetty, Jurema Oliveira, Karpouzi, Kbdank71, Kierandobson, Kittybrewster, Kman543210, Kobrakid, Kwiki, LAX, Legis, Lightmouse, Luk, M.nelson, MRSC, MaesterTonberry, Malik Shabazz, Marky-Son, Martinmunroe, Mausy5043, McTrixie, Merqurial, Metallurgist, Milton Stanley, Molchar, Mosmof, Mullet, NawlinWiki, NeroAxis, Neropolis, NielsenGW, Nightkey, NuclearWarfare, Nyttend, Ohconfucius, Pablo X, Paki.tv, Paul Barlow, Pdkay, Peter G Werner, Pharillon, Pharos, Phatom87, Philip Trueman, Pinethicket, Pinktulip, RFBailey, Rambam rashi, Rannpháirtí anaithnid (old), Riana, Rich Farmbrough, Rjwilmsi, Rmky87, Road Wizard, Rodhullandemu, Rossrs, Saintswithin, Sam Blacketer, Sandstein, Sardanaphalus, Setanta747, Shadowjams, Shell Kinney, Shoeofdeath, Sicar, Simesa, Sluzzelin, Smjg, Someone65, SoundStone, Soupforone, SouthernNights, Spongefrog, Steel, Steinsky, Stevvvv4444, Superm401, Supermichaeljames2, Switchercat, Tabletop, TastyPoutine, Tchoutoye, Tellyaddict, Tevildo, The Interior, The Singing Badger, TheTruthIsComing, Thelostlibertine, Therock40756, Thevanityshow, Tigermichal2, Timrollpickering, Tkynerd, Topbanana, Toussaint, Trident13, Tukes, Tyler's Boy, Ukabia, Ulric1313, Vivenot, Welsh, Wereon, Westee, Wikiaddict8962, Wikignome0530, Wobble, Woohookitty, Work permit, Wormwoodpoppies, Wxyzzz, Yahel Guhan, Yellowfiver, Zagalejo, Zleitzen, 683 anonymous edits

Mixed (United Kingdom ethnicity category) *Source*: http://en.wikipedia.org/w/index.php?oldid=389742370 *Contributors*: Agagames, Ala.foum, All Hallow's Wraith, AnemoneProjectors, Anetode, Aremsi, Aspects, Auntof6, Baje Tiger, Beckford14, Cobaltcigs, CommonsDelinker, Cordless Larry, CreativeSoul7981, D-Notice, Dbachmann, Dewan357, Discospinster, ESkog, Egard89, Escape Orbit, Freize1, Galati, Harrypotter, IDono08, Indisciplined, Indoboi, Iridescent, Izzedine, JaGa, Jagged 85, Jdrewitt, Jjj088, Jorge Stolfi, Joseph Solis in Australia, Karpouzi, MapsMan, Markparker, Mayumashu, Meritocora, Millbanks, MinnaK, Monkeynoze, Neptunes2007, Pegship, PlovG, Pondle, Radicalthinker, Ramdrake, Rannpháirtí anaithnid (old), Regancy42, Rjwilmsi, Rockfang, Rynewell91, SamuelTheGhost, Sandboxiguana, Sardanaphalus, Sheffmetro, Sir Stanley, Sixtytwohundred, Skinnysock, Stevvvv4444, Tassedethe, The Baroness of Morden, Timrollpickering, Topebrown7, Tukes, Tweeheart, Vamsipotluri, Vegaswikian, Werdnawerdna, Wickethewok, Yun-Yuuzhan (lost password), 285 anonymous edits

British Indo-Caribbean community *Source*: http://en.wikipedia.org/w/index.php?oldid=385719088 *Contributors*: 23prootie, Caribbeanproduct, Cordless Larry, DaTraveller, Jagged 85, Stevvvv4444, Woohookitty, Xezbeth, 17 anonymous edits

Classification of ethnicity in the United Kingdom *Source*: http://en.wikipedia.org/w/index.php?oldid=389936376 *Contributors*: Alejandro.a, Bobblehead, Bydand, Cordless Larry, Cronholm144, DinosaursLoveExistence, Erechtheus, Fishiehelper2, Grant65, Jagged 85, Josquius, Kenaldinho10, Lightmouse, Martin.Budden, Middayexpress, Modernist, Neelix, Tide rolls, 17 anonymous edits

Jamaicans of African ancestry *Source*: http://en.wikipedia.org/w/index.php?oldid=386339649 *Contributors*: Alexius08, Arb, Blackable2323, Blackjays1, CanuckAnthropologist, Contributor777, Cordless Larry, Cup22, Dakiiidx, Falcon Kirtaran, Fclass, Gil Gamesh, Giraffedata, Gobbleswoggler, Grafen, Guttybud, Gwen Gale, J.delanoy, Jamaicandoctor, Jmack8080, Joseph Solis in Australia, Jpeeling, Jurema Oliveira, Jwillbur, Oxymoron83, Rjwilmsi, SpaceFlight89, Stevvvv4444, Tkynerd, Totorotroll, Ukabia, Unknown789, Vgmaster, Woohookitty, 64 anonymous edits

Image Sources, Licenses and Contributors

Image:Gallery of Jamaican-British people.jpg *Source:* http://en.wikipedia.org/w/index.php?title=File:Gallery_of_Jamaican-British_people.jpg *License:* Attribution *Contributors:* User:CoCoLumps

File:Jamaicans Empire Windrush.jpg *Source:* http://en.wikipedia.org/w/index.php?title=File:Jamaicans_Empire_Windrush.jpg *License:* unknown *Contributors:* Stevvvv4444

File:Brixton riots, 1981.jpg *Source:* http://en.wikipedia.org/w/index.php?title=File:Brixton_riots,_1981.jpg *License:* unknown *Contributors:* Stevvvv4444

Image:HotPeppersinMarket.png *Source:* http://en.wikipedia.org/w/index.php?title=File:HotPeppersinMarket.jpg *License:* Creative Commons Attribution-Sharealike 2.5 *Contributors:* Carstor, Juiced lemon, Oxam Hartog, Secretlondon, 1 anonymous edits

File:Darren Bent.png *Source:* http://en.wikipedia.org/w/index.php?title=File:Darren_Bent.png *License:* Creative Commons Attribution-Sharealike 2.0 *Contributors:* http://www.flickr.com/photos/95721003@N00/

Image:Office for National Statistics logo.png *Source:* http://en.wikipedia.org/w/index.php?title=File:Office_for_National_Statistics_logo.png *License:* unknown *Contributors:* Jolly Janner

Image:ONS.JPG *Source:* http://en.wikipedia.org/w/index.php?title=File:ONS.JPG *License:* unknown *Contributors:* User:Londoneye

Image:1882 Kingston Fire.png *Source:* http://en.wikipedia.org/w/index.php?title=File:1882_Kingston_Fire.png *License:* Public Domain *Contributors:* T. Sulman

File:Jamaica hut4.jpg *Source:* http://en.wikipedia.org/w/index.php?title=File:Jamaica_hut4.jpg *License:* Public Domain *Contributors:* William Berryman

Image:Leicester Caribbean carnival.jpg *Source:* http://en.wikipedia.org/w/index.php?title=File:Leicester_Caribbean_carnival.jpg *License:* GNU Free Documentation License *Contributors:* DeansFA, Man vyi, NotFromUtrecht

Image:Seacole photo.jpg *Source:* http://en.wikipedia.org/w/index.php?title=File:Seacole_photo.jpg *License:* Public Domain *Contributors:* Original uploader was RetiredUser2 at en.wikipedia

Image:Windrush square.jpg *Source:* http://en.wikipedia.org/w/index.php?title=File:Windrush_square.jpg *License:* Public Domain *Contributors:* Oxyman, Verica Atrebatum, Zleitzen

Image:Notting Hill Carnival 2002 large.jpg *Source:* http://en.wikipedia.org/w/index.php?title=File:Notting_Hill_Carnival_2002_large.jpg *License:* GNU Free Documentation License *Contributors:* Athaenara, Hoenny, Man vyi, Okki

Image:Ridley road market dalston 1.jpg *Source:* http://en.wikipedia.org/w/index.php?title=File:Ridley_road_market_dalston_1.jpg *License:* Creative Commons Attribution-Sharealike 2.5 *Contributors:* Tarquin Binary

Image:Diane Abbott low quality.jpg *Source:* http://en.wikipedia.org/w/index.php?title=File:Diane_Abbott_low_quality.jpg *License:* Creative Commons Attribution-Sharealike 2.5 *Contributors:* User:JK the Unwise

Image:Africa shopping.jpg *Source:* http://en.wikipedia.org/w/index.php?title=File:Africa_shopping.jpg *License:* Public Domain *Contributors:* Secretlondon, Zleitzen

Image:Tate.britain.arp.750pix.jpg *Source:* http://en.wikipedia.org/w/index.php?title=File:Tate.britain.arp.750pix.jpg *License:* unknown *Contributors:* Dani 7C3, Juanpdp, Tyrenius, White-Silent-Night

Image:Dennis Seaton Singer Musical Youth 2005.JPG *Source:* http://en.wikipedia.org/w/index.php?title=File:Dennis_Seaton_Singer_Musical_Youth_2005.JPG *License:* Public Domain *Contributors:* Biho, Funke, Jkelly

Image:Goldie 2003.jpg *Source:* http://en.wikipedia.org/w/index.php?title=File:Goldie_2003.jpg *License:* Public Domain *Contributors:* AnemoneProjectors, Ardfern, Frank C. Müller, High on a tree, Libertad y Saber, Thuresson, Werckmeister, Yamavu

Image:MichaelJohnson02.jpg *Source:* http://en.wikipedia.org/w/index.php?title=File:MichaelJohnson02.jpg *License:* Creative Commons Attribution-Sharealike 2.5 *Contributors:* Struway, TuborgLight, Ytoyoda

Image:Rio Ferdinand, 2004.jpg *Source:* http://en.wikipedia.org/w/index.php?title=File:Rio_Ferdinand,_2004.jpg *License:* Creative Commons Attribution 2.0 *Contributors:* John Dempsey

Image:FourTimesNoon.jpg *Source:* http://en.wikipedia.org/w/index.php?title=File:FourTimesNoon.jpg *License:* Public Domain *Contributors:* William Hogarth

Image:PD-icon.svg *Source:* http://en.wikipedia.org/w/index.php?title=File:PD-icon.svg *License:* Public Domain *Contributors:* User:Duesentrieb, User:Rfl

Image:Altab Ali protest.jpg *Source:* http://en.wikipedia.org/w/index.php?title=File:Altab_Ali_protest.jpg *License:* unknown *Contributors:* Skier Dude, TheGreenEditor

Image:Chinatown.london.700px.jpg *Source:* http://en.wikipedia.org/w/index.php?title=File:Chinatown.london.700px.jpg *License:* GNU Free Documentation License *Contributors:* Michael Reeve

Image:IraqicelebrationsinLondon.jpg *Source:* http://en.wikipedia.org/w/index.php?title=File:IraqicelebrationsinLondon.jpg *License:* GNU Free Documentation License *Contributors:* Bazel

File:Colombianfestivaluk.jpg *Source:* http://en.wikipedia.org/w/index.php?title=File:Colombianfestivaluk.jpg *License:* Creative Commons Attribution 2.0 *Contributors:* User:Stevvvv4444. Original uploader was Stevvvv4444 at en.wikipedia. Later version(s) were uploaded by Ww2censor at en.wikipedia.

Image:Jerk chicken july 05.jpg *Source:* http://en.wikipedia.org/w/index.php?title=File:Jerk_chicken_july_05.jpg *License:* Creative Commons Attribution-Sharealike 2.0 *Contributors:* User:Secretlondon

File:Jamaica sweets.jpg *Source:* http://en.wikipedia.org/w/index.php?title=File:Jamaica_sweets.jpg *License:* Public Domain *Contributors:* C.H. Graves (The Universal Photo Art Co.)

File:Curry Goat with rice and peas (in this case kidney beans).jpg *Source:* http://en.wikipedia.org/w/index.php?title=File:Curry_Goat_with_rice_and_peas_(in_this_case_kidney_beans).jpg *License:* Creative Commons Attribution-Sharealike 2.0 *Contributors:* Original uploader was ChildofMidnight at en.wikipedia

File:Gizzada.jpg *Source:* http://en.wikipedia.org/w/index.php?title=File:Gizzada.jpg *License:* Creative Commons Attribution 3.0 *Contributors:* ChildofMidnight, Sherool, Sreejithk2000, 1 anonymous edits

File:Stamp and go and callaloo fritters.jpg *Source:* http://en.wikipedia.org/w/index.php?title=File:Stamp_and_go_and_callaloo_fritters.jpg *License:* Attribution *Contributors:* Original uploader was ChildofMidnight at en.wikipedia

File:Ackee and Saltfish.jpg *Source:* http://en.wikipedia.org/w/index.php?title=File:Ackee_and_Saltfish.jpg *License:* Creative Commons Attribution 2.0 *Contributors:* gailf548 from New York State, USA

File:Coco bread wrapped beef patty.jpg *Source:* http://en.wikipedia.org/w/index.php?title=File:Coco_bread_wrapped_beef_patty.jpg *License:* Creative Commons Attribution 2.0 *Contributors:* Jason Lam

File:Caribbean dinner plate.jpg *Source:* http://en.wikipedia.org/w/index.php?title=File:Caribbean_dinner_plate.jpg *License:* Creative Commons Attribution-Sharealike 2.0 *Contributors:* Averette, Giorgiomonteforti

File:Jamaican Irish Moss drink - in can and over ice.jpg *Source:* http://en.wikipedia.org/w/index.php?title=File:Jamaican_Irish_Moss_drink_-_in_can_and_over_ice.jpg *License:* Creative Commons Attribution 2.0 *Contributors:* Flickr user: FatherJack (http://www.flickr.com/photos/father_jack/)

Image:Ting grapefruit soda 300ml DG.jpg *Source:* http://en.wikipedia.org/w/index.php?title=File:Ting_grapefruit_soda_300ml_DG.jpg *License:* GNU Free Documentation License *Contributors:* Whitebox

Image:GilesBarnes02.jpg *Source:* http://en.wikipedia.org/w/index.php?title=File:GilesBarnes02.jpg *License:* Creative Commons Attribution-Sharealike 2.5 *Contributors:* TuborgLight

Image:Darren Bent.png *Source:* http://en.wikipedia.org/w/index.php?title=File:Darren_Bent.png *License:* Creative Commons Attribution-Sharealike 2.0 *Contributors:* http://www.flickr.com/photos/95721003@N00/

Image:Uso-show-downtown-julie-brown-pentagon-gov.jpg *Source:* http://en.wikipedia.org/w/index.php?title=File:Uso-show-downtown-julie-brown-pentagon-gov.jpg *License:* Public Domain *Contributors:* Anonymous Cow, Jorgebarrios

Image:Communion2110.jpg *Source:* http://en.wikipedia.org/w/index.php?title=File:Communion2110.jpg *License:* Public Domain *Contributors:* Original uploader was Ross Todhunter at en.wikipedia

Image:Keisha Buchanan.jpeg *Source:* http://en.wikipedia.org/w/index.php?title=File:Keisha_Buchanan.jpeg *License:* Creative Commons Attribution-Sharealike 2.0 *Contributors:* Rokfoto

Image:Deon-Burton-SWFC.jpg *Source:* http://en.wikipedia.org/w/index.php?title=File:Deon-Burton-SWFC.jpg *License:* Creative Commons Attribution 2.0 *Contributors:* Dan1980, 1 anonymous edits

Image:NaomiCampbell.jpg *Source:* http://en.wikipedia.org/w/index.php?title=File:NaomiCampbell.jpg *License:* Creative Commons Attribution-Sharealike 2.5 *Contributors:* Original uploader was Jgro888 at en.wikipedia

Image:Sol-Campbell.jpg *Source:* http://en.wikipedia.org/w/index.php?title=File:Sol-Campbell.jpg *License:* unknown *Contributors:* Original by Thom32 at English Wikipedia, modifications only by Yottanesia

Image:Errol Christie in 2007.JPG *Source*: http://en.wikipedia.org/w/index.php?title=File:Errol_Christie_in_2007.JPG *License*: Public Domain *Contributors*: Original uploader was Ross Todhunter at en.wikipedia

Image:Chriseubank.jpg *Source*: http://en.wikipedia.org/w/index.php?title=File:Chriseubank.jpg *License*: Creative Commons Attribution-Sharealike 2.0 *Contributors*: Keith Page

Image:Ben Gordon.jpg *Source*: http://en.wikipedia.org/w/index.php?title=File:Ben_Gordon.jpg *License*: GNU Free Documentation License *Contributors*: User:Jauerback

Image:Ainsley Harriott.jpg *Source*: http://en.wikipedia.org/w/index.php?title=File:Ainsley_Harriott.jpg *License*: Creative Commons Attribution 3.0 *Contributors*: DavidDjJohnson, Zipsco

Image:Naomie Harris 1.JPG *Source*: http://en.wikipedia.org/w/index.php?title=File:Naomie_Harris_1.JPG *License*: GNU Free Documentation License *Contributors*: alotofmillion

Image:Delroy Lindo cropped.jpg *Source*: http://en.wikipedia.org/w/index.php?title=File:Delroy_Lindo_cropped.jpg *License*: Creative Commons Attribution-Sharealike 2.0 *Contributors*: Mike Wooldridge

Image:Mungomacaroni.gif *Source*: http://en.wikipedia.org/w/index.php?title=File:Mungomacaroni.gif *License*: Public Domain *Contributors*: Bwithh

Image:Beverley Knight.jpg *Source*: http://en.wikipedia.org/w/index.php?title=File:Beverley_Knight.jpg *License*: Creative Commons Attribution 2.0 *Contributors*: Pieter Baert from Antwerpen, Belgium

Image:Cleo Laine.jpg *Source*: http://en.wikipedia.org/w/index.php?title=File:Cleo_Laine.jpg *License*: Creative Commons Attribution-Sharealike 2.0 *Contributors*: Michael Cohn

Image:Day three studio d 144.jpg *Source*: http://en.wikipedia.org/w/index.php?title=File:Day_three_studio_d_144.jpg *License*: Creative Commons Attribution-Sharealike 3.0 *Contributors*: User:Rustielee

Image:Allsaints8.jpg *Source*: http://en.wikipedia.org/w/index.php?title=File:Allsaints8.jpg *License*: GNU Free Documentation License *Contributors*: ger1axg

Image:Jobi McAnuff.jpg *Source*: http://en.wikipedia.org/w/index.php?title=File:Jobi_McAnuff.jpg *License*: unknown *Contributors*: Djdannyp, Sherool, WFCforLife

Image:Winstonmckenzie.jpg *Source*: http://en.wikipedia.org/w/index.php?title=File:Winstonmckenzie.jpg *License*: Creative Commons Attribution-Sharealike 2.0 *Contributors*: hubbers

Image:Jermaine Pennant.jpg *Source*: http://en.wikipedia.org/w/index.php?title=File:Jermaine_Pennant.jpg *License*: Creative Commons Attribution 2.0 *Contributors*: Agnieszka Mieszczak from Krakow, Poland

Image:Tessa Sanderson.jpg *Source*: http://en.wikipedia.org/w/index.php?title=File:Tessa_Sanderson.jpg *License*: Creative Commons Attribution-Sharealike 2.5 *Contributors*: Original uploader and author was Indianathletics at en.wikipedia

Image:Seacole - Challen.jpg *Source*: http://en.wikipedia.org/w/index.php?title=File:Seacole_-_Challen.jpg *License*: Public Domain *Contributors*: Original uploader was RetiredUser2 at en.wikipedia

Image:Frank Sinclair.png *Source*: http://en.wikipedia.org/w/index.php?title=File:Frank_Sinclair.png *License*: Attribution *Contributors*: Martyn Spencer

Image:Neville Staple Dundee 2007.jpg *Source*: http://en.wikipedia.org/w/index.php?title=File:Neville_Staple_Dundee_2007.jpg *License*: unknown *Contributors*: Citizensmith

File:TheoWalcottUnderhill.JPG *Source*: http://en.wikipedia.org/w/index.php?title=File:TheoWalcottUnderhill.JPG *License*: Attribution *Contributors*: Glyn Trebble. Original uploader was Gjt6 at en.wikipedia

Image:Francis williams.jpg *Source*: http://en.wikipedia.org/w/index.php?title=File:Francis_williams.jpg *License*: Public Domain *Contributors*: James317a

Image:Shaun Wright-Phillips warming up.jpg *Source*: http://en.wikipedia.org/w/index.php?title=File:Shaun_Wright-Phillips_warming_up.jpg *License*: Creative Commons Attribution-Sharealike 2.0 *Contributors*: John Dobson

Image:LordTaylorW.jpg *Source*: http://en.wikipedia.org/w/index.php?title=File:LordTaylorW.jpg *License*: Creative Commons Attribution-Sharealike 2.5 *Contributors*: Virtualstuart

File:Olaudah Equiano - Project Gutenberg eText 15399.png *Source*: http://en.wikipedia.org/w/index.php?title=File:Olaudah_Equiano_-_Project_Gutenberg_eText_15399.png *License*: Public Domain *Contributors*: Uploader: User Tagishsimon on en.wikipedia; Unknown artist

Image:Adewalegfdl.PNG *Source*: http://en.wikipedia.org/w/index.php?title=File:Adewalegfdl.PNG *License*: GNU Free Documentation License *Contributors*: Crissy Terawaki Kawamoto

File:Chiwetel Ejiofor by David Shankbone.jpg *Source*: http://en.wikipedia.org/w/index.php?title=File:Chiwetel_Ejiofor_by_David_Shankbone.jpg *License*: Attribution *Contributors*: David Shankbone

File:Paul Ince.jpg *Source*: http://en.wikipedia.org/w/index.php?title=File:Paul_Ince.jpg *License*: Creative Commons Attribution-Sharealike 2.0 *Contributors*: Justin Hartman

File:Naomie Harris 1.JPG *Source*: http://en.wikipedia.org/w/index.php?title=File:Naomie_Harris_1.JPG *License*: GNU Free Documentation License *Contributors*: alotofmillion

File:Allsaints8.jpg *Source*: http://en.wikipedia.org/w/index.php?title=File:Allsaints8.jpg *License*: GNU Free Documentation License *Contributors*: ger1axg

File:Estelle Swaray.jpg *Source*: http://en.wikipedia.org/w/index.php?title=File:Estelle_Swaray.jpg *License*: Creative Commons Attribution-Sharealike 2.0 *Contributors*: caporilli

File:ThandieNewtonBAFTA07.jpg *Source*: http://en.wikipedia.org/w/index.php?title=File:ThandieNewtonBAFTA07.jpg *License*: Creative Commons Attribution 3.0 *Contributors*: Caroline Bonarde Ucci at http://flickr.com/photos/caroline_bonarde/

File:IgnatiusSancho.jpg *Source*: http://en.wikipedia.org/w/index.php?title=File:IgnatiusSancho.jpg *License*: Public Domain *Contributors*: Adam sk, Patstuart, Vonvon

File:Idris Elba.jpg *Source*: http://en.wikipedia.org/w/index.php?title=File:Idris_Elba.jpg *License*: unknown *Contributors*: lukeford.net

File:Francis williams.jpg *Source*: http://en.wikipedia.org/w/index.php?title=File:Francis_williams.jpg *License*: Public Domain *Contributors*: James317a

File:Shaun Wright-Phillips warming up.jpg *Source*: http://en.wikipedia.org/w/index.php?title=File:Shaun_Wright-Phillips_warming_up.jpg *License*: Creative Commons Attribution-Sharealike 2.0 *Contributors*: John Dobson

File:Flag of England.svg *Source*: http://en.wikipedia.org/w/index.php?title=File:Flag_of_England.svg *License*: Public Domain *Contributors*: User:Nickshanks

File:Flag of Scotland.svg *Source*: http://en.wikipedia.org/w/index.php?title=File:Flag_of_Scotland.svg *License*: Public Domain *Contributors*: User:Kbolino

File:Flag of Wales 2.svg *Source*: http://en.wikipedia.org/w/index.php?title=File:Flag_of_Wales_2.svg *License*: Public Domain *Contributors*: AlexD, Cecil, Dbenbenn, Duduziq, FruitMonkey, Homo lupus, Iago4096, Pumbaa80, Red devil 666, Srtxg, Torstein, Vemanimalcula, Vzb83, 3 anonymous edits

File:Liverpool Slaves.jpg *Source*: http://en.wikipedia.org/w/index.php?title=File:Liverpool_Slaves.jpg *License*: unknown *Contributors*: Stevvvv4444

File:British West Indies Regiment Q 001202.jpg *Source*: http://en.wikipedia.org/w/index.php?title=File:British_West_Indies_Regiment_Q_001202.jpg *License*: unknown *Contributors*: Brooks, Ernest (Lt)

File:Windrush.jpg *Source*: http://en.wikipedia.org/w/index.php?title=File:Windrush.jpg *License*: unknown *Contributors*: Original uploader was Prosaic at en.wikipedia

File:St-pauls-riot.jpg *Source*: http://en.wikipedia.org/w/index.php?title=File:St-pauls-riot.jpg *License*: unknown *Contributors*: Jezhotwells

File:Harehills riot1.jpg *Source*: http://en.wikipedia.org/w/index.php?title=File:Harehills_riot1.jpg *License*: unknown *Contributors*: Muylor848, Sfan00 IMG

File:Diane Abbott, New Statesman hustings, cropped.jpg *Source*: http://en.wikipedia.org/w/index.php?title=File:Diane_Abbott,_New_Statesman_hustings,_cropped.jpg *License*: Creative Commons Attribution-Sharealike 3.0 *Contributors*: User:Rwendland

File:Seacole - Challen.jpg *Source*: http://en.wikipedia.org/w/index.php?title=File:Seacole_-_Challen.jpg *License*: Public Domain *Contributors*: Original uploader was RetiredUser2 at en.wikipedia

Image:Olaudah Equiano - Project Gutenberg eText 15399.png *Source*: http://en.wikipedia.org/w/index.php?title=File:Olaudah_Equiano_-_Project_Gutenberg_eText_15399.png *License*: Public Domain *Contributors*: Uploader: User Tagishsimon on en.wikipedia; Unknown artist

File:Shirley Bassey Wembley 2006.jpg *Source*: http://en.wikipedia.org/w/index.php?title=File:Shirley_Bassey_Wembley_2006.jpg *License*: Public Domain *Contributors*: User:Nyctc7

Image:Corinne Bailey Rae B&W.jpg *Source*: http://en.wikipedia.org/w/index.php?title=File:Corinne_Bailey_Rae_B&W.jpg *License*: Creative Commons Attribution 2.0 *Contributors*: FlickreviewR, Philip Stevens, Väsk

Image:Myleene Klass -- Greatest Britons.jpg *Source*: http://en.wikipedia.org/w/index.php?title=File:Myleene_Klass_--_Greatest_Britons.jpg *License*: Creative Commons Attribution 2.0 *Contributors*: Louise Marcus-Hamilton from London and Buckinghamshire, United Kingdom

Image:Lewis Hamilton (crop).jpg *Source*: http://en.wikipedia.org/w/index.php?title=File:Lewis_Hamilton_(crop).jpg *License*: Creative Commons Attribution 2.0 *Contributors*: User:Diniz

Image:Sir Ben Kingsley by David Shankbone.jpg *Source*: http://en.wikipedia.org/w/index.php?title=File:Sir_Ben_Kingsley_by_David_Shankbone.jpg *License*: Attribution *Contributors*: David Shankbone

File:Leonalewis.jpg *Source*: http://en.wikipedia.org/w/index.php?title=File:Leonalewis.jpg *License*: GNU Free Documentation License *Contributors*: User:Mfield

Image:Michael chopra.jpg *Source*: http://en.wikipedia.org/w/index.php?title=File:Michael_chopra.jpg *License*: Creative Commons Attribution-Sharealike 2.0 *Contributors*: wonker

Image:Raj Persaud at Humber Mouth 2007-06-30.jpg *Source*: http://en.wikipedia.org/w/index.php?title=File:Raj_Persaud_at_Humber_Mouth_2007-06-30.jpg *License*: Creative Commons Attribution 2.0 *Contributors*: walnut whippet from Hull, UK

License

GNU Free Documentation License Version 1.2, November 2002 Copyright (C) 2000,2001,2002 Free Software Foundation, Inc. 59 Temple Place, Suite 330, Boston, MA 02111-1307 USA Everyone is permitted to copy and distribute verbatim copies of this license document, but changing it is not allowed.

0. PREAMBLE

The purpose of this License is to make a manual, textbook, or other functional and useful document "free" in the sense of freedom: to assure everyone the effective freedom to copy and redistribute it, with or without modifying it, either commercially or noncommercially. Secondarily, this License preserves for the author and publisher a way to get credit for their work, while not being considered responsible for modifications made by others. This License is a kind of "copyleft", which means that derivative works of the document must themselves be free in the same sense. It complements the GNU General Public License, which is a copyleft license designed for free software. We have designed this License in order to use it for manuals for free software, because free software needs free documentation: a free program should come with manuals providing the same freedoms that the software does. But this License is not limited to software manuals; it can be used for any textual work, regardless of subject matter or whether it is published as a printed book. We recommend this License principally for works whose purpose is instruction or reference.

1. APPLICABILITY AND DEFINITIONS

This License applies to any manual or other work, in any medium, that contains a notice placed by the copyright holder saying it can be distributed under the terms of this License. Such a notice grants a world-wide, royalty-free license, unlimited in duration, to use that work under the conditions stated herein. The "Document", below, refers to any such manual or work. Any member of the public is a licensee, and is addressed as "you". You accept the license if you copy, modify or distribute the work in a way requiring permission under copyright law. A "Modified Version" of the Document means any work containing the Document or a portion of it, either copied verbatim, or with modifications and/or translated into another language. A "Secondary Section" is a named appendix or a front-matter section of the Document that deals exclusively with the relationship of the publishers or authors of the Document to the Document's overall subject (or to related matters) and contains nothing that could fall directly within that overall subject. (Thus, if the Document is in part a textbook of mathematics, a Secondary Section may not explain any mathematics.) The relationship could be a matter of historical connection with the subject or with related matters, or of legal, commercial, philosophical, ethical or political position regarding them. The "Invariant Sections" are certain Secondary Sections whose titles are designated, as being those of Invariant Sections, in the notice that says that the Document is released under this License. If a section does not fit the above definition of Secondary then it is not allowed to be designated as Invariant. The Document may contain zero Invariant Sections. If the Document does not identify any Invariant Sections then there are none. The "Cover Texts" are certain short passages of text that are listed, as Front-Cover Texts or Back-Cover Texts, in the notice that says that the Document is eleased under this License. A Front-Cover Text may be at most 5 words, and a Back-Cover Text may be at most 25 words. A Transparent" copy of the Document means a machine-readable copy, represented in a format whose specification is available to ne general public, that is suitable for revising the document straightforwardly with generic text editors or (for images composed of pixels) generic paint programs or (for drawings) ome widely available drawing editor, and that is suitable for input text formatters or for automatic translation to a variety of ormats suitable for input to text formatters. A copy made in an therwise Transparent file format whose markup, or absence of narkup, has been arranged to thwart or discourage subsequent nodification by readers is not Transparent. An image format is ot Transparent if used for any substantial amount of text. A copy at is not "Transparent" is called "Opaque". Examples of suitable ormats for Transparent copies include plain ASCII without arkup, Texinfo input format, LaTeX input format, SGML or XML sing a publicly available DTD, and standard-conforming simple TML, PostScript or PDF designed for human modification. xamples of transparent image formats include PNG, XCF and PG. Opaque formats include proprietary formats that can be ad and edited only by proprietary word processors, SGML or ML for which the DTD and/or processing tools are not generally ailable, and the machine-generated HTML, PostScript or PDF oduced by some word processors for output purposes only. The itle Page" means, for a printed book, the title page itself, plus ch following pages as are needed to hold, legibly, the material s License requires to appear in the title page. For works in mats which do not have any title page as such, "Title Page" eans the text near the most prominent appearance of the work's e, preceding the beginning of the body of the text. A section ntitled XYZ" means a named subunit of the Document whose e either is precisely XYZ or contains XYZ in parentheses owing text that translates XYZ in another language. (Here XYZ nds for a specific section name mentioned below, such as cknowledgements", "Dedications", "Endorsements", or story".) To "Preserve the Title" of such a section when you dify the Document means that it remains a section "Entitled Z" according to this definition. The Document may include rranty Disclaimers next to the notice which states that this ense applies to the Document. These Warranty Disclaimers considered to be included by reference in this License, but y as regards disclaiming warranties: any other implication that se Warranty Disclaimers may have is void and has no effect the meaning of this License.

/ERBATIM COPYING

u may copy and distribute the Document in any medium, er commercially or noncommercially, provided that this ense, the copyright notices, and the license notice saying this License applies to the Document are reproduced in all copies, and that you add no other conditions whatsoever to those of this License. You may not use technical measures to obstruct or control the reading or further copying of the copies you make or distribute. However, you may accept compensation in exchange for copies. If you distribute a large enough number of copies you must also follow the conditions in section 3. You may also lend copies, under the same conditions stated above, and you may publicly display copies.

3. COPYING IN QUANTITY

If you publish printed copies (or copies in media that commonly have printed covers) of the Document, numbering more than 100, and the Document's license notice requires Cover Texts, you must enclose the copies in covers that carry, clearly and legibly, all these Cover Texts: Front-Cover Texts on the front cover, and Back-Cover Texts on the back cover. Both covers must also clearly and legibly identify you as the publisher of these copies. The front cover must present the full title with all words of the title equally prominent and visible. You may add other material on the covers in addition. Copying with changes limited to the covers, as long as they preserve the title of the Document and satisfy these conditions, can be treated as verbatim copying in other respects. If the required texts for either cover are too voluminous to fit legibly, you should put the first ones listed (as many as fit reasonably) on the actual cover, and continue the rest onto adjacent pages. If you publish or distribute Opaque copies of the Document numbering more than 100, you must either include a machine-readable Transparent copy along with each Opaque copy, or state in or with each Opaque copy a computer-network location from which the general network-using public has access to download using public-standard network protocols a complete Transparent copy of the Document, free of added material. If you use the latter option, you must take reasonably prudent steps, when you begin distribution of Opaque copies in quantity, to ensure that this Transparent copy will remain thus accessible at the stated location until at least one year after the last time you distribute an Opaque copy (directly or through your agents or retailers) of that edition to the public. It is requested, but not required, that you contact the authors of the Document well before redistributing any large number of copies, to give them a chance to provide you with an updated version of the Document.

4. MODIFICATIONS

You may copy and distribute a Modified Version of the Document under the conditions of sections 2 and 3 above, provided that you release the Modified Version under precisely this License, with the Modified Version filling the role of the Document, thus licensing distribution and modification of the Modified Version to whoever possesses a copy of it. In addition, you must do these things in the Modified Version: A. Use in the Title Page (and on the covers, if any) a title distinct from that of the Document, and from those of previous versions (which should, if there were any, be listed in the History section of the Document). You may use the same title as a previous version if the original publisher of that version gives permission. B. List on the Title Page, as authors, one or more persons or entities responsible for authorship of the modifications in the Modified Version, together with at least five of the principal authors of the Document (all of its principal authors, if it has fewer than five), unless they release you from this requirement. C. State on the Title page the name of the publisher of the Modified Version, as the publisher. D. Preserve all the copyright notices of the Document. E. Add an appropriate copyright notice for your modifications adjacent to the other copyright notices. F. Include, immediately after the copyright notices, a license notice giving the public permission to use the Modified Version under the terms of this License, in the form shown in the Addendum below. G. Preserve in that license notice the full lists of Invariant Sections and required Cover Texts given in the Document's license notice. H. Include an unaltered copy of this License. I. Preserve the section Entitled "History", Preserve its Title, and add to it an item stating at least the title, year, new authors, and publisher of the Modified Version as given on the Title Page. If there is no section Entitled "History" in the Document, create one stating the title, year, authors, and publisher of the Document as given on its Title Page, then add an item describing the Modified Version as stated in the previous sentence. J. Preserve the network location, if any, given in the Document for public access to a Transparent copy of the Document, and likewise the network locations given in the Document for previous versions it was based on. These may be placed in the "History" section. You may omit a network location for a work that was published at least four years before the Document itself, or if the original publisher of the version it refers to gives permission. K. For any section Entitled "Acknowledgements" or "Dedications", Preserve the Title of the section, and preserve in the section all the substance and tone of each of the contributor acknowledgements and/or dedications given therein. L. Preserve all the Invariant Sections of the Document, unaltered in their text and in their titles. Section numbers or the equivalent are not considered part of the section titles. M. Delete any section Entitled "Endorsements". Such a section may not be included in the Modified Version. N. Do not retitle any existing section to be Entitled "Endorsements" or to conflict in title with any Invariant Section. O. Preserve any Warranty Disclaimers. If the Modified Version includes new front-matter sections or appendices that qualify as Secondary Sections and contain no material copied from the Document, you may at your option designate some or all of these sections as invariant. To do this, add their titles to the list of Invariant Sections in the Modified Version's license notice. These titles must be distinct from any other section titles. You may add a section Entitled "Endorsements", provided it contains nothing but endorsements of your Modified Version by various parties--for example, statements of peer review or that the text has been approved by an organization as the authoritative definition of a standard. You may add a passage of up to five words as a Front-Cover Text, and a passage of up to 25 words as a Back-Cover Text, to the end of the list of Cover Texts in the Modified Version. Only one passage of Front-Cover Text and one of Back-Cover Text may be added by (or through arrangements made by) any one entity. If the Document already includes a cover text for the same cover, previously added by you or by arrangement made by the same entity you are acting on behalf of, you may not add another; but you may replace the old one, on explicit permission from th previous publisher that added the old one. The author(s) ar publisher(s) of the Document do not by this License giv permission to use their names for publicity for or to assert or imp endorsement of any Modified Version.

5. COMBINING DOCUMENTS

You may combine the Document with other documents release under this License, under the terms defined in section 4 above f modified versions, provided that you include in the combination a of the Invariant Sections of all of the original document unmodified, and list them all as Invariant Sections of yo combined work in its license notice, and that you preserve all the Warranty Disclaimers. The combined work need only contain on copy of this License, and multiple identical Invariant Sections ma be replaced with a single copy. If there are multiple Invaria Sections with the same name but different contents, make th title of each such section unique by adding at the end of it, i parentheses, the name of the original author or publisher of tha section if known, or else a unique number. Make the sam adjustment to the section titles in the list of Invariant Sections i the license notice of the combined work. In the combination, yo must combine any sections Entitled "History" in the variou original documents, forming one section Entitled "History likewise combine any sections Entitled "Acknowledgements", an any sections Entitled "Dedications". You must delete all section Entitled "Endorsements".

6. COLLECTIONS OF DOCUMENTS

You may make a collection consisting of the Document and othe documents released under this License, and replace th individual copies of this License in the various documents with a single copy that is included in the collection, provided that yo follow the rules of this License for verbatim copying of each of th documents in all other respects. You may extract a singl document from such a collection, and distribute it individuall under this License, provided you insert a copy of this License int the extracted document, and follow this License in all othe respects regarding verbatim copying of that document.

7. AGGREGATION WITH INDEPENDENT WORKS

A compilation of the Document or its derivatives with othe separate and independent documents or works, in or on a volume of a storage or distribution medium, is called an "aggregate" if the copyright resulting from the compilation is not used to limit the legal rights of the compilation's users beyond what the individual works permit. When the Document is included in an aggregate, this License does not apply to the other works in the aggregate which are not themselves derivative works of the Document. If the Cover Text requirement of section 3 is applicable to these copies of the Document, then if the Document is less than one half of the entire aggregate, the Document's Cover Texts may be placed on covers that bracket the Document within the aggregate, or the electronic equivalent of covers if the Document is in electronic form. Otherwise they must appear on printed covers that bracket the whole aggregate.

8. TRANSLATION

Translation is considered a kind of modification, so you may distribute translations of the Document under the terms of section 4. Replacing Invariant Sections with translations requires special permission from their copyright holders, but you may include translations of some or all Invariant Sections in addition to the original versions of these Invariant Sections. You may include a translation of this License, and all the license notices in the Document, and any Warranty Disclaimers, provided that you also include the original English version of this License and the original versions of those notices and disclaimers. In case of a disagreement between the translation and the original version of this License or a notice or disclaimer, the original version will prevail. If a section in the Document is Entitled "Acknowledgements", "Dedications", or "History", the requirement (section 4) to Preserve its Title (section 1) will typically require changing the actual title.

9. TERMINATION

You may not copy, modify, sublicense, or distribute the Document except as expressly provided for under this License. Any other attempt to copy, modify, sublicense or distribute the Document is void, and will automatically terminate your rights under this License. However, parties who have received copies, or rights, from you under this License will not have their licenses terminated so long as such parties remain in full compliance.

10. FUTURE REVISIONS OF THIS LICENSE

The Free Software Foundation may publish new, revised versions of the GNU Free Documentation License from time to time. Such new versions will be similar in spirit to the present version, but may differ in detail to address new problems or concerns. See http://www.gnu.org/copyleft/. Each version of the License is given a distinguishing version number. If the Document specifies that a particular numbered version of this License "or any later version" applies to it, you have the option of following the terms and conditions either of that specified version or of any later version that has been published (not as a draft) by the Free Software Foundation. If the Document does not specify a version number of this License, you may choose any version ever published (not as a draft) by the Free Software Foundation.

ADDENDUM: How to use this License for your documents To use this License in a document you have written, include a copy of the License in the document and put the following copyright and license notices just after the title page: Copyright (c) YEAR YOUR NAME. Permission is granted to copy, distribute and/or modify this document under the terms of the GNU Free Documentation License, Version 1.2 or any later version published by the Free Software Foundation; with no Invariant Sections, no Front-Cover Texts, and no Back-Cover Texts. A copy of the license is included in the section entitled "GNU Free Documentation License". If you have Invariant Sections, Front-Cover Texts and Back-Cover Texts, replace the "with...Texts." line with this: with the Invariant Sections being LIST THEIR TITLES, with the Front-Cover Texts being LIST, and with the Back-Cover Texts being LIST. If you have Invariant Sections without Cover Texts, or some other combination of the three, merge those two alternatives to suit the situation. If your document contains nontrivial examples of program code, we recommend releasing these examples in parallel under your choice of free software license, such as the GNU General Public License, to permit their use in free software.

Lightning Source UK Ltd.
Milton Keynes UK
175242UK00001B/12/P